THE WAY OF THE
RUNNER

THE WAY OF THE
RUNNER

A JOURNEY INTO THE FABLED WORLD
OF JAPANESE RUNNING

Adharanand Finn

PEGASUS BOOKS
NEW YORK LONDON

THE WAY OF THE RUNNER

Pegasus Books Ltd
80 Broad Street, 5th Floor
New York, NY 10004

First Pegasus Books hardcover edition June 2016

ISBN: 978-1-68177-121-2

10 9 8 7 6 5 4 3 2 1

Printed in the United States of America
Distributed by W. W. Norton & Company, Inc.

'Before enlightenment, I chopped wood and carried water. After enlightenment, I chopped wood and carried water.'

ZEN PROVERB

Prologue

It's February 2001. I'm standing by a school wall in the small town of Hongō in western Honshu, Japan. I have a hangover.

The night before, my brother, who is a teacher at the school, took me straight off the plane from London, to what he referred to ominously as a naked festival. It involved drinking lots of saki, wearing nothing but a *mawashi* loincloth like a sumo wrestler, standing out in the freezing night with around two hundred similarly dressed men, and trying to grab hold of a long piece of cloth. As we all fought to get hold of the cloth, priests threw cold water over us. The scrum of two hundred men kicked, pulled and barged around in the dark for hours before someone finally, mercifully, emerged triumphantly with the cloth and disappeared up some steps to a shrine.

The next morning there is a picture of the melee in one of Japan's national newspapers, featuring my pale backside right there in the middle. I can tell it is mine because in my dazed, drunken state I asked someone to write 'Flash' across my back. I was thinking I was Flash Gordon, for some reason. A man on another planet wrestling his way through a scrum of men. We've had barely four hours' sleep before my brother is up again.

'I'm running an ekiden,' he says. 'You want to run?' I have no idea what an ekiden is, but running is the last thing on my mind that morning. I was once a keen runner, but years of working in the office of a London publishing company have left me all soft and pudgy. My running days are long behind me.

'No,' I say, scratching the back of my neck.

Instead he positions me by the school wall, gives me a raincoat to protect me from the drizzle, and goes off to join his team. An ekiden, it turns out, is a long-distance relay race. Every town in Japan seems to have one, and everyone gets involved in some way or another. If they're not running, people offer to help marshal, or at the very least they come out to cheer the runners on.

I stand by the wall nodding and bowing as people bustle by under umbrellas, the race officials all wearing matching yellow raincoats. Behind me, in the school yard, everyone is gathering. I watch through the railings as athletes in shorts and singlets sprint up and down on the soggy gravel, preparing for the race. Many of them seem to be high-school students, but there are men and women of all ages taking part. They line up and then, after the bang of a starting gun, swarm off out of the school grounds and into the town.

The rain is soaking through my thin shoes, making my feet cold as I stand waiting by the empty road. The first-leg runners wear a sash called a *tasuki*, which they have to pass on to their team-mates further along the course, in the same way sprinters pass a baton in relays on the track. At some point the race will come back past me again, with my brother among them.

I decide to walk up and down to keep warm. Across the road an elderly couple stand under matching umbrellas, occasionally glancing up the road. It's almost an hour later before the runners come back into view, scampering down the street, people along the course calling out to them, cheering them on. My brother, when he appears, towers over everyone, all six foot four inches of him, his face flushed, the rain in his eyes, grinning to me as he lopes by.

'Go on, Vinny,' I shout, wishing suddenly I was out there too. It looks fun. More fun than hanging around here by this wall with my freezing hands stuck under my arms. I have an urge to throw off my jacket and start running. I get this whenever I find myself watching a race rather than running it, wondering why I'm not out there too. This is such a friendly, communal event, with the whole town busily involved, that I feel left out standing here by the wall.

It's not until many years later that I get another chance to join a team and line up for an ekiden in Japan. But this time I'm primed, two stone lighter and raring to go.

1

I enter through the revolving doors of the Tower Hotel, by the river Thames in London. It's a warm April morning just a few days before the 2013 London marathon. My legs feel strong and bouncy. I'm ready to race and I can sense the quiet buzz of anticipation here at the elite athletes' hotel.

Just inside the door, by a curving marble staircase, a small group of people are in discussion. I recognise one of them. It's Steve Cram, my childhood running hero. He's older now, of course, his hair shorter, flatter than in his heyday, but the same man I used to watch on television many years ago, his yellow vest whizzing around the track in pursuit of world records. I walk on, into the lobby.

As I stand there, runners walk by. Two Kenyan women in large puffer jackets wander past, their matchstick legs looking as though they might buckle under the weight of the jackets. They speak to each other so quietly it's hard to know if they are actually talking. By the reception desk, two Dutchmen with big laughs are chatting to a man in sunglasses with his hood up. It's only when I hear his voice that I realise it's Mo Farah.

A lot has happened in the twelve years since I stood hungover by that school wall in Japan. Somewhere along the line I started running again. Slowly, at first. I ran my first 10K race in 47 minutes. For two years it remained my best time. But gradually I began to take things more seriously, joining a running club, heading out for longer and longer runs. Then I went to live in Kenya, to train with the great Kalenjin runners of the Rift Valley. I went partly to improve my running, but also I went on a mission to understand and unravel the mystery that surrounds these great runners. I wanted to know who they were, what they did, and what moved them. When I came back I wrote the book *Running with the Kenyans: Discovering the Secrets of the Fastest People on Earth*.

In a few days a battle will rage between a group of Kenyans and Ethiopians to win the most prestigious city marathon in the world. I'll be running too, somewhere among the sweating throng of people strung out along the streets behind them. I'm hoping to beat my best time and run under 2 hours 50 minutes. I've trained hard for it, eaten the right food, bought the right kit. But today, as I stand in the Tower Hotel lobby, it's neither me nor the Kenyans I'm interested in. Today, I'm looking for the Japanese.

*

Something is going on in Japan. From the outside, it's easy to miss. Virtually every big road race around the world is won by a seemingly endless succession of superfast Kenyans and Ethiopians. No one else gets a look in.

But on one small group of islands in east Asia, they're at least putting up a fight. In 2013, the year in which our story is set, only six of the hundred fastest marathon runners in the world were not from Africa. Five of those six were from Japan.*

In the women's marathon, eleven of the top hundred runners in 2013 were from Japan. Again, that was clearly the third highest number after Kenya and Ethiopia.

In the same year, the year following the 2012 London Olympics, not a single British runner managed to complete a marathon in less than 2 hours 15 minutes. In the USA, twelve men ran under that time. Yet in Japan, a nation with less than half the population of the US, the figure was more than four times higher, with fifty-two Japanese men running a marathon in under 2:15.

And in the half-marathon, Japan is even stronger. On the morning of 17 November 2013, at a half-marathon in Ageo, a small city squashed in among the sprawling northern suburbs of Tokyo, hundreds of university students lined up hoping to impress their team coaches ahead of the important Hakone ekiden in January. Ageo is one of the main try-out races for the teams, but still many of the best university runners were missing that day, while virtually all Japan's hundreds of professional road-runners were also absent. Yet, watching the end of the race on blurry YouTube footage** something amazing unfolds.

The winner, getting his nose ahead in a five-way sprint

---

* I have excluded the year's seventy-fifth fastest marathoner, France's Abraham Kiprotich, because he was born and grew up running in Kenya, only switching nationality after serving in the French Foreign Legion; and also no. 87 on the list, Nicholas Kemboi, from Qatar, who was also born and raised in Kenya.
** See http://youtu.be/5THRBUH0MdY

finish, crosses the line in 62 minutes 36 seconds. This is pretty fast, but the real story is what happens next. Usually, if you watch a top-level race anywhere else in the world, the first few runners will finish with clear daylight behind them. Often they have time to get changed, do interviews, have a drink and do a warm-down before more than a handful of other runners have crossed the line. But not here. The amazing thing is how they just keep coming. Runner after runner, one behind the other, crossing the line, sometimes in big groups, turning and bowing to the track, some collapsing on their knees. All of them checking their watches. All of them running fast.

In the final breakdown, eighteen runners finished the race in under 63 minutes that morning. In one race. In the whole of 2013, only one British runner ran a half-marathon that fast. Only twenty-one US runners, in the whole year, managed it.

The student finishing way down in 100th position in Ageo still completed the course in 64 minutes 49 seconds. That would have ranked him in eighth position overall in the UK in 2013. In many other European countries he would have been the national champion. That's a remarkable depth of running talent.

So, something is going on in Japan. My mission with this book is to find out what it is.

I'm intrigued not only as a writer, but also as a runner. After my six months in Kenya I returned to England and broke all of my personal best times, from 5K to the marathon. For six months I was on one long, jaunty upswing, breaking ten PBs in a row.

But in the last two years I haven't gone any faster. I'm about to turn forty, and I can't help thinking, is this it? Have I passed my peak? Is it time to give up on the thrill ride of chasing personal bests, the buzz of breaking new ground, and instead begin on that calmer, post-peak journey of simply enjoying running? In some ways I look forward to those days, when running becomes a gentler pursuit, less determined and obsessive, when I'll simply enjoy the sensation of my heart pounding, and the feel of the cold, fresh wind on my face without worrying about training plans and tapering and stopwatches.

But the competitive gremlin in my gut wants one last hurrah. Surely 2:55 is not going to be my final marathon time? Seventy-eight minutes for the half-marathon? It's OK, but I'm sure I can go faster. I learnt much in Kenya, but perhaps the lessons in Japan will be different. Perhaps I can learn something new from those swarms of talented half-marathon runners in that fuzzy YouTube footage, something to push me on that one, final step further. My journey to find out begins here in the Tower Hotel in London.

*

A man is walking towards me, his white teeth gleaming across the lobby. It's Brendan Reilly. Everyone I've spoken to about running in Japan has mentioned his name. He seems to be the linchpin for everything, the gateway between Japan's insular running world and the outside. He has arranged a three-way meeting with me and a respected Japanese coach, Tadasu Kawano. Kawano trains the Otsuka Pharmaceutical ekiden team, based in the city of Tokushima on the island of Shikoku. A couple of his athletes are running the London marathon in a few days.

'Hello,' says Reilly. 'How are you?' A firm, American handshake.

He takes me to sit down at a table in the hotel café. Kawano is there, waiting. An elderly man, he looks tired, leaning over to one side. He nods his hello as I sit down.

'Hajimemashite,' I say in my best Japanese. *Pleased to meet you.* He smiles. 'Ah, hajimemashite,' he says, as though it's a game. But that's as far as we're going. My full Japanese repertoire is already used up, so we switch to English, with Reilly translating.

'I want to join an ekiden team,' I say. 'Can you help?'

Japan is unique in offering long-distance runners a salary to join a team. Big companies such as Honda, Konica Minolta and Toyota keep teams of professional road-runners who live and train together and compete in ekiden races. My plan is to join one. Not as a competitive runner – I'm too slow for that – but to embed myself with a team, like a war reporter embedded in a military unit. It seems a good way to get close enough to the athletes to understand how it all works. To learn the secrets of Japanese running. Although finding a team to take me on is proving more difficult than I'd imagined.

I've read that these corporate road-runners are huge sports stars in Japan. In fact, it was after reading an article written by Reilly, in *Running Times* magazine in the US, that I first realised what a big deal running was in Japan.

'Chat with your taxi driver or sushi chef on a night out

in most Japanese cities,' he wrote, 'and it becomes apparent that Yuko Arimori, Naoko Takahashi and Mizuki Noguchi are national icons even among the sedentary. Likewise, the employees of the corporate sponsors of distance teams are as fervent as fans of the Beautiful Game. The stands at a national ekiden relay championship are a rainbow of corporate colors and logos, as employees garbed in their company hues give raucous support to their runners.'

He goes on: 'In Japan, live broadcasts of marathons and ekiden events, which carry all the expert analysis and technical quality given the NFL here at home [in the US], garner staggering numbers. While US marathon broadcasts rarely creep above 1% ratings, in Japan a 10% rating for a major ekiden or marathon would be a disappointment; certain athletes and events can bring Super Bowl-like 40%-plus ratings.'

One of these corporate ekiden teams is Otsuka Pharmaceuticals, and I'm sitting face to face with the coach. I'm hoping he will invite me to come and run with his team. He nods when I ask him, but it's not the certain, definite nod that leads me to shake his hand and arrange my arrival date. It's more of a wait-and-see, non-committal nod. He says he knows other people who may be able to help with my research. Reilly knows people, too. I've been emailing him about this for months. He keeps telling me everything will be simple to arrange, that it's just a matter of picking the right team. But the ekiden season is looming, and still nothing concrete has been arranged.

In the end I leave Reilly and Kawano with little more than another two business cards to add to my collection. Rather than head home, I decide to hang around in the hotel lobby to sample some more of the pre-race atmosphere. Sitting quietly on a low wall beside some potted shrubs is another Japanese man. He's checking his phone, but I notice him glance up occasionally at me, so I go over to talk to him.

'Hi,' he says, standing up. 'I saw you talking to Mr Kawano.' He speaks good English. I tell him about my plan to travel to Japan for six months to experience an ekiden season. He nods along thoughtfully as I tell him I want to embed myself in a professional team. When I say I also want to train with them, though, he laughs. 'No, no, not possible,' he says dismissively, as though it's a foolish idea.

I tell him I ran with the great Kenyan runners in the Rift Valley. I'm sure I can cope with the Japanese runners. But he just smiles. 'No, no,' he says. Despite his insistence that a core element of my plan is impossible, he offers to help me. He says he has connections throughout the Japanese running world, and that I can call him if I get stuck. He gives me his business card. His name is Mr Ogushi.

*

Over the next few months, Reilly tries in vain to find me a team to join, contacting everyone he knows. But at the end of June I get an email from him telling me he has given up.

'While the coaches generally think it is a great idea for a story, not one of them has come through with any enthusiasm to host you or to let you be a regular part of their training,' he says. 'There is a lot of reluctance to make any commitment that will allow you to really get in and see a team over an extended period.'

He adds pointedly: 'It [Japan] can be a maddeningly closed society at times, and this is unfortunately one of those times.'

But by then my house has already been let, my job has agreed to give me six months off to complete my research, and my children's school has arranged for them to have time off to come with me. The ekiden season begins in September, just a few short months away, and lasts until February. If I'm going to witness it, we need to leave soon. And so it is, that with absolutely nothing arranged, on a sunny Monday morning in July, we set off for Japan . . . on the train.

2

Gorky Park in Moscow is a seething mass of posturing men and women. We're waiting in a line to hire bikes. The August sun is slow-roasting the back of my neck. I've forgotten to put suncream on and I don't have a hat. But I dare not move. I've been queueing for forty minutes already. My children are hanging off my legs.

Across the Moskva river, the women's world championship marathon is taking place. I want to go and see it, but I've promised the children I'd get them bikes. Eventually we make it to the front of the line. The sign, in English, says tourists have to show their passports, so I hand them over to the man on the till. Without even looking at me, he shakes his head and looks at the people behind me, asking them what they want.

'Passports,' I say. Maybe he didn't see them. I hold them up so he can't miss them.

'No foreigners,' the man says, and returns to the customer behind us.

I'm on the verge of turning into Basil Fawlty. No foreigners? All these signs everywhere in English. 'Welcome to Gorkey Park Cycle Hire' etc. etc. Who put those up? I've got three small children here, we've been queueing for an hour in the stupid Russian sun. And I'm missing the marathon.

'Rule change,' he says, looking at me through the squint of his eyes, as though he's surprised I'm still there.

So we all walk away, defeated, cursing. 'What happened?' my children ask me, confused by the lack of bicycles. 'Why can't we get any bikes?'

*

I leave my wife, Marietta, to get them ice creams while I weave my way through the crowds to the marathon. I can still catch the lead runners as they come by for the last time if I'm quick. To cross the river there's a huge pedestrian bridge. I rush up the steps, my camera swinging around my neck, my shirt dripping in sweat. It's 27°c. I don't know how they're running a marathon out there.

The bridge is full of people heading to the park. Everywhere there are long bare legs; down in a riverside bar women are sunbathing topless. The air is charged with an intimidating mix of wealth and anarchy. It's like *Sex in the City* meets *Mad Max*. Up on the bridge, two women are walking casually over the top of the huge, arched steel girders that hold the bridge up in the air. Nobody seems to pay them any attention, as though it's a normal thing to do. At the top of the arch, they sit down to admire the view, their long dresses billowing out behind them.

And then I'm out of it. Down a steel staircase back onto street level. The road is barricaded off and here on this side of the river everything is quiet. A set of pipes spray water in a shower across the empty tarmac, while a handful of people lean patiently on the railings under the shade of the bridge.

Under a small gazebo, a couple of television technicians are sitting with a bank of electrical equipment and a television screen. On it is a small group of runners. An Italian woman is leading. Right behind her is the usual cast: a Kenyan, an Ethiopian, and two Japanese runners.

I watch the screen quietly, wishing I had some water to drink. As I stand there, I hear the distant whirl of a helicopter. It must be following the runners. From across the river drifts the rambunctious noise of the park in full flow.

Suddenly, as though they've popped out of a hole, two Japanese women appear beside me. They're both wearing Japanese national tracksuits and are talking excitedly to each other, glancing anxiously up the road towards the helicopter. Across the street I notice a few people have draped a Japanese flag over the railings. They all start cheering in high-pitched voices as the runners come into view. The Japanese women on my side are leaping around and screaming at their teammates as the five women race by.

'*Gambare, gambare,*' they say, before rushing off, presumably to catch another glimpse of the runners somewhere else further along the course.

*

It was my wife's idea to travel to Japan overland. After I took my family to Kenya for six months, I got endless comments about how understanding Marietta was. People told me only half joking that if they'd suggested such a thing to their partners, they'd have faced divorce proceedings within the hour. What they didn't realise, however, is that she was a born adventurer and was delighted to be heading off to Kenya.

Japan didn't initially hold the same appeal. Perhaps it wasn't wild enough. It was only when she came up with the overland plan that she became fully enthused about the project.

'Flying is so weird,' she said. 'You get lifted up from one part of the world and then dumped in a completely different environment and time zone. It's a shock to the system. You have no idea about the time and space, the world, in between.'

It feels more natural, she reasoned, to traverse the world by land. Besides, the children love trains. It would be fun. Think of all the places we'd get to visit along the way.

I looked at her nervously. I wanted to feel as enthused about travelling nine thousand miles overland with three small children, but the idea filled me with blind panic.

*

So it was with sweaty palms that I climbed on board the 9.06 a.m. train from Tiverton Parkway in Devon on a Monday morning in late July, en route to Kyoto in Japan.

We took a route around the north of the Baltic Sea, through Denmark, Sweden and Finland. Scandinavia was a joy to travel across with children. When catching the train from Turku to Helsinki in Finland, the woman in the ticket office noticed I had children. 'Would you like seats near the playroom?' she asked. It had a slide, and a toy train to sit in, and a library of books. The time flew by.

But everything changed when we hit Russia. After less than a minute in Moscow, before we'd even left the station, my youngest daughter, Uma, looked0 at me and said: 'Dad, I think I liked Finland better.'

I didn't want to make hasty judgements, but I knew what she meant.

Our sense of foreboding is confirmed over the next few weeks. Friendly service seems to be an alien concept in Russia, with most staff in cafes, on trains, and everywhere else apparently sharing the view that customers are to be ignored and, if they persist in their stupidity, given exasperated shrugs.

By happy coincidence we arrived in Moscow just as the world athletics championships were rolling into town. Most of the city seems oblivious to the event, although I do spot a few Usain Bolt posters on bus shelters here and there.

Bolt himself, it turns out, is no more taken with the city than Uma, noting in one interview: 'They [Russians] don't smile a lot.'

After watching the women's marathon – where in the end the two Japanese runners finish third and fourth – I rejoin my family in Gorky Park. The sun has cooled down a bit by the time I find them languishing in a dusty playground. Luckily for them, I have another treat lined up – an evening in the Luzhniki Stadium watching the athletics.

The stadium is half empty despite the appearance of Bolt in the 100m heats. We find ourselves sitting surrounded by flag-waving Brits from Basingstoke and Cheltenham. It's somehow comforting to hear their familiar accents and complaints about the Russian service.

In front of us sit a couple of elderly Russians who look like they've wandered in from some remote village, bits of hay still poking out from under their shirts. I love the way athletics attracts people like this. It's an old-fashioned sport at heart, despite the pumped-up razzmatazz of some of its sprinting stars.

Tonight, the big race is the men's 10,000m. I'm as excited as anyone to watch Britain's Olympic champion Mo Farah race against the best Kenyans and Ethiopians. Propping up the field are the other Europeans and a few Japanese runners. Despite their prowess on the roads, the Japanese have a poor record on the track and it's no surprise to see their three runners drop off the back of the group as soon as the pace starts hotting up.

Farah toys with the field, running around right at the back for a while, before taking over and winning comfortably in the end. After the race I head down to the trackside to catch him on his lap of honour, and I arrive at the same moment his coach, Alberto Salazar, pops up to congratulate him. After their hugs and smiles, Salazar walks past me.

'Good work,' I say to Salazar. He is one of the most brilliant coaches in the world. As well as Farah, who won double gold in the 2012 Olympics, his other runner Galen Rupp from the US came second in London and fourth here tonight. If anyone is showing the world that the Kenyans and Ethiopians can be beaten, it's this man.

'Thanks,' he says, and walks off.

*

Ever since we began planning our overland trip to Japan, the bit that has been giving me the knotted feeling in my stomach is the seven-day journey on the Trans-Siberian Railway from Moscow to Vladivostok.

We start the journey on a bright Sunday morning. Families loll around on the station platform surrounded by huge piles of luggage. Once the train pulls in, we climb on board and find our compartment, taking turns with everyone else to run bags down along the narrow corridor. Lots of people are outside wiping down their windows. Part of the appeal of the journey is to sit and watch the world chug by, but the windows are thick with grime. Marietta pulls out some wipes, finds our window and joins in with the mass clean-up.

A few minutes later, she's being hurried onto the train by the attendant, and we're off. We roll slowly out through Moscow, past wooden houses and grey apartment blocks, on past small villages, endless woodland, through into days and nights, up across the Ural mountains and then on to Siberia. The countryside along the way is surprisingly pretty, full of little fairytale houses with pointy roofs and wooden wells in the garden.

Russians are often amazed that tourists choose to take this train for fun. To them it is a means of transport and nothing else. The glamour aboard is certainly negligible. On our train the compartments are musty, the bathrooms consist of nothing but a grimy metal toilet and basin, while the restaurant car is all chipped wooden tables and faded curtains. It's also mostly full of German tourists or drunk Russian men with sad eyes. When we visit, the waiter hands us a menu with pages of tasty sounding dishes, virtually all of which are unavailable. 'Borsch,' she tells us, which evidently means it's that or nothing.

After a two-day stop halfway at Irkutsk, where we sit eating ice creams and skimming stones by Lake Baikal, the deepest lake in the world, we re-board to find ourselves on an even older, more decrepit train. The air on board is sweltering and reeks of cigarette smoke as we realise to our horror that the windows are sealed shut. As we rumble out of the station, I'm stripped to the waist, sweating, trying to make up the beds. I begin counting down the hours to Vladivostok almost immediately.

I spend the next three days opening the door between our carriage and the next one to let the fag-end air out through the tiny gap there. But someone always shuts it again. For three days we dig in, keep our door closed to protect our air, and spend time together, reading, playing chess, watching films. It's not exactly ideal preparation for my Japanese running adventure. Apart from a steady jog around Amager Fælled in Copenhagen, I haven't managed to fit in any training the entire trip. Usually I enjoy running when I'm away from home, using it as a way to explore new areas, but when we haven't been cooped up in train compartments, we've had other things to do, such as find something to eat, or somewhere to sleep.

I think I'm finally going to go mad when on the last day the train grinds to a complete stop in the middle of the baking Siberian taiga. As the hours begin to tick by, the thought of missing the ferry and getting stuck in Vladivostok is enough to have me chewing the bed rails. Luckily the children, now tragically used to the smoky air, are happily running up and down in the corridor, playing with the other children.

Finally, when I'm not sure I can take any more, the train jerks back into life and resumes its slow crawl across the world.

The next morning we're all giddy with excitement to be boarding the Korean ferry out of Russia. As we sail away from Vladivostok, the fresh air and warm sun on our faces, it feels like we're breathing out again. Two easy days of sailing later, we arrive in Japan.

3

We travel to Kyoto, our final stop, on the bullet train. Inside it's wide like an aeroplane, with the seats in threes. The train is packed, but virtually silent, full of people returning from work. A quiet unwinding from the day. I sit with Lila, my eldest daughter, who is reading. Outside the window, glancing over the lap of a man playing a game on his phone, cities fly by in the blueing dusk. We ride along the rooftops. Out beyond the streetlights and buildings, forested mountains rise up, hulking black shapes dashed with white brushstrokes of mist.

'Argh, stop it,' I hear Uma yell, sitting further back in the carriage somewhere. 'That's naughty, Ossian. *Umbaya.*'

Her admonishment is met by a gut-wrenching yowl.

'Oh, god,' I say to Lila. She smirks, thinking it funny that her siblings are the only noise rising over the gentle hum of the train.

A full-scale fight is breaking out. Lila glances back down the train and then looks at me giggling.

'They're so loud,' she says.

It's four weeks since we hauled our bags onto the train at Tiverton Parkway in Devon. Finally, finally, we have arrived.

'We will soon make a brief stop at Kyoto station,' the train says helpfully in English as it begins to slow down. 'The doors on the right-hand side will open.'

*

We drag our bags up from the illuminated belly of the station, through huge underground shopping-mall avenues, and out into the warm night. Thirteen bags in all, some of them so heavy you could almost see the carriages sinking down every time we hauled them aboard a train. Ossian, our youngest, sits on his suitcase and looks up at the tall buildings. 'Where are we going now?' he asks.

'We're here,' I say. 'Just one last taxi ride and we've done it.'

We've come out beside a huge car park. Taxis pull up one at a time, but without properly stopping. They look at us, with all our bags and children, and move on. They're all small, saloon-type cars, with white lace-covered seats and uniformed drivers wearing white gloves. The illuminated taxi signs on the roofs of the cabs are in the shape of hearts. Finally a car stops and the driver gets out.

'Hoteru?' he asks.

I give him a piece of paper with an address on it in Japanese. We're staying with an old friend called Max. The driver grimaces at the piece of paper for a while, then nods, picks up the biggest of our bags and loads it into the boot of his car.

It's a squash getting everything in, but the driver is game, packing bags in around our feet, on our laps. Once we're in, we drive north through central Kyoto, past the old Imperial Palace, the car moving gently, the streets full of upright bicycles, people strolling around in groups like tourists, young men standing in the windows of convenience shops reading comic books.

Inside the car the children watch the little sat-nav tinkling instructions in Japanese. The driver switches it to a television. A game show. Lots of laughter and people falling over. Outside the streets get gradually quieter, and smaller, until after about twenty minutes we stop. A figure stands in the street. An Englishman in linen trousers and a white shirt.

I first met Max in London about twelve years earlier. We were both following the teachings of an Indian man called Prem Rawat who talks about the essence of life, the beautiful reality of human existence. Things like that. Max was floating around like an enlightened soul, meditating for four hours a day. He had a sereneness about him that was slightly unnerving.

I don't remember what he was doing for work, if anything. At sixteen, Max had seemed like just another lost cause. His parents had broken up when he was young and the teachers at his school in Leeds thought he was a troublemaker. Having flunked his GCSEs, when he said he wanted to stay on and do A-levels, they told him he was wasting his time.

'It was a challenge,' he tells me. 'And that's just what I needed.' Two years later he was at the prestigious Somerville College, Oxford, studying biology.

One evening, in a cafe in London, he told me he had applied to teach English in Japan and had been offered a post. He was thinking of taking it. The next thing I heard, he had gone. Twelve years later, here he was, standing outside his house in the expensive Kamigamo neighbourhood in northern Kyoto, looking slightly concerned at where the taxi driver was stopping his car, telling him in Japanese to move it forward a bit.

Max is not only fluent in Japanese, but has written books in the language and gives lectures about childhood, lifestyles, dreams; anything people want him to discourse upon. He seems to have his own little following of devoted Max-ites.

'Come in,' he says, taking a bag and leading the way into a small entrance porch, where we take off our shoes. His wife, Maduka, and his two-year-old son, Sen, greet us as we all pile in, up some steps and into a small room with a tatami-mat floor, a low table and some cushions. The evening is still hot, so we're not too disturbed when Max starts spraying us with a slightly strange-smelling water.

'Effective microorganisms,' he explains. 'Good bacteria. It's good after a long journey.' The children are giggling, enjoying the coolness of the spray. Microorganisms, we soon learn, are one of Max's favourite subjects. They seem to be good for everything. He drinks them, bathes in them, and sprays things with them. Including people.

Later that evening Max takes me for a walk around his neighbourhood. In the warm night, my head still racing after our journey halfway across the world, everything seems to take on a cartoon quality. The streets seem so neat and quiet, the street-lights drawn in coloured pencils, the leaves from the encroaching forest, each one picked out and quickly sketched. Every now and then a person wobbles by on a squeaky bicycle.

At the end of Max's road there is a shrine set back among the trees. He bows sincerely at the red-pillared entrance, and instructs me to do the same. Inside, the stillness of the night seems to become even stiller, as though you could almost touch it. We walk up a gravel pathway to the shrine itself, its jutting roof and dark recesses emerging from the foliage like a place long forgotten. The melodic clicking of cicadas fills the air. Without either of us speaking, I follow Max through a simple ritual of washing hands, ringing a muted bell, and then bowing.

'Now you can make a wish,' he whispers. As I stand there, the engulfing silence seems almost magical. Is it coming from the shrine? Later I decide that through all the bowing and ritual, we had bestowed a sense of reverence on the shrine. Perhaps with everyone who visits, the reverence lingers and grows. I know I should wish for something grander, more worthwhile, but in that moment all that comes to me is my reason for coming to Japan: ekiden.

The words are not clearly formulated, but I ask for help to find an ekiden team. We throw a five-yen coin into the box, and then turn, bowing, back out onto the street, leaving the wish enveloped by the trees, to be digested and turned over at their leisure by the Shinto gods.

*

The next evening, I head out around the same streets for my first run in Japan. Max comes with me. He's not a runner, but he says he might try to run while I'm here. He was once the captain of his school football team. 'Yorkshire champions,' he says proudly.

We set off at an easy pace. Although I've hardly run in the last month because of all the travelling, the lack of food on the Trans-Siberian train means at least I'm feeling quite light, and I find myself skipping along easily next to Max.

It's almost 11 p.m. by the time we set off, but the air is still thick with humidity. After the bustle of the day, the streets have returned to their nocturnal stillness, only occasionally ruffled by a slow-moving car or a bicycle. A man buzzes slowly by on a scooter motorbike with his dog on a lead scampering next to him.

Max tells me that his wife has been in touch with a man she used to work with called Kenji Takao. He is a former professional runner and has contacts in the ekiden world. He also has an amateur running team, which we've been invited to join. The first training session is in Osaka that Friday evening.

Once I realised I didn't have a professional ekiden team to join, we were free to live anywhere in Japan. I was still hoping to get interviews and perhaps convince a team to let me join them, so one option was to live in Tokyo where many of the teams are based. But from the point of view of my family, this wasn't ideal, as we'd struggle to find anywhere to live bigger than a storage container.

The next best location seemed to be Kyoto. There may not have been as many ekiden teams as in Tokyo, but there were still a few. In any case, it was only two hours to Tokyo on the bullet train, and we had our friend Max living there, who had offered to help us settle in and to help me with translations. Kyoto was also a beautiful city and close to Mount Hiei, home to the famous marathon monks. These Zen Buddhists use running as a way to reach spiritual enlightenment, traversing an incredible thousand marathons in a thousand days as part of a punishing challenge few men have ever completed. I didn't know if it was possible to meet any of them, but I was hoping to try.

Kyoto also happened to be the birthplace of ekiden running. During Japan's Edo period (1603 to 1868) couriers ran messages between Tokyo and Kyoto, the old Imperial capital. They used to stop at stations dotted along the way to rest and get refreshment, often passing the message on to another courier to carry along the next leg of the journey. It was from this that the idea for ekiden races originated.

The word 'ekiden', in fact, is made up of the Japanese characters for 'station' (駅) and 'transmit' (伝), and to symbolise this idea of passing something on the runners wear a sash, called a *tasuki*, over one shoulder, which they pass on to the next runner. The first-ever organised ekiden race began in Kyoto in 1917 and ran all the way to Tokyo, 508 km away. Somewhere in the city there is a plaque marking the spot where it all started.

The final thing that tipped us towards moving to Kyoto was a school. In England, my children go to a Steiner school, which has a different curriculum. We hoped that if they went to a Steiner school in Japan, it would feel familiar to them and provide a sense of continuity.

Steiner schools exist all over the world and there are a few in Japan. One of the biggest and most established of these is in a satellite town of Kyoto called Kyotanabe. So we decided to go there.

*

We've only been jogging for about twenty minutes when Max has to stop. He's dripping in sweat and clutching his sides. I hop around on my toes for a few moments, to see if he'll recover, but he shakes his head. We start walking back to his house together without speaking. After a while Max gets his composure back. He tells me that Kenji, the former runner his wife met, who has the amateur team, is actually from Kyotanabe, the town where the school is. He will be our neighbour once we get there.

Before we get back to Max's house, we stop at the shrine again, to sup the clear water and gather ourselves. At the entrance to the shrine is a small children's playground. A young couple sit awkwardly on a little bench holding hands, trying to look invisible as Max walks over to the swings.

He has been telling me about his friend, a yoga teacher, who has taught him some moves. He wants to show me one. Pulling himself up onto the top bar of the swing, he spins around on it on his stomach so his legs are in the air. With a steely look, he takes a deep breath and starts swinging his legs up into the sky and over, back into his starting position. Up and around he goes, blowing out deep, forceful breaths. The couple on the bench try not to look. After a few more, he stops swinging, but stays hanging upside down on the bar.

'I was told by an old university sprinting coach,' he says, 'that if you can do ten of these in a row, you can run 100m in under 12 seconds. Even to do one takes great strength.' He fixes his eyes ahead and does one more, while I stand there watching. Then he drops down, brushing the dust off his hands. 'I haven't been practising,' he says, 'so right now I can only do six.'

*

As a family from England, finding a house in Japan to rent for six months is not easy. I'm told by numerous sources that Japanese people are wary of renting to foreigners. Japan is often characterised as a homogenous island nation unwilling to engage with outsiders. For over two hundred years it was the North Korea of the world, banning people from entering or leaving the country on pain of death. Some of that isolationist feeling still lingers. A few years ago, the Japanese transport minister, whose brief included the promotion of tourism, had to resign after saying that Japanese people generally did not like foreigners. And a recent survey found hundreds of hotels in Japan that admitted they would actually turn away foreign guests.

In 2002, the Harvard Institute of Economics, in the biggest study of its kind, found Japan to be one of the most homogenous countries on earth. The whole concept of Japan as a unique, isolated island has been written about so much, both by Japanese writers and foreigners, that the genre even has its own name: *Nihonjinron*. The idea is dismissed by some academics as an outdated form of cultural nationalism, but even before I get to Japan I seem to be running into endless closed doors in my search for a team to join. As Brendan Reilly wrote in his email: 'Japan can be a maddeningly closed society at times.'

But then, just as we were about to head into the tunnel on the Eurostar at the beginning of our journey to Japan, Max called me on my phone.

'Dhar, I've found you a place to rent, but you need to tell me now if you want it.' The Kent countryside flickered by outside the window. Uma was asking me to read something. Ossian was singing excitedly at the top of his voice and bouncing on his seat.

'It's nice. Not expensive. And it's near the school,' he said.

'We'll take it,' I said. It was the first concrete news we'd had on anything since I'd started trying to arrange things in Japan. I didn't want to lose it. Besides, everything already felt so random, so disconnected, that one place was as good as another right then. I felt we had little option but to trust in the gods on this one. And Max.

Seconds later our train nosedived into the Channel Tunnel, and the phone reception died.

'Looks like we have a house to live in when we get there,' I told Marietta in the seat in front.

'Really? What's it like?'

'I don't know.'

*

The house is narrow and tall, neatly fitted in between two similar houses in a steep little cul-de-sac in suburban Kyotanabe. To get there we cram into Max's little red sports car. As soon as we sit down he sprays us in effective micro-organisms, and then he sprays the car. He even sprays the tyres, explaining patiently how it prolongs their life.

We drive down through the city, past the Imperial Palace, out into the suburbs of southern Kyoto and onto the motorway, which rises up into the air on concrete stilts. The roads curve and cross each other in large spaghetti junctions, before we descend once again to ground level, driving through some desolate-looking flatlands, rice fields dotted with unused warehouses, barns, peeling billboards.

After about ten minutes we arrive into another built-up area, full of large warehouse shops, parking lots, a drive-through McDonald's.

'Welcome to your neighbourhood,' says Max, as Marietta and I look at each other nervously. The children get excited when we pass a fire station. The fire engines, glistening red in their sheds, are about half the size of the ones in England. There is also a mini-ambulance parked outside.

As we drive on, I find myself looking in vain between the gaps in the buildings for any sign of a park, somewhere green to play, to run, some respite from the endless concrete.

At a Lawson convenience store we turn right up a steep hill, past the Steiner school and into a residential area. It's still the summer holidays, and the streets are quiet. The temperature is around 30°C. The houses sit side by side close to the road, with barely the width of a person between them. Most of them have the blinds drawn closed.

Finally, we stop outside our house. Our home for the next six months. We get out. We must be quite an unusual sight around here, but there's no sign of life, of anyone watching us. Max unlocks the front door. Inside it's dark, with the blinds down, and completely bare. No furniture, or pots or pans. Not even a fridge or washing machine.

'Let's go shopping,' says Max.

4

And so our new life in Japan begins. Before we left England, I read *The Wind-Up Bird Chronicle* by the Japanese writer Haruki Murakami. It's set in a nondescript, suburban Japanese community, just like this one. But under the calm veneer of normality lies a dark, twisted and surreal reality. I wonder, as we roll our new futons out across the bare, wooden floor, what we'll find in our little cul-de-sac.

The first neighbour to introduce herself is a lady called Rie who lives next door. She's a solid woman with a big, friendly smile. And she speaks English. She spent six months living in London when she was younger, before she got married and had children. Over the next six months she becomes our own fairy godmother. Whenever we're in trouble, when we don't know how to read the mail in our mailbox, or don't know how to pay our bills, or get books from the library, or find a doctor, she arrives in a cloud of sparkles, tinkling on our door, offering to help.

One time a few months after moving in we accidentally order a big box of shellfish. The doorbell goes and there's a man on the step with a box and a piece of paper. I've no idea what he's saying, or what the paper says, so I take them both from him. My kids come to see what it is. We lift the lid and inside it's full of ice and bags of water filled with still squirming shellfish.

'Marietta,' I call. 'Do you know anything about this?'

The only thing to do at a time like this is to go and see Rie. She looks at the paper and tells us we must have ticked the wrong box on a form or something. We use a local food-delivery service and do this a lot. One time we mistakenly order a box of about a hundred onions. We've barely made a dent on them when the following week, another huge box of onions arrives.

But this shellfish needs eating pretty quickly, judging by the way it's wriggling around in the bags of water. The problem is, we're all vegetarians. Rie, as always, giggles and tells us not to worry. She will buy the shellfish off us and eat them for supper that evening.

'My children will be very happy,' she says, as though we're doing her a favour somehow.

The other people we meet in the first few days are a family who live across the street and have three children at the Steiner school. They have one daughter in Lila's class and one in Uma's, which is a happy coincidence. They also have a fifteen-year-old son. They don't speak a word of English, but when they hear I've come to Japan to write a book about running, the mother, Yoshiko, gets very excited. It takes us a while to work out what she's saying, but it turns out her son goes running with his friends. Every morning before school. At 5.30.

I think I must be misunderstanding her. A group of fifteen-year-old boys running at dawn every morning. Really? They're not part of a team, they just do it for fun, she says. I can't quite imagine it, so I ask her if I could join him one morning. She looks at me as though I'm a holy man offering her a free pass to heaven.

'Thank you,' she keeps saying, while I wonder what I'm letting myself in for.

*

The next day, at 5.20 a.m., my alarm goes off. I pull on my running clothes and step outside the door into the quiet morning. It's already warm. The boy from across the street, Ryohei, is waiting on the road, wearing a white mask over his mouth. He has his bike with him. He bows humbly and nods to the bikes lined up in our drive. We've managed to get hold of one for everyone except me, so I clamber onto Marietta's and follow him down the road.

Outside the Lawson convenience store he stops, gets off his bike and starts looking around furtively in all directions, as though his friends might be hiding among the bushes. Nothing moves in the grey half-light of the morning. It's still very early. Then we see another young boy cycling along the empty road towards us. He pulls up beside us without saying anything, hopping off his bike. He doesn't look surprised to see me. A few minutes later a third boy arrives. He smiles and says hello, in English, before turning to the others and talking to them quietly. They're all wearing shorts and T-shirts. Nothing specifically for running, just cotton T-shirts and regular shorts.

It's hard to imagine teenagers in England getting up this early in the morning to go running together. I don't know how common it is in Japan, either. It could be just some crazy coincidence that of all the back streets in Japan, I happen to have moved to the only one where teenagers go running at 5.30 a.m. But that seems unlikely. On another day, leaving the house early, I find a young boy in the street practising baseball. He's throwing it repeatedly against a wall and catching it. Another time, returning home late one night, I find two men practising baseball with about two hundred shuttlecocks. The street is covered in them, like a spillage of little paper lanterns. What the two men, the young boy, and these teenagers I'm with this morning all have in common is the earnest intent of their practice. They are not 'playing', they are clearly training. This is serious. It's an attitude to sport I will encounter repeatedly during my time in Japan.

After waiting a few more minutes without anyone else showing up, the three boys climb on their bikes and we ride off. They've got whizzy mountain bikes that glide smoothly through the quiet streets. Marietta's bike is a clunky old sit-up-and-beg bike with no gears and a rattly child seat on the back. It's also too small for me, so I have to work hard to keep up with them.

After about five minutes' riding we pop out of the suburban streets into a wide, flat area of parcelled-up, cultivated land. The sun is just rising, landing golden across the rows and rows of aubergines and orange trees. Suddenly it makes sense to be up and outside this early, riding like four pioneers across the new earth.

We ride in silence, between the fields, until we get to a river. We then follow the river and come to a stop below a huge bridge. Above, the first cars of the day are purring by, the occasional lorry. Here, by the road, are warehouses, a car showroom, some apartment blocks. A few elderly people are out walking along the river path. Not strolling gently, or walking a dog, as they would in England, but in sports gear, swinging their arms purposefully, taking exercise.

We leave the bikes by the grass bank. There's no need to lock them. Then we head up to the starting point, up on the bridge by the road.

It seems a shame to stand by the road to warm up, with all the space out along by the river, but this is their starting point, a line painted on the ground right here. 'Five kilo,' Ryohei tells me, meaning five kilometres, and I don't doubt that they have it marked out exactly. In any case, they don't warm up for long. *Ich, ni, san* . . . and we're off.

They sprint away from me as though it's a 100m race. My old legs creak into action. It hurts my still sleepy tendons to run this fast this early. I need to do some jogging first, but they're running off along the river into the distance. Are they really this fast? I try to get my body moving, to catch them up.

After a few minutes, the first of them comes back to me. He's barely jogging as I go by him. Ryohei and his other friend are coming back to me, too, running much slower now. As I catch them, though, Ryohei suddenly surges again. We reach a mark on the path and they both turn around. We run back towards the start together, moving at a decent pace, with Ryohei constantly surging and slowing. Eventually he drops off the pace and his friend and I push on. I'm feeling warmed up now and running easily, but I don't want to race away from them. We finish together back up by the road, everyone stopping their watches. Ryohei has finally cast off his mask and I get to see his face for the first time. He is breathing heavily, but smiling.

'Thank you,' he says, bowing to me.

They're all much more chatty now. Ryohei's friend, the faster one, speaks some English. I ask him why he gets up so early every morning to train.

'It is my hobby,' is all he says.

As we pull ourselves onto our bikes and set off home, it's barely 6.30 a.m., but training is done for another day. Until tomorrow, when their *hobby* will get them out of bed early yet again.

On the way home they talk to each other, riding slowly, lazily, leaning their elbows on the handlebars. They've left themselves plenty of time, so there's no need to rush back. At every set of traffic lights they stop and wait patiently, even in the wide open spaces when there isn't the faintest murmur of a car anywhere.

This willingness to follow rules is something I notice a lot here in Japan. Even among teenagers, expressions of rebellion are usually limited to clothes or hairstyles.

One day I board a local train in my area and three teenage boys are sitting on the floor of the carriage. They're wearing ripped jeans and talking loudly to each other. It's probably the most anti-social behaviour I witness in my entire time in Japan. They're not being rude to anyone, but it's quite shocking, after months sitting on silent trains, to see people chatting loudly and sitting on the floor.

However, as the journey progresses and the train begins to get more crowded, I notice the three boys stand up to make room for the other passengers, and they begin to talk more quietly. They're so well behaved, in fact, that one of them is wearing a face mask. He probably has a bit of a cold, and doesn't want to spread any germs.

Of course, crime exists in Japan – although it is lower than in any other industrialised country – and teenagers rebel, but my overriding sense is of an eagerness to conform, to abide by the rules, to fit in.

At the heart of it is a fundamental difference in the perception of a person's place in society. One saying I hear repeatedly in Japan is *The nail that sticks out gets hammered down*. To western ears, this sounds terrible. It says, don't stand out, don't try to do anything different, but keep your head down and work together.

In her book *Understanding Japanese Society*, Joy Hendry writes about how this concept of social harmony and co-operation is ingrained in Japanese children from an early age.

The annual sports day at the kindergarten where she worked, she says, emphasised co-operation over individual competition. She says popular events 'included tug-of-war and the three-, five- or seven-legged races where co-operation is vital for success'.

She adds: 'Television programmes for children often reiterate the theme of co-operation, as a single hero tries unsuccessfully to defeat the monster, or other alien force, until he gains the co-operation of other victims of the danger.'

Among adults, more activities are carried out in orderly groups than I'm used to in the UK. Wherever you go, especially if it is a tourist attraction, but even often in nondescript suburbs of unremarkable towns, you are likely to see groups of people being ushered around in an orderly fashion by people holding flags in the air. Often they'll all be wearing the same jacket or hat.

This conformist streak may explain in part why ekidens are so popular in Japan, why the particularly individual sport of long-distance running has been turned into a team sport.

Many of Japan's top ekiden teams were formed in the aftermath of the Second World War as part of the country's rebuilding process. Races were seen as a way of bringing people together and boosting morale and community spirit after the terrible events of the war. In this period many of Japan's most famous marathons were started, such as Lake Biwa (first run in 1946), and Fukuoka (1947), as well as many of the top ekidens, which were initially thought of as a way to prepare athletes for running the more serious marathons.

The main races were sponsored by newspapers – most of them still are – so people got to read about the teams and runners, and follow the results. This helped make them popular with the public. As Japan's economy grew in the post-war period, the companies began to spend more on their teams, signing up the best university runners and giving them time off work to train.

All this support and focus on distance running paid off, and by the 1960s, as Japan was growing into one of the world's economic powerhouses, its runners began to dominate marathon running almost in the way the Kenyans and Ethiopians do today. In 1965, ten of the top eleven times worldwide were run by Japanese men. In 1966, it was fifteen of the top seventeen.

A widely admired characteristic of Japanese society at this time was its concept of *wa*, or group harmony. It was championed by the coach of the most famous Japanese baseball team ever, the Yomiuri Giants team that won nine consecutive national titles from 1965 to 1973.

Even more than ekiden, baseball is the most popular sport in Japan, and according to William W. Kelly, a professor of anthropology and Japanese studies at Yale University, the Yomiuri Giants' success 'was celebrated as a powerful synecdoche for the confident, industrious society and competitive, resurgent economy that Japan saw itself becoming. Directed by a marshal-general-like manager . . . the Giants projected a player image and a playing style that was coordinated, committed, and collective.'

Many of Japan's booming firms held the Giants up as an ideal and used them to foster a spirit of self-sacrifice in which workers were expected to commit to the harmony of the group – in this case, the company. This meant putting their jobs first, their families second and their own self-interest last. The typical image of the salaryman, or *sarariman* as they're known in Japan, was a person who would get to work early, leave late, and go drinking with his colleagues, before grabbing a few hours' sleep and rushing in to work early again the next morning. The number of sleeping men in suits I saw on late-evening trains suggests this approach, while perhaps not as prevalent as it once was, is still fairly common.

Many companies adopted *wa* as their company slogan and Japan's continued economic rise in the post-war period was put down in large part to this spirit.

Robert Whiting, in his book about Japanese baseball *You Gotta Have Wa*, first published in 1989, writes: 'In Japan, the word for individualism, *kojin-shugi*, is almost a dirty word . . . The concept and practice of group harmony, or *wa*, is what most dramatically differentiates Japanese baseball from the American game. It is the connecting thread running through all Japanese life and sports.'

'Even the bees have it,' Max says to me one day as we drive around the Kyotanabe suburbs in search of a second-hand washing machine.

'The bees?'

'They once tried to introduce European honey bees to Japan,' he explains, 'but they were wiped out by the giant Japanese hornets. The European bees had no defence. When the hornets arrived at the hive, the worker bees would rush out one by one to fend off the attack. But they were no match for the giant hornets, which used their sharp claws to rip the heads off the European bees one by one. A small squadron of hornets can massacre an entire hive in a matter of hours.

'The Japanese bees, however, take a different approach. Rather than rush out in a hopeless flight to the death, they wait for the first scout hornet to enter the nest. Then, in unison, all together, they swarm around it in one tight cluster. Rather than attempting to sting the hornet, they all vibrate their wings until the temperature begins to rise, and the carbon dioxide they produce fills the hive. The hornet, unable to survive such high temperatures or levels of CO_2, has no chance and dies.

'The power of the group,' he says, pulling in at another recycling shop, rows of bikes and washing machines lined up outside.

Ekiden embodied the spirit of *wa* perfectly. A relay team could only succeed if all its component parts did their bit.

Everyone had to pull together for the good of the team. It suited the spirit of the time, and gradually ekidens began to overtake marathons in popularity.

Of course, it's too simplistic to attribute the rise of ekiden solely to the conformist nature of Japanese society. Indeed, even this widely held view of Japan as a collectivist society begins to come apart at the seams under scrutiny.

'If the Japanese are such conformists,' asks Brian Moeran, a professor of business anthropology at the Copenhagen Business School, 'how come all their sports – judo, karate, sumo and so on – are so individual?'

It's a good question. Roland Kelts, the Japanese-American author of *Japanamerica: How Japanese Pop Culture has Invaded the US*, says ekiden suits Japan in part because it maintains an emphasis on individual performance.

'While there is a tendency in Japan to prioritise the harmony of the group over the desires of the individual,' he writes, 'that doesn't mean that individuality and individual performance and responsibility are devalued. In fact, the concept of *amae*, or the need to be interdependent and to remain in good stead with others, places a very high value on individual behaviour and performance. You have to be a better person as an individual if others are relying upon you.'

In this way, he says, ekiden is an ideal sport for the Japanese, for while each individual has to perform at a high level, the goal is success for the group.

Baseball also contains at its heart this battle between individuals – in this case the pitcher versus the batter – fighting for the team.

It's not so much conformity, or not sticking out, that

characterises both of these sports, but rather an emphasis on individual responsibility, each person playing their part for the success of the team. In ekiden, even more than most other team sports, one poor performance can ruin everything. Indeed, the word I will hear most often when people talk to me about ekiden over the coming months is 'responsibility', which holds succinctly within it the great play between the individual and the group.

With all these thoughts milling around in my head, a few days later I finally get a chance to meet some ekiden runners.

5

My first stop in the Japanese running world is the amateur team run by Max's contact, the former professional runner Kenji Takao. His team is called Blooming. 'Isn't Blooming a swear word?' Uma asks me when she hears the name. I think they mean blooming as in a flower opening up, or a person realising his potential, rather than *what a blooming mess*. 'Oh,' she says, disappointed.

The team meets in a place called the Dawn Centre in Osaka. I go there with Max, who is planning to join in with the training session. Despite struggling on our runs from his house, Max says his goal is to be outrunning me by the end of six months. He's not joking, or trying to rile me, but says it as though it's already a factual certainty. In the same voice he tells me which platform to head to at the train station, he tells me that in six months he will be running quicker than me.

Part of his confidence comes from the fact that he knew me in my non-running days. These memories have clearly clouded his view of me as a runner.

'I had no idea you were interested in sport,' he says. 'I couldn't imagine you running.'

On one of our first runs he offers to lend me a pair of his shorts. 'I don't think they'll fit,' I say, holding them up.

'Come on,' he says. 'I'm sure you can squeeze into them.'

He can't quite believe it when I try them on and they're way too big.

We emerge out of the subway station in Osaka beside a huge road junction with concrete bridges arching over our heads. The Dawn Centre is nearby, a tall glass building full of meeting rooms like a kind of convention centre.

'Up on the fourth floor,' says Max, pointing to a board in the reception. The board is covered in what looks to me like random squiggles. I'm glad he came.

The Blooming meeting room is full of tables set facing a whiteboard along one wall. It looks like a classroom. Kenji, a short, skinny man, rushes over when he sees us, all smiles and bows. He tells us to sit down. The room is full of men, most of them older than me. They all sit in layers of running kit despite the heat outside, chatting quietly, not acknowledging the presence of the two tall *gaijin* who have just walked in. On another table at the front, Kenji has laid out some things for sale, mostly products to treat injuries.

After a few minutes the door opens and the women come in, filtering into the empty seats. Kenji makes some jokes, but everyone else sits quietly. Max looks around, grinning, as though he finds it all amusing.

Kenji is saying something about me, Finn-san. Max says we need to go up and introduce ourselves. I stand next to Kenji as Max translates. The lights of Osaka are coming on outside the window as the day begins to wind down.

I tell them I wrote a book about running in Kenya, and now I've come to Japan to learn about Japanese running, and especially ekiden. Everyone in Japan is surprised that I've come here to learn about running. They don't realise that the Japanese are one of the world's best distance-running nations, or that ekiden is a sport unique to Japan.

They give me a round of applause. After we sit down, one man comes over to speak to Max, crouching down at our table. He asks what my best time is for 10K. When I say 35 minutes, they look at each other, evidently impressed. The man says he is one person short for an ekiden team in a few months time, at Lake Biwa. Would I like to run?

I jump at the chance. This is what I was hoping for. *Arrigato*, I say, bowing my head. He nods, his mop of hair almost covering his eyes. He looks different to the others. More calculating, aloof. Not so awkward and self-deprecating. For some reason he reminds me of Charles Bronson. Max tells me that his name is Morita. He is the Blooming 'ace', the team's fastest runner.

Before we set off for the night's training, Kenji gives a talk to the group. They pay good money to run here and part of the deal is that they get some wisdom and insight from the former champion runner. Kenji also runs with them, though he has just had an operation on a long-term injury, so right now he can't do much more than hobble. Even this he does pretty quickly, though. All his movements are quick. His talking, too.

I don't know if it's for my benefit or not, but he talks to them about ekiden. He tells them that ekiden is more popular in Japan than marathon. It's more than a race, he says, it's about people coming together and working towards the same goal.

'No nails sticking out,' says Max, with a see-what-I-mean look. 'No one trying to go their own way.'

The most popular ekiden, Kenji tells the group, is the Hakone ekiden, raced between men's university teams. This, he says, is because it is so dramatic. It is longer than most other ekidens, running over two days, on a tough course, and the lead is always changing. The professional, corporate teams, he says, are too slick, too organised, too machine-like. They always run as expected, exactly on pace, with no surprises. But in Hakone, where all the runners are university students, anything can happen.

I take lots of notes. This is all excellent stuff. Kenji Takao's Guide to Ekidens.

Finally it's time to start running. Kenji's team of coaches – he has three – explain the session on the whiteboard. They call it 'forty-minute build-up'. Basically, we run slowly for twenty minutes and then get faster.

Once the coaches give the word, we make our way, a shuffling mass of mildly decrepit-looking runners, along the strip-lit corridor and into the lifts. As the lifts open downstairs, I make the apparent faux pas of walking out first. Max tells me I should have let Kenji out first, as he's the most important member of the group.

'It's OK, you didn't know,' he says. It's hard to tell how offended everyone is by this. They don't seem to hold it against me, but carry on chatting to each other as we head out into the muggy night, jogging along a delivery alley at the back of the building and across a road to the entrance gates of a park. Rising out of the dark foliage in the near distance is a huge, multi-layered building, lit up against the sky.

'Osaka Castle,' Kenji says proudly. It's a fine sight. '*Sugoi*,' I say. *Amazing*.

The park is crawling with runners, all running back and forth along the same stretch of road that partly circles the castle. They run in groups mostly, jogging slowly.

We join the flow of other runners, sticking together in a big group. The pace is very slow. A few of them venture to ask me a question or two, which Max responds to in great detail. I have no idea what he's telling them, but they *ooh* and *aah* and look at me as though I've done great things. I give up asking Max to repeat everything and trust to the wind the image he is building of this man from England who is writing a book, and walks out of lifts first.

After exactly twenty minutes, the pace begins to pick up and the group starts to stretch out. The road curves around the castle for about a mile and so we simply run back and forth repeatedly along the same stretch. I'm feeling easy and so I stick with the fastest group, led by Morita. I'm expecting the pace to continue to increase, but it stays the same, at around seven minutes per mile. I can't help it, but with about a minute to go, I take off, leaving them behind. Over the years I've joined many different running clubs and it's always tricky on those first few nights. Each running club has its established pecking order, and the last thing anyone likes is for some upstart to appear and run roughshod all over it.

I remember when I first joined my club in Devon after I came back from training in Kenya. The man in charge asked me if I ran much, and I told him I'd just been in Kenya for six months. I'd run a marathon there in 3 hours 20 minutes. But it was a hot day. On sandy trails. At an altitude of over five thousand feet.

'I'll put you in the threes,' he said. I'd read on the club's website that they had five groups with the ones being the slowest and the fives being the fastest. The threes seemed a little slow.

'I was training with Wilson Kipsang in Kenya,' I protested. 'For six months.'

He looked at me dubiously. 'OK,' he said, 'You can come with me in the fours.'

We set off in a small group at a relaxed pace, down to the seafront in Torquay. Fresh from six months' training at altitude, I was tripping over myself wanting to go quicker. Just then we started to get overtaken by lots of faster runners, skipping onto the road to pass us.

'Who are they?' I asked the man in charge.

'The fives,' he said. They looked like they were going more my pace. It was quite a big group, too. I felt I was missing out.

'Can I run with them?'

'They won't wait for you if you can't keep up,' he said. 'We will.'

I hesitated for a moment. I knew I was annoying him, thinking I knew better. I admit, 3:20 wasn't the most impressive marathon time, but it was in tough conditions. Before they were out of sight, I made up my mind.

'I'll take my chances,' I said, and raced off after the fives.

In the end, it was fine. It was a good group but I was able to stay with them easily. Afterwards, though, the man in charge gave me a dark look, but didn't say anything. It was months before he fully forgave me.

Here in Osaka, I tell myself to sit back, to run with the group. It seems disrespectful to go blazing off on my first session. But the urge to just go, to let the legs do their thing, is too strong. At the end they all stand shaking their heads in disbelief at how fast I ran. Max, who dropped out a lap before the end, stands there laughing. The only one who doesn't say anything is Morita. He looks at me from under his hair, almost scowling.

I must admit, I'm surprised to find myself so far ahead. I'm not in great shape and I'm still finding the humidity difficult. It makes me wonder where all the faster runners are. Are they all professional? There are around 1,500 professional runners in Japan, signed up by companies to run for their ekiden teams. In the UK, which has roughly half the population of Japan, there are probably fewer than twenty professional distance runners – people who make a living from running. This means many of Britain's most talented athletes find themselves with normal jobs and paying to run with athletics clubs in the evenings. Would these top club runners be professional in Japan? If I were Japanese, could I even have made a career out of it?

The level of professionalism in Japan in part explains the disparity in results between the two nations. With more time and resources dedicated to training, many of Britain's top runners would likely be faster, while many more would have an incentive to nurture their talent. Instead, most runners have to squeeze their training in around jobs and family. In most cases they're not encouraged to run, to get up early for extra sessions, to spend money on massages, on core workouts in the gym. In the UK, even for very good runners, it's a hobby. In Japan, for those at the same level, it can be a viable career, with coaching, sponsorship and recognition.

On the way back to the Dawn Centre, our backs and brows now dripping in sweat, Max tells me he's happy with his run. He says it's a good start. 'I can feel it, right now my body is making haemoglobin. I've always been good at that. In six months . . . you better watch out.'

Back in the conference room the men get changed back into their office clothes, wiping themselves dry with small towels, turning themselves back into accountants, doctors, sales executives. Only Kenji and I remain in our running clothes. When the men are ready, the women return, also turned back into civilians. Someone hands around delicately wrapped biscuits as Kenji gives them a debrief. Max doesn't bother to translate. I think he's too tired.

*

While things have started well for my ekiden research, with a spot on a team already lined up, back in Kyotanabe my daughters have the rather more daunting task of settling in to a Japanese school.

They're both amazingly sanguine about it as the first day approaches, and on the first morning they get up and get ready without fuss. They even seem to be looking forward to it.

'Lila says it's good to go to school because it gives you something to do when it's raining,' Uma informs me.

Bags on their backs, with new shoes, dresses and pencil cases, they skip ahead of us as we make the short walk to school through our suburban homeland. It's only when we get within about fifty metres of the school that Uma starts to slow down, pulling me back by the hand.

'I want you to come into the classroom,' she says. We've already told them we'll do this. We've even talked it through with the teachers. I'm imagining a bit of staring from the other children, perhaps a few giggles behind hands. But nothing like the commotion they experienced at school in Kenya.

'Of course,' I say. 'It's going to be fine.'

*

As we enter the school compound, all hell breaks loose. It's the first day back for the children after the summer break, so they're excited anyway, but when they see us they start whizzing around, sliding across the wooden floors, yelling and pointing as we make our way to the entrance. It's like entering a house full of excited puppies as they rush up to us, stop, confused, then whirl away yelping.

We have to push our way through the melee to get to the classrooms. Marietta and Ossian go in with Lila, while I go with Uma. She is keeping her head down, holding tight to my hand. The children show us to Uma's desk, but even I'm finding it hard to cope with the chaos. They keep tapping on my arm and asking me questions I can't understand. The teacher doesn't seem to be anywhere in sight.

We work out where Uma's desk is and she sits down, still holding on to my arm, waiting for the storm to pass. I stand there awkwardly, smiling at the children as they continue to rush around. I wish I knew how to say 'I don't understand'. But I can't even say that.

Finally, the tinkling of a bell signals the teacher's arrival.

It quietens the children down, but they're still chattering as she comes over to us, smiling. She takes Uma's hand and talks to her in English. Uma, looking up for the first time, smiles weakly. I tell her I need to go now and she looks at me through moist eyes. She lets go of my arm and I slip out, hoping she will be all right.

*

When I pick them up later that day, they seem happy enough. I tentatively ask how it went and they both say 'good', which is their standard answer when they aren't in the mood for retelling events. That afternoon they play outside with the other children from the street, happily throwing water balloons in the air so they burst open on the ground. As easy as that, it feels like we've made it. Our little suburban house, the children at school, already making friends, our neat row of bikes in the front yard. Our life in Japan, it seems, is up and running.

But that evening, as we sit in our 'Japanese room', with its sliding paper doors and tatami-mat floor, the remains of supper on the low table, Lila sits playing with her chopsticks, moving the last few grains of rice around and around in her bowl. 'Uma says she doesn't want to go to school tomorrow,' she says, looking up at us. And then suddenly they're both crying, saying it's horrible, that the children keep staring at them and asking them questions they can't understand. They had the wrong lunch, they say, the wrong hats, the wrong shoes. 'I don't like being different,' says Uma, breaking my heart with her sobs.

That night, after they're asleep, Marietta and I stare at each other. This wasn't the plan. We feel for the children, but we can't give up after one day. I feel that if they can come through this and make it work it will be an important life lesson. They'll know and understand what it feels like to be different. And if they can cope, and even begin to fit in, speak some Japanese, learn to adapt to the situation they find themselves in, well, it will be an achievement they'll carry with them through their entire lives. I have a vision of them one day arriving at the school, greeting their friends in Japanese, sliding happily into their seats, laughing at one of the boys' jokes. But is this really possible?

The next morning, as I sit in on Uma's class for ten minutes to try to help her settle, I find it hard to believe it is. Words fly scattergun back and forth across the room. Trying to make sense of them seems impossible. After the ten minutes, I leave her sitting at her desk with a stoical look on her face. She doesn't protest as I sneak away, realising perhaps that there's nothing I can do to help.

The next few days we have more protests, but gradually they begin to subside. Marietta tells me not to reason with the children or plead with them to go to school in the mornings, but to simply stay strong in the assumption that they will go. So while they say they're not going, we calmly make up their lunches, and help them pick out their clothes, find their books for them. It seems to work. While I worry that I'm ignoring their concerns, I know we'll all be disappointed if we give up without making a real go of it. Besides, we've moved to this nondescript suburb to be beside the school. We've paid six months' rent in advance on a house with no garden. If they don't go to school, we could all end up facing a serious case of cabin fever.

*

My daughters' troubles settling in at school leave me reassessing why I've come all this way to Japan. I haven't met any of the great runners yet, but from the results I've seen someone somewhere must be doing something right. I just have to dig deeper and find it. But why is it so interesting?

Partly, I'm intrigued that long-distance running is so popular as a spectator sport here. In other parts of the world, only the most dedicated fans get excited about long-distance running races. Most people watching marathons in Europe or America don't know the names of the elite runners at the front. They are only interested in the progress of friends or relatives toiling away gamely further back. The leaders are only relevant as a benchmark, an illustration of what is possible. It's impressive to see them run by, but their names, their histories, their rivalries, are irrelevant. But in Japan, these elite runners are stars.

The other reason the running culture in Japan is fascinating is the possibility that maybe I can learn something that can help me continue to improve as a runner. People often ask me how my running changed after six months in Kenya. The truth is that, mostly, it didn't. I was inspired by Kenya to run more often, to channel the passion and enthusiasm I witnessed there into my own practice. But some of the key things that make them great, I simply can't replicate. I can't conjure up a rural upbringing for myself, running every day to school, to the river, to the fields, all in bare feet and at an altitude of over two thousand metres.

But nobody in Japan has that either. Society, in terms of comfort and convenience – those things such as TVs, cars, offices, that weaken our ability to run – is fairly similar to the UK. At least on the surface. But yet in Japan there are thousands of super-fast runners. Why? It's an intriguing question, and the next stop in my quest to find the answer is Ritsumeikan University in Kyoto.

6

As you arrive at Ritsumeikan University on the outskirts of Kyoto, the first thing you see is the running track. It sits in a grass-banked bowl below the road level, in front of the main buildings. Everyone arriving and leaving on the endless shuttle buses to and from the train station can see the track and the athletes running around on it, a regular reminder of the central role of sport, and particularly running, in university life here in Japan.

As well as organising his Blooming amateur team, Kenji recently started coaching the men's ekiden team at Ritsumeikan University. This is one of the biggest teams outside the Tokyo region.

In Japan, the most popular ekiden teams are the university teams. This is partly because, as Kenji pointed out to the Blooming runners, the professional teams are too well drilled and the racing just isn't as exciting. But mainly it is because of Hakone.

At the centre of the Japanese running world sits one race, one event that towers above all else: the Hakone ekiden. Already its name has been popping up everywhere, but by the end of my time in Japan, even the sound of the word 'Hakone' seems to echo with drama and meaning. I can see people react when I mention it, their eyes widening. '*Ikimasu* [I'll be there],' I tell them, reverential, as though it's a holy place of pilgrimage. As though, now, when they hear this, they'll know just how serious I am.

Hakone is not only the biggest race on the Japanese running calendar, it's the biggest annual sporting event in Japan. Run over two full days, it regularly draws television audiences of close to thirty per cent. The viewing figures are similar to those of the Super Bowl in the US, and more than the FA Cup Final in the UK usually gets. And this is on 2 and 3 January, prime viewing time, when people are still off work after New Year.

In addition to those watching on television, the streets along all 217.9 km of the course are lined deep with spectators. It really is epic.

For months before the race, we receive junk mail through our letter box in Kyotanabe selling Hakone merchandise: towels, jackets, baseball caps. Sapporo even bring out a commemorative beer for the occasion.

The Hakone ekiden reaches beyond the running world to those who usually have no interest in running. It is a national event. It may well be the most watched foot race in the world.

But like a black hole sucking in everything that gets too close to it, the popularity of the Hakone ekiden brings with it many problems for Japanese running.

Hakone is only open to men's university teams from the Kanto region of Japan, the region around Tokyo. It is, essentially, a local university race. So the first problem is that it excludes all the universities from the rest of the country, including Kenji's Ritsumeikan in Kyoto, which is in the Kansai region.

All the best high-school runners want to run Hakone. This means that a coach like Kenji, scouting for runners for his non-Hakone university, has to work with what is left after the Hakone teams have finished creaming off the top talent. Of course, there are some late bloomers, or runners who were injured in high school, or not focused on their training, who come good later, but generally the top high-school runners go on to become the top university runners.

The result of all this is an insurmountable two-tier system: those in the Kanto region and those not in Kanto.

The extent to which Kanto universities are willing to go to win Hakone is illustrated by the unveiling, shortly before I arrive in Japan, of a building for the 2012 Hakone winning team from Toyo University. The university has built its ekiden team its own state-of-the-art base, complete with gym, hot and ice baths, a dining room and enough dormitories to house a hundred people. The building is right beside the university track, although all the bedrooms face out over a nearby park.

'If you can see the track all day long it keeps you from relaxing properly,' explained the Toyo head coach, who had a key role in the design of the building.

Interestingly, in women's ekiden running, Hakone has the opposite affect. With the Kanto region universities obsessing over their men's teams in the hope of shining at Hakone, their women's teams become neglected. In the rest of the country, however, with no Hakone to play for, the universities put more time and effort into their women's teams, and the result is that the best women's ekiden teams come from non-Hakone universities. And the very best of them all is Ritsumeikan, the national champions in 2012 for a record seventh time.

The first time I arrive at Ritsumeikan it is in the back of Kenji's car. He picks Max and me up from the train station. He has a young high-school student with him in the front seat. 'Osaka, number two,' he says proudly. Apparently she's the second fastest 3,000m runner for her age in the nearby city of Osaka. Kenji has taken her under his wing and has high hopes for her. 'Tokyo Olympics,' he says, his eyes popping with excitement. The girl just smiles politely.

As we drive in through the campus gates, the women's team is lapping the track in a big group. They all run with the same shuffling style so distinctive of Japanese women runners. It may be effective, but it never looks particularly impressive. From a distance it could be a group of joggers, rather than one of the most powerful women's running teams in the world.

Unfortunately, the coach of the women's team has banned her athletes from talking to Kenji or any of the men's team. She doesn't want them being corrupted or led astray. One time, months later, we bump into two of the women runners in the Ritsumeikan canteen. They are friendly, but keep looking around to check that they're not being watched. In the end they get too nervous about being spotted and leave us.

Kenji laughs when I ask him if I would be able to interview any of them.

'No, no,' he says, shaking his head. He parks his car and we walk down the banked concrete seating to the track, where the men's team are loitering, chatting and stretching casually on rubber mats laid out on the floor. '*Os*,' they all say as we approach, muttering it under their breaths mostly. Kenji, carrying an armful of folders and clipboards, makes a joke, giggling away to himself. A few of the runners give a wry smile, but mostly they just carry on with what they're doing.

I'm not sure if they're expecting me. Max tells me that Kenji is happy for me to chat to the team and possibly run with them, so I've come in my running kit. Max, too, is ready to run.

'Let's see what happens,' he says.

Once Kenji has said hello to everyone, he introduces us to the team captain, Daichi Hosoda. He has a big, swooping haircut and a wide boyish smile, and shakes hands and bows politely, welcoming us to the training session. In all, there are around thirty runners in the ekiden team. Tonight's session, Kenji explains, is a 15km timed run in a big group. He asks us if we'll join in. '*Ju kilo*,' he suggests as a lighter session for Max and me. *Ten kilometres*. 'OK?' They're planning to run at a pace of four minutes per kilometre, which is considerably faster than the fast pace at the Blooming group. But not so fast I shouldn't be able to keep up for 10km. I have a couple of weeks' running under my belt since our month-long journey and I'm beginning to feel the semblance of some fitness returning. The route is back and forth along a 1.25 km stretch of road, so we'll pass back by the start every 2.5 km, giving us ample opportunities to drop out if we need to. It's a hot evening, but the humidity has died down a little from the previous few weeks.

Before we start, we gather in a big circle and Kenji formally introduces Max and me. He tells them not to be shy and to speak to us, and one immediately ventures to ask us both how old we are. Max tells them I'm thirty-nine and that he's thirty-five. The runner says something in response, Max replies, and they all laugh.

'What did he say?' I ask Max.

'He said I look much younger,' Max tells me, with a smile.

With no such compliments for me, we head over to the start line, and after lining up quickly, everyone setting their watches, a few last-minute head counts, a few words of encouragement, we're off. I tuck myself into the middle of the group. Out at the front, the captain leads the way. It's been a while since I ran at pace with a big group and it feels nice to be back among the pack, our feet clattering the road together. Everyone is running easy, but nobody speaks. The challenges lie further ahead, for now we need to be patient.

The road meanders around the back of the university, past the tennis courts, a few large car parks, and then, at a marked spot on the road, we circle around and head back.

We pass Max coming the other way. He has dropped off the pace, but is pushing hard enough, his face concentrated, ignoring us as we rush by. As we turn around again to begin lap two, back where we started, a team of managers and coaches stand calling out our times. One of them, the team trainer, is taking pictures with an iPad.

Out and back we go for a second time. It's only now that I notice that it's a slight incline on the way out. The muggy night seems to be closing in on me as I run, pressing on my face, my shoulders, draining the energy from my legs. I can feel myself drifting to the back of the group. On the downhill section back to the start I make a special effort to stick close to everyone, but my body is feeling the strain.

As we head out for the third lap I suddenly find myself adrift, together with one other runner. I look across at him. He glances back, his head tilted to one side slightly, an anxious look on his face.

For me, I can drop out whenever I want. Everyone is expecting me to. I'm not a runner, I'm a writer. For me, it's just a bit of fun. This thought is always a comfort at moments like this, when the crunch begins and my legs burn to slow down; although it also brings with it a tinge of sadness. In my own mind, I *am* a runner. Until, that is, I run with real runners. The experience can be deflating.

My friend here, though, is running for his future, for his place on the team. He likely got his place at university based on his running performances at high school. He probably hopes to become a professional athlete. Before the run began, one of the other runners told me that most of the members in the team hoped to go professional after university. This was the path they were on. But not all of them will make it.

We run together for the third lap, my worried friend and I, at which point I drop out exhausted. He turns around, to start lap four, running valiantly on. Others are dropping off the tail end of the group now, which is beginning to pick up speed. The captain still leads the charge.

I check my watch. I've run 7.5 km in 30 minutes. I vow to stay with them until 10km next time.

While we wait for them to come back, Kenji asks me if the Kenyan runners train like this. Not really, I have to tell him. Instead of lapping up and down a short piece of road, they prefer to run off for miles along dusty trails. In fact, they never run on concrete if they can help it.

Kenji says it's important for ekiden runners to train on the roads because it prepares their legs for racing on the roads. When I point out that the Kenyans still seem to race pretty well on the roads,* he says they would be even better if they trained on concrete.

It's a subject Kenji and I will return to again, but for now I just nod that I acknowledge his rationale, even if I don't fully agree with it.

Before we leave him that evening, Kenji tells us that the next week they are off on a week-long training camp in the mountains, and he invites us to come along. I quickly accept. I seem to have found myself a serious ekiden team to hang out with after all.

*

While Hakone is the pinnacle of the men's university ekiden season, in the build-up to it there are two other major races, the Izimo ekiden and the All-Japan national ekiden. Teams from across the country are able to compete in these races, with only the final Hakone race being restricted to the Kanto region.

For teams across the rest of the country, it means they have two opportunities to get amongst the glory, racing against the more glamorous Hakone teams and if they can, trying to beat them.

* That year, 2013, thirteen of the top twenty marathon runners in the world are Kenyan. The other seven are Ethiopian, who also prefer to train on soft ground.

So Kenji's job is to make his Ritsumeikan men's team as strong as he can for these two races, and to show that there is life outside Hakone.

In order to get his team into shape for the challenge, he has taken them up into the mountains for a week-long training camp. Max and I join them on the third day, driving six hours along the curved highways from Kyoto north to Nigata. Up here the air is less muggy. The altitude is nine hundred metres, not particularly high, but enough to get the lungs working a bit harder.

We arrive mid-afternoon and join the runners at the track. A few other teams are here training, too. The track they're using has only three lanes and there's no sign of any long-jump pits or throwing cages. It's a track purely for long-distance running. In the summer months, this whole area is set up to host ekiden teams, with tracks and cross-country trails laid out everywhere. Because the snow gets so deep in the winter, not many people live here, so apart from the runners it's largely deserted. It's a running paradise.

The Ritsumeikan team has already done a morning run, and they are now off to do what they call 'free running'. This is basically each person setting his own pace, route and distance. Kenji tells the captain to take us out with him for a run.

Although the mountains stretch off for miles, we run along a short, zig-zagging trail marked out in the woods beside the track. With the twists and turns it's probably half a mile long, and so we just go around and around it until the captain decides he has done enough. The other athletes all do the same, like little steam trains on a model railway set, chugging back and forth.

I ask the captain if he hopes to become a professional ekiden runner when he graduates. As far as I can see, the incentive of a career in running is part of the driving force behind all this training. In the UK, the prospects of becoming a professional runner are so slim that most people give up on the idea by the time they're at university. In Britain, unless you're Mo Farah, becoming a full-time professional distance runner means scraping by on maybe some Lottery funding, if you are lucky, some free kit from a sponsor, and the pittance you can earn in prize and appearance money at races. But with Kenyans and Ethiopians winning most of the road races across the world, for most British runners it's a case of picking up the odd hundred pounds here or there. In Japan, even the slowest professional runners can earn as much as a regular office worker, while for the top athletes the incentives are much greater.

So I'm surprised when the captain says he doesn't want to be a professional runner. He wants to be a firefighter. He says his father is a firefighter. But surely, as the captain of the team, he's one of the best runners. Why wouldn't he want to be a professional runner?

He smiles bashfully, as though he doesn't like being pressed on the question. It turns out, he isn't one of the best runners. He's the captain partly because he's the oldest in the team, and partly because he's a bright, popular student with good social skills. The type of person who can handle questions from a foreign journalist.

'The life of an ekiden runner is short,' he says. 'When

your times slip, you get put to work in an office. That's in a good company. Some companies just get rid of you.'

I have to admit, it doesn't sound great when you put it like that. As we run back past the track, a group of three professional women runners are churning along at full pace. Their faces are a study in anguish, each one seemingly on the brink of a tearful breakdown.

We pass them and head back into the woods.

'Will you run ekiden for the firefighters' team?' I ask him.

'Yes,' he says.

I ask him why he runs. What motivates him to keep training, to be part of the team? He looks at me blankly, running on in silence for a moment. Our feet sound soft on the trail. After a minute, he glances over at Max, as though hoping the question has gone away.

'I don't like running that much,' he says. He lets out a quick smile, relieved perhaps, finally to say it. 'I did lots of sports at school, but this is the one I was best at. People supported me, cheered me on.'

A few months later, he does indeed get his job as a firefighter. I'm happy for him. Perhaps finally he can stop running. Or maybe he will continue doing it, against his will, to make others happy.

*

After the run we head back to the team's lodging house. Owned by an old couple, it's a pointy wooden building with a couple of dormitory-style bedrooms full of bunk beds for the athletes. We take turns to pile into the bathroom, three or four at a time getting into the big, tiled bath full of hot water. There's lots of excited chatter and laughing now the training is over for the day.

After we're washed, we gather in a strip-lit dining room. Long tables with green floral tablecloths, laden with food. Bowls of sauce and sliced raw vegetables. In the middle of each table are small heaters with pots of fish and seaweed broth steaming on them. Max and I are the last two to arrive. Two seats have been left vacant opposite Kenji, the chopsticks neatly resting on their holders on the table.

I'm vegetarian, but I'm going to have to bend a little with the wind here. The pots are full of vegetables, noodles and fish. I do my best to avoid the chunks of fish, scooping up the rest and placing it in my bowl. There's plenty of rice to fill up on. And miso soup. And natto – a pungent helping of fermented soya beans. I first tried natto when I visited my brother twelve years ago, when he ran the ekiden at his school the morning after the naked festival. I couldn't stand it then, and Japanese people delight in offering it to unsuspecting foreigners to taste. As well as smelling like soggy, smelly boots, it's covered in an offputting layer of slime. But tonight, the second time I try it, it tastes quite nice. It's full of good bacteria, Max tells me. As is the miso. 'The Japanese diet is full of fermented foods like these,' Max explains, 'which increase the "good" microorganisms in your gut. This makes digestion more efficient, which is linked to overall health, but is also particularly good for athletes because it makes it easier to absorb energy.'

All the athletes I meet in Japan eat a fairly traditional Japanese diet, with rice, miso soup, natto, seaweed, fish,

[66]

buckwheat noodles, tofu and vegetables forming the main body of their daily food intake. They eat a combination of these things for breakfast, lunch and dinner every day. It's an incredibly healthy diet that contributes to the fact that Japan is one of the healthiest nations on Earth. Not only do they famously have one of the longest life expectancies of any nation, but in a list of the world's fattest developed countries, compiled by the UN in 2013, Japan was right at the bottom, with just 4.5% of adults considered obese. In comparison, the UK was ranked twenty-third, with 24.9% of the adult population obese.*

Another large study in 2013, by the American Heart Association, found that children in the developed world today take on average ninety seconds longer to run a mile than their counterparts did thirty years ago. Some decline in fitness was recorded in every developed nation except one: Japan, where the children today could still run as fast as their parents had done. While this may in part be down to the central role given to sport in school, combined with the obesity figures it's likely that a healthy diet also plays a part.

In Japan, processed breakfast cereals, sandwiches, burgers, pizzas and all those unhealthy things exist, but they are not as prevalent as in most western countries, and they certainly don't form the basis of most people's diets.

Wheat, that great staple of Europe and America, which has come in for some bad press in recent years as an unhealthy, problematic food source, is consumed a lot less in Japan. If you want to buy a loaf of bread in the super-

*The fattest nation in the world was Mexico with a 32.8% obesity rate, followed by the USA with 31.8%.

market, it comes in a packet with only three slices in it. For my children, who love to eat toast in the morning, it means virtually cleaning out the shelves each time we go shopping.

The portions of most things are generally smaller in Japan. One time in a restaurant I notice you can order a meal with a side portion of chips and I can't resist. When it comes, there are just three chips in a tiny bowl.

Numerous studies have looked at the effect of portion size on eating habits and have all concluded, perhaps not surprisingly, that offering someone a bigger portion of something results in the person eating more. In one study, even when the food on offer was stale, fourteen-day-old popcorn, those given the bigger portion ate more, even though afterwards they freely admitted it tasted terrible.

Small portions and restricted calories are buzzwords in the western health world right now, yet these things have been widely practised for years in Japan. The common Japanese phrase *hara hachi bu* means 'Eat until you are eighty per cent full.'

Eating with chopsticks also helps prevent over-eating because it forces you to eat slower, which means you feel fuller on less. Now that I'm used to chopsticks, whenever I get the chance to eat with a fork, I feel like I'm shovelling the food into my mouth like some monster intent on devouring everything before my time runs out.

Refined sugar, one of the worst things you can eat, which basically strips your body of vitality and health and has been famously categorised as a poison by the scientist Robert Lustig, is also less abundant in Japan – it is not typical to ritually finish each meal with a dessert like in the west. At the Ritsumeikan training camp, sugar is not on the menu at all.

Of course it's not perfect. Japan is riddled with convenience stores on every street corner packed to the rafters with gaudily packaged junk food. But even here, the chocolate bars and bags of sweets are generally smaller than in other countries. And the savoury snacks are not pasties and crisps, but rice balls filled with fermented plum or fish, and wrapped in seaweed or tofu.

I asked eminent sports and diet scientist Tim Noakes what he thought about the Japanese diet and whether it could help with athletic achievement. His response was simply that it sounded 'fabulous'.

Dr Kevin Currell, head of performance nutrition at the English Institute of Sport, agreed.

'This is a good mix of foods for any athlete. There is a combination of carbohydrate, protein and vegetables, and most importantly I would guess the food is of good quality and freshly cooked. This is how we would encourage all athletes to eat.'

By the end of my six months in Japan, eating mostly traditional Japanese food – except for breakfast, for which my taste buds are just too used to having something sweet so I would eat toast or porridge – I would weigh less than at any time in my adult life (sixty-seven kilograms – down from seventy-three kilograms when I left England). Though I did spend a lot of the six months running, I wasn't training any harder than I had done during the previous two years in England. Even when I was training for the London marathon and running much more, my weight never dipped below seventy-one kilograms.

*

After dinner, the athletes disappear off to their rooms. Max and I have been given a room to share. In typical Japanese style, it consists of a tatami mat floor and a cupboard full of bedding. It feels too early to shut ourselves in, so we shuffle around in our slippers. Downstairs they've set up a treatment room. The door is open and so I poke my head in. On a table, one of the athletes is getting a massage from the trainer. One of the assistant managers, a female student, is giving another runner a massage on the floor. A stocky student in glasses is moving an ultrasound machine around in circles on his knee, while the rest of those in the room sit on the floor chatting. Kenji, who is also seated on the floor, has his laptop open and is filling in the day's times on a spreadsheet.

'Come in,' they chorus, shifting around to make room. I sit down. My presence has brought a temporary silence to the room. I can tell someone is trying to think of something to say in English.

'*Itai?*' I ask the runner with the ultrasound machine. *Does it hurt?* They all laugh. I'm not sure if it's at my attempt at speaking Japanese, or the idea of the machine hurting. Or just general awkwardness.

Fortunately, Max appears soon after and everyone relaxes as the lines of communication are reopened. They go back to chatting, laughing and joking with each other. People wander in and out, leaving their flip-flops at the door. Everyone is just hanging out, seemingly enjoying each other's company.

All this joking, and the relaxed atmosphere, is part of the team spirit Kenji is trying to foster. Other coaches are more serious, he says, much stricter. I ask him if he enjoyed going on running camps when he was a runner. His eyes widen.

'No,' he says, shaking his head. 'It was very, very serious. Not fun.'

He says something to Max. He wants us to watch a video on his computer. We gather around as he pulls up some old, fuzzy footage of a track race. It's the Asian Games 10,000m final from 1998. A young Japanese man wearing a tight necklace stands on the start line, an anxious look on his face, blowing out his cheeks. It's Kenji.

He skips impatiently through the video of the first half of the race, in which a group of six runners, including the young Kenji, pull away from the rest of the field. 'OK,' he says, sitting back as the runners on the screen approach the halfway point in the race. As they pass 5,000m, exactly, Kenji surges to the front and starts to push hard, his shoulders rocking as he runs. It's a long bid for home.

We crowd around the screen. Kenji keeps piling on the pace until there is only one runner left following him. A tall runner from Qatar.

'Rival,' Kenji says, pointing at the man. While the young Kenji is straining, pumping his arms, his eyes full of fright, the Qatari runner looks poised, relaxed, waiting for his moment. We've all seen this scenario countless times before. It's nearly always the runner sitting behind who wins.

With a lap to go, the Qatari keeps coming alongside Kenji, but Kenji keeps speeding up. Around the last bend, they both attack, their legs flying now, the Qatari level with Kenji, in full flow. But Kenji won't let him past. It's like he has an arm out, holding the other man back. They race with everything down the finishing straight, side by side, past lapped runners who seem to be standing motionless, and still it looks like the Qatari runner will pass. But Kenji somehow digs out one more surge and crosses the line first, arms raised. The Japanese commentators can be heard simply applauding. Not saying a word. It's an amazing run.

The others have obviously seen this before, as they say very little, and go back to what they were doing.

'Great race,' I say to Kenji. 'I thought he was going to pass you at the end.'

'I won because of ekiden training,' he says. 'In ekiden, you never let anyone pass.'

7

It's 5.45 the next morning. I'm standing sleepy-eyed out on the road beside the lodging house, waiting for Max. The runners from the team are climbing into the back of their two minibuses, their shoe bags on their backs. Nobody is speaking. The forest surrounds us on all sides, dark and silent.

Max comes bounding out, excited. The buses aren't waiting for us. We're thirty seconds late, so they drive off, up the hill.

'Don't worry,' says Max. 'We'll catch them in seconds.'

He revs up his car and we screech around a few sharp turns, following the road up through the forest, waking up any animals still left sleeping.

The minibuses lumber ahead of us. We follow on behind them, the road snaking its way through the trees. Max is talking about snowboarding. He's going to come back here in the winter, he tells me. He keeps pointing out how high the snow will get. For now, though, it's a still, warm morning. We come out of the trees to see the peaks of mountains all around us. Ahead, on a flat piece of open ground, is a building with an empty car park in front of it.

The minibuses pull up and stop outside the building. As the runners pile out of the buses, no one laughs or makes a joke. Each person is quiet, with his own thoughts, wandering off in separate directions around the car park. This is partly because it's so early, but also because later today they have a time trial. In the recent regional Kansai ekiden, it turns out Ritsumeikan only finished in third position. Kenji had only just begun working as the team coach at that stage. The result meant they didn't qualify for the first of the three big university ekidens, the Izimo ekiden. As they are ineligible to run Hakone, it leaves them with only one big race to contest – the All-Japan national ekiden, in early November. It's now mid-September, so all the focus is on that one race. Today's time trial, Kenji tells me, will go a long way to deciding who makes it onto the team of seven runners.

Kenji calls everyone into a circle. We stand with our hands behind our backs as he tells them he wants them fresh for the time trial that afternoon. He says he has picked some of the team already, but not all of it. There are places still to fight for.

After he has finished speaking, the runners start stretching and putting on their running shoes. It surprises me to see them stretching so deeply, so early in the morning. In Kenya, the runners rarely stretch before their morning run, while in Europe the advice is clear that stretching a cold body, one that hasn't been already warmed up with some gentle running, can weaken the muscles and cause injury.

Many coaches, in fact, advise against doing any static stretches like the ones the Ritsumeikan runners are doing – in other words, holding each stretch for longer than a few seconds. Instead, western coaches prefer dynamic stretching, where you are moving while you stretch.

I ask Kenji why his runners stretch so much before training, telling him that in the UK we're always advised against it. He laughs.

'It is the old-fashioned Japanese way,' he says. 'We believe a flexible body prevents injuries. But I have my doubts.'

As soon as they're ready, the runners head off. They don't say anything, they just start running, one at a time, out along a marked course. This one is bigger than the previous day's back-and-forth trail next to the track, instead disappearing off across the wide, lower mountain slopes and away down enticing forest paths. Up beyond the trees, the rocky peaks catch the morning sun.

At the official start point there's a big metal map of the various routes. Although it's used for cross-country skiing in the winter, this is primarily a running course. The motif on the map is of two runners, and the wooden markers along the way also have pictures of runners on them. There may be permanent, purpose-made running trails like this in other parts of the world, but I've never seen any.

Kenji suggests I run with the assistant team manager, Nomura. Nomura is a student at the university, too, and in his first year he was part of the ekiden team. But he always thought his future lay in coaching rather than running. At high school, he says, the training was too intense. It burnt him out. But he loves ekiden, so when the opportunity arose for him to become a team manager, he took it.

Every morning, back at Ritsumeikan, he gets up with the athletes at 6 a.m. to make sure they head out on their runs. Often he runs, too, but only at an easy pace. His days of stressing himself to make the team are over.

We set off together at a gentle pace, our feet pat-patting softly on the pine-covered forest floor. After some stilted conversation, I can't resist speeding up, wanting to make the most of my run. I don't have a time trial later to save myself for. Nomura runs beside me as we twist and turn along the path, passing by the other Ritsumeikan runners, who emerge here and there, jogging alone like wandering spirits lost among the trees.

Nomura seems to keep up with me easily, but when we reach the finish, or the 'goal' as they call it, back where we started, he collapses on the floor, crying out in shrieks of pain. Kenji stands there giggling, jogging on the spot, testing out his sore leg. He is clearly itching to run again, but he is still limping after the operation. He starts stepping up and down on the verge.

Behind him, in the car park, Max has the team physio and the two other assistant team managers trying out his yoga moves while they wait for the runners to get back. They're lined up, synchronised, with one arm on the floor, the other in the air. Kenji looks as though he's doing his best to ignore them, and instead comes over to us, asking how far we ran. When Nomura tells him, he looks at me, impressed. 'Good, good,' he says.

I feel like I'm getting fitter. More of this focused training and hopefully I'll be back breaking my PBs again before too long. When I tell Kenji I want to beat my best times, he says he's convinced I can.

'Yes,' he says. 'Thirty-three minutes [for 10K] is OK.' He's probably just being polite, but I'll take all the encouragement I can get.

*

After another meal of rice, vegetables and natto back at the lodging house, the runners get up one by one to leave the dining room, fixing themselves protein shakes from big buckets of powder on one of the tables. There's no joking this morning. They do everything with a studied seriousness, not even catching each other's eyes as they move around the room scaled in their own thoughts, each one focusing, gathering himself for the time trial.

Kenji, meanwhile, has got himself another bowl of rice and doesn't seem to be in a rush to leave. I ask him about when he first started running.

'I wasn't a top runner in high school,' he says. It was his friend who got him into running. They were both second-year students at the school, and his friend wanted to try out for the ekiden team.

'We didn't make it,' he says. 'But when we were in the third year, we were both selected to run.' He waits for Max to translate, watching me for my reaction.

'*So desune*,' I say. This is a useful stock phrase which I haven't quite got the hang of. The sports commentators on Japanese television use it constantly when talking to each other. It means 'It is, isn't it?' and is broadly used to show you're listening and agree with what's being said.

Kenji laughs at my clumsy use of the phrase. Then, after a pause, he says: 'A few days before the race, my friend was in a car accident and died.'

I hold my chopsticks in my hand, poised over my still unfinished tub of natto, not sure what to say. All the students have left the room now. Behind Kenji, the television is showing ice skating.

'We never got to run an ekiden together,' he says. 'But I've remembered my friend before every race during my whole career. Every ekiden, he ran it with me.'

The spirit of togetherness, of teamwork and companionship that ekiden embodies, clearly had a strong hold over Kenji after his friend died. It pushed him to great heights and continues to drive him.

'In Japan,' he says, 'running is ekiden. First ekiden, then everything else.'

*

Back at the track that afternoon, however, the spirit of togetherness is momentarily replaced by rivalry as the runners know they are racing each other for a place on the team. Kenji has planned a 10,000m time trial. He wants them to run together at a controlled pace for the first 5,000m. Then, he says, they can start to race.

Feeling good after my morning run, I decide to join in for the first mile or two. I promise to keep out of the way, at the back of the field.

We arrive at the track a full two hours before the time trial is to begin, and they all start warming up immediately. I think if I warm up for two hours I'll be too tired to do anything else, so I sit in the warm sunshine and wait. As the time ticks by, I can feel the tension mounting. Even I begin to feel nervous about running. The day seems too still, as though something's not right. Nobody else is at the track that afternoon. No cars even drive by along the road.

Eventually, Kenji calls us to the start. They're all wearing short racing shorts and vests, rather than their usual long shorts and T-shirts. It's the first time I've seen them in their stripped-down racing outfits. They sprint up and down the track like serious athletes, slapping their legs and arms. I keep out of the way as they line up. The team's ace runner, Yoshimura Naoto, is told to run at the back, while it's the captain's job to lead. The rest of the team line up one behind the other and we file off out on our first lap.

Right from the start it feels frantically fast. Kenji has set them off at a pace of 3 minutes 20 seconds per kilometre, but I keep drifting off the back, and then having to surge to catch up again. The ace, running just in front of me, keeps doing the same, dropping off and then catching up, which is putting me off my rhythm even more. It's like I've forgotten how to run, and now my legs are aching, my arms are getting heavier. After only four laps, I have to stop. They still have twenty-one laps to run.

At the 5,000m point, like a hound who has finally been let off the leash, the ace comes racing from the back of the line past everyone and starts stretching away at the front. I realise this is the same way Kenji ran the Asian championships back in 1998, the race we watched on his computer last night. The same template. He's passing it on. Surge at halfway, and run for your life.

Each lap now, the faces of the runners become more contorted and anguished. Later, looking back at my photographs, it looks almost comical, as though they're auditioning for parts in a zombie movie. The ace wins comfortably, by a hundred metres or so, in just over 31 minutes. Behind him comes a young second-year runner in a duel with the number two ace, Shota Nagumo – the team's second fastest runner. The second-year pips Nagumo in a desperate sprint finish, his eyes straining, his head to one side.

In fourth place is a first-year student they call the Professor. The reason is not that he's particularly clever, but because they say he doesn't look like a runner. What they mean is he's short and doesn't have such a handsomely chiselled face as some of the others. But he's clearly fast.

The captain struggles in around sixth or seventh. I ask Kenji if his place on the team is in jeopardy, and he sort of waggles his head non-committally, which suggests it could be.

After the training, I join the team in what is for them a well-earned trip to the local *onsen*, or communal public baths. Inside, they sit chatting by a large window, waist-deep in steaming hot water. Outside the mountains are dark in the fading light. The students talk in lowered voices, some of them reclined against the stone sides of the bath with soaked flannels over their faces. Max comes in too, but I sit quietly, leaving them to talk undisturbed. This is not the time for my questions.

Kenji says that while they come to the training camp for the cooler weather and the benefits of running at altitude, the main reason for the camps is to foster a sense of togetherness, a feeling of belonging to the group.

'The most important thing in ekiden is your strength as a team,' he explains. 'When you train together with your teammates, all focusing on the same target, it gives you strength mentally. The physical state is less important.'

8

Back in Kyotanabe, our next-door neighbour Rie and her family are waiting on their bikes as we hustle our children into their shoes. Marietta is trying to brush Lila's hair, Ossian has run outside in his socks and is clambering up a small tree. Uma is ready as always, standing with her arms crossed, surveying the rest of her family with a look of despair.

'*Chotto mate*,' I say, as I slip my shoes off and run back in to the house for my wallet.

Rie and her family are taking us to the local sports day, at the nearby shrine. It was supposed to happen the previous week, but it rained, so they postponed it until this week.

We're not quite sure what to expect. I'm wearing my running kit, just in case. Ryohei, the fifteen-year-old from across the street, and his friends have been training for the last few weeks for today's race, running along the course every morning before school. I went with them one morning. They keep inviting me along to train with them, but 5.30 a.m. is just too early. I don't know how they do it every day.

Finally we're ready, tumbling out of the door, grabbing our bikes. I still don't have one, but as the sports day is only around the corner, I'm going to jog along beside the others.

'*Ikimashoka*,' says Rie cheerfully, while her husband nods, and they roll off down the hill in convoy.

'*Ikimasho*,' says Ossian, sitting regally on the back of Marietta's bike, his sunhat pulled down over his mop of blond hair.

*

At the front of the shrine is a gravel square about the size of a small football pitch. It's swarming with children when we arrive. The shrine itself is hidden among the bamboo trees that rise up the hills on three sides of the square. In one corner there are some swings and a slide, while along the back a few gazebos have been set up.

At the entrance to the square we're given a complimentary roll of household bin bags to welcome us. This is a surprisingly common gift in Japan. Rie tells me this event has been going for sixty-two years, and every year there is a big race. I should run it, she tells me. Of course, I already know about it. I'm itching to run.

Rie introduces me to the man who won the race the year before. He's a local policeman. She tells him I will be his rival, and he smiles, friendly, telling me he is sure I will beat him. I try to be as modest, telling him I'm very slow and tired, but it sounds a little disingenuous. I've been training with one of the top university teams in the country. I should win easily.

A man on a megaphone is getting everyone to join in a mass warm-up. Children line up in rows and follow the leader's instructions, waving their arms up in the air, or bending over to touch their toes. My children, still unsure about the whole occasion, decide against joining in, and stand watching from the sidelines.

Once the racing begins, however, the sight of prizes being handed out to everyone who takes part gets them up and over to the start line. Ossian's race is a sprint. It's only about 30 metres long and he runs it holding Marietta's hand. Two of the bigger boys are already finished before he even starts to run, but this is a friendly day, and he gets his prize at the end: a little packet of sweets. He comes back grinning from ear to ear as though he has pulled off some ingenious heist.

I spot my young neighbour Ryohei and his early-morning group standing together among the melee. They look serious. Ryohei has his mask on and is doing some stretches. This is the moment he has been waiting for. The big race is about to start.

I join them on the start line feeling far too keen in my running shorts and quick-dry T-shirt. Even at the Blooming training sessions, nobody wears short running shorts. Instead they play down their intentions and status, hiding their legs under long shorts or leggings.

Here I'm surrounded mostly by children. The few adults entered loiter around at the back, joking about how slow and unhealthy they are. Lila is joining the race, too, skipping around excitedly with our neighbours from across the street. I try to look disinterested as we're called to the line. *Oh, are we running now? I didn't realise.* But secretly I'm plotting my route past all these kids, down one side of the path that leads out of the shrine and onto the road. There are fewer bushes on that side.

A gun goes and we're off. I see Ryohei racing away at the front like he's fleeing a crime scene, his arms pumping. His friend who speaks English, the faster one, starts more slowly, but I manage to catch them both by the start of the first hill. I have a half-baked plan to let them win, to run with them and then let them beat me at the end. But now we're running, that seems silly. It could even be embarrassing for them. I'm sure they don't want to win because I let them. Besides, as our shadows merge temporarily, my competitive urge kicks in and before I know it I'm racing hard up the hill, trying to get a lead on them both.

It's a while since I've had that feeling of leading a race, the course empty and quiet ahead, the rest of the field strung out behind in pursuit. It can sometimes feel like you're running for your life, but today it's easy. I know they won't catch me.

On the way back, I begin to pass the children, who are running a shorter loop. I bundle through them like a mad cow on the charge. It feels odd passing Lila, red-faced and running next to her friend. 'Well done girls,' I say, as though I'm just standing watching. And then into the shrine, a patter of applause as I cross the line. I make out that I wasn't trying, acting as though it's no big deal, but really I'm chuffed to bits to win.

Ryohei, mask in hand, comes in second, punching the air. His friend is just behind him.

Ten minutes later, I somehow find myself in another race. This time I have to drink a bottle of beer through a straw while my team-mate, Rie's seven-year-old daughter, drinks up a sugary sports drink. Neither of us is any good, but we still win a roll of tin foil.

Lila enters every race going and comes home with a stash

of prizes, from chocolates to bottles of soya sauce and rolls of clingfilm. For my victory in the day's main race, I get presented with a metal beer mug, flanked on either side by Ryohei and his friend: the early-morning team. The policeman, last year's winner, our vanquished rival, hands out the prizes.

*

I may have won the local sports day, but my efforts to infiltrate the Japanese corporate running world, the land of a thousand (and more) professional runners, are not going so well. Kenji has asked some of the coaches he knows whether I can visit, but he's getting the same response that Brendan Reilly got: thank you, but no.

Mr Ogushi, whom I first met in the lobby of the Tower Hotel in London, contacts me to suggest I come to the national corporate track championships in Tokyo.

'All the coaches will be there,' he says when I speak to him on the phone. 'You will get a chance to talk.' It sounds like a good plan, so I do as he says and take the bullet train from Kyoto to Tokyo, whizzing past Mount Fuji along the way. I'm not the only person on the train holding up my phone to take a picture.

Mr Ogushi meets me as I step off the train. He has paid to come on to the platform to find me, scared I'll get lost if he arranges to meet me out in the station. As soon as we say hello, he turns on his heels and I follow him through the gates and into the city. He walks fast, and seems to be constantly checking his phone as he goes. In fact, he seems to have two phones. He's calling someone on the other phone now. I follow behind feeling like a child being picked up by an overworked chaperone.

We wander through some busy, narrow streets into an underground shopping mall, and then into a bookshop. I follow him to what looks like the map section, where he finally puts down his phone.

'First, you need a map,' he says. A map? 'A map of Japan. So you can see where all the races are. I will email you a list.' I'm not sure I need a map, but maybe he's right. The kids will enjoy looking at it, at least. We can put it up on the wall in our unfurnished house.

He's not sure about that idea, and so I end up buying two maps. One fold-up map, and one wall poster map.

'OK, let's go,' he says, as I stuff the maps into my backpack. He's already halfway out of the door.

On the way to the race, we meet an old friend of his on the train, a newspaper reporter. He looks at me out of the corner of his eyes, unsure how to treat me.

Later at the track, after Mr Ogushi has gone off to talk to some colleagues, the reporter sidles up to me.

'Twenty years ago, these championships were a big event,' he says, 'with a packed stadium. But as ekiden has grown more popular, the interest in track running has waned to nothing.' I look around. The huge stadium, built for the Japanese national games, is mostly empty. Full of rows and rows of yellow folded-up seats.

We're standing down by the trackside, where all the team managers have gathered, dressed in their dark suits and white shirts, with mobile phones and lists of the runners, like racehorse owners checking the form of their horses. They're establishing fitness levels after the summer training camps, assessing the form of their athletes before the ekiden season begins. Mr Ogushi tells me they don't really care if their runners win tonight.

'It's nice to win, of course,' he says. 'But it's not a big deal.' Unlike the ekidens and the big marathons, these track championships are not televised. With all the officials and athletes milling around, as well as team managers and coaches, the whole thing feels like a show with no audience. A dress rehearsal, perhaps. Although the real show will take place on a different stage.

However, up in the stands, a few groups of supporters are belatedly unravelling banners and flags. The newspaper reporter says they are probably employees from companies who have offices nearby. 'They're probably made to come,' he says. They have bugles and clappers and make a lot of noise when their runners go by.

Later, when I venture up into the stand, I notice a few other people watching who seem unconnected to the teams. Mostly smartly dressed young women with expensive handbags. They sit in twos or threes, or sometimes alone, and seem unmoved by most of the races.

Mr Ogushi says they're here to see Ryuji Kashiwabara. He was the big star of recent Hakone ekidens and is known as God of the Mountains after he broke the course record for the tough mountain stage of the race three times, singlehandedly dragging his unfancied Toyo University to three Hakone victories. 'He's like David Beckham,' Mr Ogushi ventures as a comparison I will understand.

The big races of the evening are the men's and women's 10,000m. In the British national championships a few months earlier, just thirteen men entered the 10,000m and, bizarrely, only one woman ran in the women's race. Here in Japan, while the crowds may be no bigger, the field of runners certainly is. I count seventy-five men and fifty women across the A and B races.

On the start line of the women's A race, the runners spend a lot of time slapping their arms and legs, even their faces. I noticed the Ritsumeikan runners doing this too. To fire themselves up, they told me. The women's race features two Kenyans running for two of the corporate teams, Hitachi and Kyudenko. They are noticeably not hitting themselves.

Many of the corporate teams sign up Kenyan and Ethiopian runners to boost their chances in the big races. The Africans live, train, and often work in the company offices, along with the other members of the team. Over the last ten years or so, some of the very best Kenyan and Ethiopian runners have lived and competed in Japan, such as the 2008 Olympic marathon champion, the late Sammy Wanjiru, and the 2011 world 10,000m champion, Ibrahim Jeilan.

As soon as the starting gun goes, the two Kenyan women fly to the front, and by the end of the second lap they have a 40-metre lead on the pack of chasing Japanese athletes. As well as the daylight between them, their running styles clearly distinguish the two sets of runners. The Kenyan runners have a loping, easy style, while the Japanese runners all share the same shuffling, short stride, their arms pumping back and forth like clockwork toys. It almost looks as though the Japanese runners have had their legs tied together by an invisible string so they can't move as much, which doesn't seem fair.

In one of the rare moments I get to speak to one of the Ritsumeikan women runners, when their team manager is not around, I manage to ask Natsuki Omori, one of the country's top young runners, why most Japanese women run with such a short stride.

'Because we have shorter legs,' she tells me. 'It is more efficient to run like that.' She says the coaches tell them to run this way.

As the corporate 10,000m race progresses, the Kenyans get further and further ahead. Are they really that much better? In the end, it turns out that they're not. In the last few laps they begin to tire, and the lead group of Japanese runners, still lapping consistently at the same pace, begin to catch up. It's a frantic race for the line over the last 200m, with the Kenyans finishing first and second, but only by a whisker.

The race makes for an interesting illustration of two different approaches to racing. Later I meet the manager of the fourth-placed runner, who is very happy with her performance. When I ask him about the Kenyan women racing off at the beginning, he laughs. 'No,' he says. 'That is not the Japanese way. The Japanese way is even pace.'

Of course, even pace is more sensible, and you're less likely to end up jogging pathetically down the home straight, being overtaken by your more even-headed rivals, but the two Kenyans still ended up finishing first and second. Were they more talented, or just braver?

It wasn't naivety on their part, either. Later I find the winner of the race with some of her Team Hitachi team-mates, conversing in what to me sounds like perfect Japanese. I ask her about the race and she tells me she worked together with the other Kenyan runner to share the lead.

'She took one lap, then me,' she explains. Even though they are on different teams, they worked together as Kenyans, as runners who share the same racing philosophy. Of course, racing off at the front doesn't always work, and tonight it almost didn't, but it reminds me of something the great marathon coach Renato Canova once said to me. He said: 'To win a big city marathon, you need to be a little wild. Not an accountant.' You have to take risks, throw caution to the wind and run free from the shackles of the watch, the counting machine. Who knows, *before* the race, what your even pace should be? You may think you do, but that's placing a limit on yourself. A limit that can stop you winning.

Talking as a man who has started too fast and suffered for it in nearly every race I've ever entered, I must wave the flag of caution here. In most cases, starting like a wild man or woman will end up with you coming unstuck at the end, struggling through the last few miles like you've suddenly aged forty years. But when you look at the results from races like the 2013 Ageo half-marathon, where over a hundred Japanese university runners ran under 65 minutes, you have to ask why did the winner only manage 62 and a half minutes. Surely with that quantity of talent going in at one end, a few sub-60 runners should be popping out the other end?

Paula Radcliffe once broke the marathon world record by

almost two minutes. Usually records are broken by seconds, because the mindset of the runner is to run just faster than world-record pace. This is, of course, completely reasonable. If you're looking at the fastest anyone has ever run a particular distance, then to attempt to run even slightly quicker is fairly wild in itself.

But that day, Radcliffe told me when I spoke to her about it, she didn't even know how fast she was running.

'I never plan to run at a certain pace,' she said. 'All my career my motto has been "no limits". I don't try to run with a set time in mind, sticking to set splits, because what happens if you're ahead of your splits, are you going to slow down?'

Yes, most people would, I think. But to run times that are off the scale, like Radcliffe, like the Kenyans, sometimes you have to forget about the watch. I can't help wandering how many of those Japanese runners were holding themselves back in that 10,000m race because the watch was telling them what pace to run. Is the 'Japanese way', meticulously counting lap times like accountants, limiting the very fastest runners, stopping them from beating the Kenyans? It is an intriguing thought.

*

The next day I head back to the track, but without the high quality of the long-distance events it feels more like an inter-company sports day than a serious competition. It's a sunny afternoon and everyone is in good spirits, bowing, laughing and swapping business cards.

I'm wandering around aimlessly, bored with watching the hammer throwers, when I spot Mr Ogushi talking to a man in a tracksuit. I'm not sure if he wants to be left alone. He keeps disappearing on me, saying he has business to attend to. He hasn't introduced me yet to any of those corporate team coaches he told me about. I try to walk by close enough for him to see me, but not too close that he has to if he doesn't want to. It's a difficult line to tread without looking like I'm stalking him. Luckily, he spots me and nods, which I take to mean he wants me to come over.

'This is the coach of the Nissin Foods team,' he says. 'New Year ekiden winners last year. National champions. Very good team.'

Mr Ogushi tells the coach that I live in Kyoto, laughing a little, as though it's a funny place for me to live. The coach tells me that he is originally from Kyoto.

'South of Kyoto,' he says. 'A place called Kyotanabe.'

'That's where I live.'

He's clearly amazed. 'Kyotanabe?'

I nod, pleased with this little piece of serendipity.

'Why, of all the places, did you decide to live there?' He looks at Mr Ogushi, who nods that it's true, I do live in Kyotanabe.

I tell him about the school. He says he knows it. His cousin's children go there.

'You must come and see us in Tokyo,' he says, referring, I assume, to his team. The national ekiden champions. This is great.

'I'd like that,' I say, wondering how far I can pin him down right here and now. 'I can come any time.'

'Welcome,' he says.

'*Arrigato gozimasu,*' I say, bowing.

Finally, I'm in. I think.

9

We enter the grounds of the Tafukuin temple through a small side door. It's only four feet high, so we have to duck down.

'To be humble,' Max explains. The door forces you to bow. Even the samurai were expected to leave their fighting egos outside when they entered a temple.

Inside we're met by a beautifully dressed woman with big eyes and hair brushed back in a striking grey quiff. She speaks to us in a hushed voice, almost a whisper.

'What did she say?' I ask Max, who is standing there smiling at her and nodding. I'm not sure whether to take my shoes off or not.

'She said I'm very handsome,' he says, giving me a disarming grin. He slips off his shoes and steps up onto the raised floor of the temple. I do the same, getting left behind as I fiddle with my laces. I shuffle up the steps after them, the ancient wooden floor wonderfully smooth under my feet.

Inside we're led into a large tatami-mat room, with windows all along one edge looking out on a perfectly manicured Japanese garden. It has been raining and everything is bejewelled in water drops. We sit on the floor and wait quietly as our host leaves us alone.

Up in the mountains somewhere around Kyoto live the marathon monks. Legend (and numerous television documentaries) has it that the monks of Mount Hiei run a thousand marathons in a thousand days in their quest to reach enlightenment. Those who succeed become hugely respected and revered, as human Buddhas or living saints. It is rare that a monk chooses to embark on the thousand-day challenge, or *Kaihogyo*, and even rarer that one completes it. In the last 130 years, only forty-six men have achieved it. And I'm hoping to meet one of them.

However, I can't just walk up the mountain and knock at his door. Visits are strictly by invitation only. But Max has been working on it. He thinks the woman here at this private temple in northern Kyoto could be our key contact. She's married to the priest here, and she knows one of the marathon monks. But before she will agree to take us to see him, she wants to meet us. So I'm wearing my neatest shirt, and Max has combed his hair in a tidy side-parting. We both sit looking as enlightened as we can, surveying the garden outside with an air of serenity. A stillness seems to pervade the temple, as though time inside its walls has been stopped. I almost feel like lying down and going to sleep. I was awake in the night putting cream on Ossian's insect bites. They seem to savour his young, foreign blood and he goes to bed each night with fresh marks all over his skin, and then spends half the night wriggling around itching them. Marietta, too, has been suffering from itchiness, the heat aggravating her eczema.

My tired eyes are starting to close when our host comes back with a companion. She carries a tray laden with bowls of bright green tea and some small sweets so beautifully made it seems almost wrong to eat them. They both sit down. She asks me why I want to visit the monks.

I tell her I've often found myself questioning why I run. Running is difficult, exhausting, my legs get tired, sometimes I find it hard to get myself off the sofa, or out of bed, to go for a run. Nobody is forcing me to do it, or asking me to. Nobody else cares if I run or not. But I always go. Something makes me do it.

I know some people run to lose weight, to get fit, or maybe they're running to raise money for a charity. But for me and many other runners, these are just by-products. Running itself has its own raison d'être. But ask most runners why they run, and they will just stare back at you blankly.

The more I thought about it, the more I began to realise that we run to connect with something in ourselves, something buried deep down beneath all the worldly layers of identity and responsibility. Running, in its simplicity, its pure brutality, peels away these layers, revealing the raw human underneath. It's a rare thing to experience, everything stripped bare, and it can be confronting. Some of us will stop, almost shocked by ourselves, by how our heart is pumping, by how our mind is racing around, fighting our attempts to leave it behind.

But if we push on, running harder, further, deeper into the wildness of it all, away from the world and the structure of our lives, the tiredness seems to lift, we begin to float, even if the pain still aches in our muscles. Our minds begin to clear and we begin to feel strangely detached, yet at the same time connected, connected to ourselves. We begin to experience some form of self-realisation.

'Of course, most of this is happening at a subconscious level,' I say. 'But when I heard there were monks who did

this consciously, who used running as the path to enlightenment, I wanted to meet them.'

She is smiling, as though she knows what I'm saying. She
lets the silence back into the room before speaking again.

'It is a shame,' she says, 'that now running is all about racing, not for fun.'

'But in this modern world, we need excuses,' I say. I'm on
a roll now. Max is egging me on with his nods and smiles as
he translates.

The world is set up to cater for the rational, logical mind,
which needs to see tangible reasons and benefits behind any
effort. We need to dangle the carrots of marathons and best
times in front of ourselves, to justify this strange habit of
getting up, running around outside, coming back having
not actually gone anywhere. We need to find some rationale
to it. Some structure. It needs to fit into the narrative of our
lives, which is one of striving, of chasing goals. This is what
we have been taught. I do it myself. Beating a best time or a
set target, no matter how arbitrary, gives me a warm tingle
of achievement, I can't deny it. And this, on some superficial
level, motivates me to run. It gets me out there. But, really,
deep down, I know it's just a front. What I really want to do
is get away from all this structure, the complexity and chaos
of my constructed life, and to connect with that simple human being that lies buried away under everything else.

The woman smiles and nods. She pours me some more
tea. I take a deep, slow breath. Talking like this, in this place,
seems to imbue running with an almost religious quality. It
doesn't feel wrong. If I was talking about football or tennis
in this way, it would feel out of context. But here the others

nod in agreement. They want to run now, I can sense it.

The woman tells me that she used to run, but that she doesn't any more.

'I used to love the feeling of running,' she says.

Her companion, too, who has been sitting listening quietly, tells us how he likes to run.

'Children love running,' the woman says. 'It is natural for them.'

'Yes, and the more excited they are, the more they run around. They can't help it.'

She smiles. '*So desune*,' she says. *I agree.*

Max gets up to visit the bathroom. Without him there to translate, the conversation stops. Outside it starts raining, a smattering on the window. Max comes back and sits down.

The woman tells me that the monks run their thousand marathons in straw sandals. She once met a monk on the last day of his thousand-day challenge and she expected to see his feet all swollen and sore.

'But they were smooth and clean,' she says. 'As though he had been floating over the ground. Not touching it.'

I ask her about the stories I've heard, that if the monks can't complete the challenge for any reason, if they have to quit, they must kill themselves.

She says she doesn't know. This used to happen, yes, but now it is not clear. Nobody asks the question. In fact, a lot of secrecy surrounds the marathon monks. I'm told we won't be able to see the exact route they take, as it is too sacred.

The woman's companion gathers the tray of bowls and plates. Bowing, he leaves the room. It is our cue to leave, too. She says she will talk to one of the monks she knows.

We will have to wait to see if he will agree to meet us.

Back outside, the world trundles by as before, taxis looking for customers, people in suits off for lunch, bicycles waiting for traffic lights to change, a man arranging items outside his shop. Max opens the door of his car for me.

'You getting in?' he asks as I stand there.

'Yes,' I say. I glance back at the temple, but the wooden gates have now been closed. I get in the car and we drive off.

*

Back in the world of competitive running, the Ritsumeikan University squad are having another try-out for the ekiden team, at a track race in the nearby city of Shizuoka. These try-out races are taken very seriously and often slews of fast times are recorded. Just the week before in Tokyo, the Hakone champions, Nittai university, held a similar time-trial meeting on their campus open to all universities and high schools. Incredibly, there were forty-five separate heats of the 5,000m, starting at 7.30 on a Sunday morning and not finishing until 9.20 that evening. The heats averaged forty-two runners in each race. That's 1,890 runners. Just in the 5,000m. On the Saturday, there were almost as many runners in the 10,000m heats.

When I went along to an equivalent track open meeting at Bristol University in the UK shortly before heading out to Japan, there was only one heat, and I was one of only four runners in it. The women's race didn't even start because nobody turned up to run.

The quality in the Tokyo races, too, was impressive, with

even the very slowest runner in the slowest 5,000m heat running around 19 minutes. In the final race of the day, thirty men ran under 14:05. Only twenty men in the UK ran that fast all year.

Ritsumeikan's race in Shizuoka, without any of the Hakone universities nearby, won't be quite as big as one of the Tokyo time trials, but I'm interested to see how it all works.

The race is held in a giant stadium built for the 2002 football World Cup. I arrive at around 4 o'clock in the afternoon. It's still warm as I approach the stadium. Tracksuited runners are jogging around the perimeter of the huge concrete wall of the stadium, swishing past each other without comment, eyes focused.

Here and there the teams have laid out large bits of tarpaulin on the ground, sometimes covered with blankets, for the runners to sit on while they wait for their races. Even here they carefully remove their shoes before treading on the blankets.

I've been told to call Nomura, Kenji's assistant team manager, when I get into the stadium. There is no charge to get in or any security, and before I know it I'm stepping out onto the trackside. A group of women are racing by, pain distorting their faces, full of anguish, as though they're being slowly dragged down into a fiery hell.

I walk along beside the finishing straight. Here again, lots of teams are sitting on squares of tarpaulin. Team managers in suits stand looking concerned, eyes fixed on the race, stopwatches in their hands. The bell goes – the runners are on the last lap. Along the back straight I can hear team-mates, coaches, yelling support at the runners. High-pitched shrieks echo in the mostly empty stadium as the runners come around the final bend and battle down the home straight, crossing the line one after the other in a pile of agony and despair.

The last runner has barely crossed the line when I hear a gun go. At the opposite end of the track the next race has already started.

I call Nomura on my phone.

'*Finn desu*,' I say. *It's Finn.* '*Doku desu ka?*'

He tells me where he is, but I don't understand, so I try to tell him where I am. Down by the 100m start. On the track. 'Eh?' He doesn't understand. 'Usain Bolt,' I say, clutching at straws, realising as soon as I've said it that I've completely confused him.

'Bolt?' he almost screeches, as though the great man is here in the stadium.

Eventually he spots me. He's up in the stand behind me, waving. I head up to join the team. They're all waiting for the 5,000m races, which are set to start soon. They seem surprised to see me, but nod and say '*os*'. Kenji is on his way, they tell me. One of the first-year runners, Takumi Kasahara, speaks a little English. He's a 1500m runner, but in Japan that's not much use to anyone, so he's usually pushed to run longer distances in an attempt to make the ekiden team.

The Japanese 1500m record is just 3:37, set almost ten years ago. I keep comparing the Japanese favourably to the British, but here the contrast is the other way around, with three British runners breaking the Japanese record in 2013 alone. The fastest Japanese 1500m runner ever would only appear thirty-ninth on the UK all-time list.

One key reason for this is that people like Kasahara are channelled away from the 1500m almost as soon as they start running. In Japan, if you can run, then you're pushed into ekiden. Which is a shame, because Kasahara is clearly built for 1500m. He is taller than most of the other runners, his legs are chunkier. He doesn't have that light frame of a distance runner.

So today, earlier in the morning, he ran in one of the slowest 5,000m heats. He ran 15:50 – over a minute quicker than my best time – and came near the back.

'It's very far for me,' he says, resigned to his fate. 'But I try.'

A short time later, as the moon begins to rise unnoticed beyond the stadium like a paper lantern, Kenji arrives in a bustle of smiles and excitable jokes. He's wearing a neat black suit. The serious racing, the ten fastest heats of the 5,000m, is about to begin.

The Ritsumeikan runners who haven't run yet head off to warm up, while I head down to the track with Kenji and Kasahara, who has agreed to translate.

The races are graded according to the runners' best times, with the last race being the fastest of the night. The Ritsumeikan runner in the first heat powers through his race, burning up the last lap to win easily. He has a determined, focused air about him, often looking at the others in annoyance when they joke around with each other.

'Secret bomb,' says Kenji, delighted. Nomura, lurking behind my shoulder, steps in. 'Secret weapon,' he says.

'Secret weapon,' Kenji repeats, nodding. This runner was nowhere in August, and now suddenly he looks bionic. The team is taking shape, Kenji says. 'Top ten,' he says. This is his prediction for the team in the upcoming national ekiden. It would be quite an achievement – in the twenty-four years they've run it, Ritsumeikan have only finished in the top ten once, in 1984, when they finished tenth. Last year, before Kenji joined, they finished thirteenth.

Each time a race ends, a swarm of new runners rushes onto the track, the gun goes, and they're off again. Altogether there are twenty races for women and seventeen for men, with about forty runners in each race. They're mostly high-school and university runners, but a few professional runners are here too, as well as the odd plucky amateur.

As each race whirls by, we stand in lane four along the top bend of the track with many of the other coaches and managers. Kenji leans out offering advice as his runners go by. But he's also networking with all the other managers. Many of them know him and come over to say hello, everyone bowing to each other. Lots of exchanging of business cards takes place.

The Professor and the Captain are in the same race, but this time the Captain shows his credentials, hanging on to the leader almost to the end, claiming second place, while the Professor, his face twisted, his neck cranked to one side, his eyes squinting with the effort, finishes about halfway back.

'He's the fastest first-year,' Kasahara tells me, slightly in awe of his friend's running ability.

Lots of the runners wear headbands that trail down their backs. These are the high-school runners. In some ways, high-school running is even more serious than university or professional running.

'At high school, the training is too hard,' Kasahara tells me. As a first-year, he has only recently graduated himself. 'It's like the military.'

I ask him if he prefers university.

'Yes,' he says, grinning for emphasis.

The high-school students all have shaved heads and stern, determined looks on their faces. Even though they're younger, they hold their own in the races. Even in the fastest races, they're there, battling for the lead, their team-mates screaming them on as though lives depended on every second they gained. One high-school student next to us even has a megaphone to blast out his encouragement above the noise of everyone else. At the 200m point, halfway around the lap, squads of women with stopwatches call out the lap times to their runners. All at the same time. It's chaos.

The last race of the night features the ace and the number two ace. Kasahara tells me the ace, Yoshimura, is going for a new best time of 13:55, which is 20 seconds faster than his current best. 'He can do it,' says Kenji's assistant, Nomura, who has joined us at trackside. He tells me everyone in the team has been running best times in the last few weeks. It's all coming together nicely.

'Next year,' Kenji says, bristling with excitement, 'top five.' He's talking about the national ekiden again. He holds up five fingers and laughs, knowing it's ridiculously optimistic.

In the hush before the race starts, Kenji introduces me to a manager from another team. Kenji tells him I ran in Kenya, and that I told him the Kenyans prefer to train on dirt trails rather than on concrete. The man looks surprised.

'In Japan,' he says, in English, 'in Japan, there is only concrete.'

Almost all the training I have done so far has been on concrete or on the track, but surely the whole of Japan can't be cemented over?

We have no time to discuss it further, however, as the race is starting. The ace, tall and lean, like a greyhound, seems to be holding himself back, running on the heels of the leader, a stocky high-school runner in glasses and a purple headband.

They're cranking the laps out in 65 seconds – about 13:30 pace – when after about four laps the ace starts to drop back. At first it's just a small gap, but then it starts getting bigger. The other runners dart past him, as though he's a discarded object drifting along on the track. The number two ace, Nagumo, goes past, moving slowly through the field as the ace drops further and further back.

We find out later that his achilles tendon started hurting. Rather than stop, though, to protect his injury, he keeps on to the end, limping home in over 16 minutes. I glance over at Kenji who looks more than a little concerned. His mouth has tightened and I decide it's best not to ask him his thoughts just now.

Later, up in the dark gods of the stadium, they have a team debrief, standing in a circle. I've no idea what Kenji tells them, but the mood is downbeat after the ace's injury. We seem to be the last team leaving the stadium, making our lonely way to the train station along the wide avenue of flags that were first put up to welcome the football fans in 2002.

I find myself walking with Kasahara and the Professor, whose real name is Masato Doi. They're talking to each other, and seem to want to ask me something.

'Do you like Japanese manga?' Kasahara asks, as the Professor looks on. Comic books are incredibly popular in Japan. If you go into a manga shop in Japan, it's full of all sorts of people, from businessmen to young women. Nobody is ashamed to be seen reading a comic on the train. However, I'm not really a fan. I can't read them, of course, but I feel I'm letting my two friends down somehow, not having anything to say about them.

Then I remember that when we first arrived in Japan, straight off the boat and sinking into the concrete with exhaustion, we were taken by a tour guide to a place called Monster Road in the port town of Sakaiminato. It's a whole street celebrating the work of a well-known manga artist called Shigeru Mizuki, who came from the town. I tell them this. Mizuki's most famous character is a boy with one eye called Kitaro.

The Professor gets excited when Kasahara tells him all this. 'His nickname at high school was Kitaro,' Kasahara explains.

'Do you like manga?' I ask them. The Professor's eyes widen.

'Yes,' he says, in English. 'I like a lot.'

They're right, he doesn't seem like a runner, though I'm not sure he's like a professor either. Kitaro is a short, ghost boy who wears his long hair over his missing eye. He does look a bit like the Professor. He also wears jet-powered sandals. It's a much better nickname for this speedster.

With only a few weeks left until the national ekiden at the beginning of November, the team's preparations are now mostly complete. But with the ace injured, they may need a few runners in jet-powered sandals if they're going to live up to Kenji's predictions of a top-ten finish.

10

Up on a hill in the city of Nagasaki, nine runners stand in a line on the spot where the world's second and last atomic bomb landed sixty-eight years ago. The TV cameras are pointed at them, while a small crowd of spectators wave flags in the bright early-morning sunshine. A gun fires and they're off, racing down the hill on the first leg of the world's longest relay race: the 740km Grand Tour Kyushu ekiden.

We barely have time to watch them go by when we have to run for the media bus. This is my first experience of watching a top-level ekiden and I'm excited just to be here. A reporter friend of Kenji was so taken with the idea that I had come all the way to Japan to learn about running that he invited me to watch the race. His newspaper was sponsoring it and so he arranged all the credentials. I could ride on the media bus, he told me, by which I imagined he meant we'd ride in front of the leaders watching the race unfold behind us. But it isn't quite like that.

Ekidens can be of varying distances and split between teams of various sizes, with the Grand Tour Kyushu ekiden being the longest of them all. The race is also unique in that it features teams made up of professional, university and amateur runners. Each of the nine regions on Japan's third-biggest island has a team, and they race each other around the island's entire perimeter. At least, that's what they did, covering 1,064km, until the race was slightly scaled back a few years ago. It's now a mere 740km. Each day, six of each team's twenty-five runners take turns to cover distances of around 15km each.

Set up after the war in 1951, as Japan and particularly Nagasaki was attempting to rebuild itself from the devastation caused by the atomic bombs, the race is laced with symbolism and history. Which is why, at the opening ceremony the day before the start, there were lots of sad faces and speeches, as this is the last time the event will ever be staged.

In some ways, the race is simply a victim of market forces. As Japan's economy continues to struggle following years of recession, the Kysuhu ekiden has failed to quite capture the imagination – and more importantly, the national television coverage and accompanying advertising revenue – in the same way as some of the country's other ekidens.

This may be because ten days of running – or now, in its scaled-down format, seven days – is just too long to hold people's attention. Leisure time is hardly an abundant commodity in Japan. Part of Hakone's popularity can be put down to the fact that it takes place during one of Japan's few national holidays.

Another reason the Kyushu ekiden has suffered could be that it's essentially a regional event far from Tokyo, and only two teams have ever won it.

The official reason for cancelling the race is that the police say the roads have become too busy and it's too hard to police a race on such a grand scale. The roads are not closed during the race and life carries on around the runners as usual. At one point on the first day, a runner has to stop at a railway crossing, losing vital ground on his rivals.

I'm also told that some of the professional teams have been lobbying for the race to end, fearing that it is too dangerous, but also too arduous, for their runners. Most of the top runners have to run at least two, and sometimes three legs over the seven days.

Kenya's late former Olympic marathon champion Sammy Wanjiru, one of the greatest road-runners in history, ran the Kyushu ekiden numerous times when he lived and trained on Japan's southern island. The locals remember him fondly. 'We used to shout out that he was breaking the speed limit,' one jokes.

At the opening ceremony an almost tearful organiser recalls all the past greats from the race, including Wanjiru. Among the roll-call I hear Kenji's name mentioned. Kenji ran the Kyushu ekiden seven times, his team winning on all seven occasions – on one occasion he was also anointed the race's best runner, or most valued player (MVP).

He says he first ran the race when he was an eighteen-year-old high-school runner, and that it taught him about how hard ekiden was – he only won one of his four legs that year. 'It was this experience more than anything,' he says, 'that prepared me for the professional ekidens when I joined a corporate team the following year.'

The last ever Kyushu opening ceremony takes place at the train station in Nagasaki and initially it looks like a big crowd has turned out to witness it. However, as the athletes file into their seats, all wearing their team tracksuits, and the speeches begin, most of the crowd moves away, drawn by the arrival of a new, luxury train pulling into the station at the end of its maiden journey. The guests of the train, all elderly VIPs, are treated to a Chinese dragon dance in the station concourse, while the runners sit straining to hear the sponsors and coaches of the ekiden lamenting on about the demise of the race.

It seems a sad way to go out, overshadowed by the arrival of a luxury train.

I stay loyally watching on as the various coaches and team managers get up to give their view on proceedings. When the Fukuoka team coach gets up, my contact, the newspaper man, leans over and whispers: 'He won the silver medal at the Barcelona Olympics.'

Fukuoka are one of the two teams ever to have won the race, winning it twenty-five times to the thirty-six victories notched up by Miyazaki.

The Fukuoka coach, though, has plans to wipe out that deficit in one final flourish.

'It doesn't matter how many times you have won the race,' he says. 'The last time is the most important. We will do our best to claim the final victory.'

*

The media bus takes us to the first changeover point at the end of the first leg. I seem to be one of only about three journalists on the bus. My friend, the newspaper man, is sitting with his head in his hands. He looks a bit green. When the bus stops he leaps off and disappears inside the nearest building. Not sure what else to do, I wait around in the sun for the runners to arrive. All along the course, people have come out of their houses to cheer the runners on. It reminds me of the Tour de France. There are lots of families waving Kyushu flags, and old ladies in aprons who, you imagine, have left something cooking on the stove and are just popping out for a moment as the runners go by.

'For me, ekiden is one of the most exciting, interesting and thrilling of all sports,' says one man I manage to talk to briefly. At the changeover point, the next leg runners are pacing around, ready to go, waiting for their team-mates to appear. And then suddenly they're here, struggling through the last few yards, reaching out, handing over the sash, the tasuki, the symbol of ekiden, the chain that links everyone together.

The finishing runners tumble in over the line, urging the new men on, collapsing on the floor. Team-mates run over to help them up, wrapping them in towels. It's all very dramatic.

The changeovers are key to the spectacle of ekiden, and part of what makes this race format so appealing. The TV cameras dwell on these points, and viewers get to watch the most exciting parts of any race, the runners starting and finishing, many times over. At each changeover the whole dynamic of the race shifts, as new runners take to the stage. It's as though the race is picked up and given a good shake every 20km or so.

Today, with only nine runners in the race, the action at the first changeover is soon over and we're back in the bus racing to the next stop. The newspaper man only just makes it, collapsing back in his seat, closing his eyes. I later find out that to celebrate the ekiden, his team of reporters went out drinking the night before. This is the fallout.

The bus is not really a media bus, but more of a sweeper, collecting up all the runners after they've finished. We don't manage to make it to any of the other changeovers ahead of the runners, so I spend the rest of the day stuck in a traffic jam, a jam caused by the race I'm supposed to be watching. About halfway through the first day, the newspaper man disappears completely, leaving me alone in the ever-crowded bus. I try a few of the athletes, but no one speaks any English. I sit back and close my eyes.

I'm drifting off when I hear the familiar tones of a Kenyan runner. He is being interviewed by a reporter in Japanese, which he seems to speak fluently. After the reporter has grilled him, I move over to talk to him.

'Hi,' I say.

He looks at me warily. He was probably hoping he had done his last interview and could sit back now and relax.

'Is it OK to talk English?' I ask.

'Yes,' he says, looking around, trying to work out my presence there. I tell him I'm writing a book. That I went to Kenya. I'm trying to get him onside. He tells me he is a university runner. He has been in Japan for three years. He grew up in Kenya just a hundred metres away from the house of Sammy Wanjiru, the Olympic marathon champion who lived in Kyushu and raced this ekiden many times.

'I came here to Kyushu because a friend of mine had finished university here and he needed replacing. He recommended me.'

He says he was happy to come to Japan, it was a great

[113]

opportunity for him. But when I ask him about the training here, he gets suddenly animated. He can't stop talking.

'The training, not good,' he says shaking his head. 'Here, they love athletics, it is amazing. More than any other country. More than Kenya. But the training is not good.

'If they trained like in Kenya, all the world records would come from Japan.'

That's quite a statement. Up to now I've been trying to find out why the Japanese are so good at running, but perhaps the question should be why they are failing to compete with the Kenyans and Ethiopians. He's right, in terms of infrastructure and support, things are better here than anywhere else in the world.

But what is wrong with the training?

'They train too much, too young,' he says. 'My best time in Nairobi was 28:52 [for the 10,000m]. After three years in Japan, it is only 28:32. I was the fastest on my leg today, but in two days, on Wednesday, I have to run another leg. Another 17km. Then on Sunday I have a big university ekiden.

'By twenty-five years old, in Japan the runners are finished. They train too hard as children. And all of it on tarmac.'

Is that a problem, I ask him?

'Big problem,' he says. 'And, you know, Japanese men are like dictators.'

He says he can't say any of this to the people here, so instead he has to adapt. But you can tell he is worried about the effect it will have on his future prospects as a runner. Yet many Kenyans and Ethiopians have come to Japan to train and have done very well.

'But Kenyans who do well here,' he says, 'they go back to Kenya before a big race to reduce their training.'

It seems perverse to say the Japanese are slower because they train too hard. Many runners across the world have this idea that if you can run 150 miles a week then you will be a better runner, and it's just laziness that stops people achieving their goals. But the Kenyans are not obsessed with running lots of miles. In my time there I was surprised more by how laid-back they were about running than by how much they ran. Of course, they run a lot. Twice a day on most days. But they rest a lot, too. Most runners in Kenya take one full day's rest each week, and they'll often skip a session, or run easy, if they're feeling tired.

In Japan, runners are expected to follow their coaches' instructions without question, and most coaches are ingrained with the belief that success comes only through hard work. That the more miles you run, the better you will be. Feeling tired is not considered a valid reason to skip training. This is why this Kenyan runner in Kyushu feels the Japanese coaches are too overbearing, because they tell him what to do all the time.

Britain's second fastest female marathoner ever, Mara Yamauchi, married a Japanese man and spent five of her best running years living and training in the country. But she never joined a team.

'When you join a team in Japan,' she says, 'you have to do what the team managers and coaches tell you. But I'm not the sort of person who can follow instructions blindly, I need to know why I'm doing something.'

Despite Japan being at the forefront of global technological developments, the traditional approach to sports training is far from rooted in scientific understanding.

In his book about Japanese baseball, *You Gotta Have Wa*, Robert Whiting writes: 'The Japanese believe that only through endless training can one achieve the unity of mind and body necessary to excel . . . The traditional view in this rich but cramped and resource-poor land is that nothing comes easily, and that only through *doryoku* (effort) and the ability to persevere in the face of adversity can one achieve success.'

He goes on to point out that in a poll by Japan's national broadcaster NHK, *doryoku* was the country's 'most-liked' word.

Mara Yamauchi's coach and husband, Shige, says that from a running point of view, Japan's adherence to a strong work ethic can cause problems, because in running it is important to train intelligently, and not always harder.

'In Japan, there is often a clash between science and the concept of hard work,' he says. 'Because it is conceptual, this idea that to achieve success you must work hard, it has to be removed from science. For it to work, you mustn't reason, you mustn't question why am I doing this. You must just accept it.'

But sometimes it is better to do less. Always doing more, at least in running, can be ineffective and can lead to injuries and burnout.

Stephen Mayaka was one of the first Kenyan runners in Japan, arriving back in 1990, when he says there were only fifteen Kenyan people living in Japan, and most of those were in the embassy.

'When I walked into a shop, people would squeal,' he remembers. Almost twenty-five years later, he's still here. Today he acts as a scout, returning to Kenya on regular trips to find new talent for the Japanese corporate and university teams.

However, he seems to have adopted the Japanese approach to training.

'Kenyans don't want to train hard,' he says. 'But they don't realise that you need to train harder if you're at sea-level.' He says most Kenyans are given their own training schedule, so they don't have to run so much.

While his point about training harder at sea-level may be valid, the amazing results of the Kenyans, both those in Japan and elsewhere, make it hard to argue with their more relaxed approach to training.

Kenji says he believes in taking a more measured, rational approach. He complains that in Japan everything is based on tradition and the whims of coaches, not science. He is a big fan of the US coach Alberto Salazar, whom I bumped into briefly in the Luzhniki stadium in Moscow. Salazar is the man who helped Mo Farah win the 5,000m and 10,000m world and Olympic titles, beating all the Kenyans and Ethiopians.

'Lots of what Salazar talks about is very precise,' Kenji tells me, 'using data and percentages, not just general ideas. Science, not intuition.'

He says the first thing he did when he became coach of the Ritsumeikan team was to cut down their training. Before they used to do two days hard, followed by one day easy, but he changed that immediately to one day hard followed by two days easy.

He also explains his training sessions to his athletes. He wants them to know why they are doing the sessions they are doing, not just blindly follow his instructions.

Kenji is standing at the crossroads of a new path, one where the traditional model of the autocratic coach with his dedication to endless practice, to *doryuku*, to running until you drop, is questioned. It is a path he is not usually encouraged to venture down. Kenji tells me he is constantly being criticised for his coaching methods.

'I'm the nail that sticks out,' he says. 'But I wish I had known what I know now when I was a kid. I would have won gold [at the Olympics]. But back then I just did what I was told.'

*

The media bus rolls into a car park and stops. Everyone gets out. I assume we're at the finish. After hours stuck in traffic, the race has long ended. We appear to be in some sort of fake Dutch town, complete with windmills, canals and plazas full of cafes selling overpriced baguettes. I feel like one of the exhibits when a group of women dressed up as vampish nineteenth-century noblewomen wave me over and ask to have their picture taken with me. I'm getting a little flustered by all the attention when my contact from the newspaper suddenly reappears and rescues me.

He's looking in better health now. He wants me to meet one of the coaches, Koichi Morishita. 'He got the silver medal in the Barcelona Olympics,' he says, watching me closely. I nod. He told me that already. As well as coaching the Fukuoka team here in Kyushu, Morishita is also the coach of a professional ekiden team. This could be my chance to finally gain access to the corporate running world. The Nissin Foods coach I met at the Tokyo track meeting, the one from Kyotanabe, hasn't been replying to my emails asking when I can visit his team.

The newspaper man takes me into the fake town's gift shop, where two of his colleagues are also waiting. The coaches are all having a debrief upstairs, I'm told. They're hoping to catch a few words with them when they appear. One of the colleagues leans over.

'Morishita-san is upstairs. He won the silver medal in Barcelona,' he tells me.

I nod, impressed, as though I didn't know that. All around us small children pore over the shop's toys. There are lots of pirates for some reason. I pick one up. I'll bring one back for Ossian. The newspaper man is pulling my arm. They're here. We rush over.

The newspaper man stops Morishita, bowing and ushering with one arm over to where I'm standing. He looks at me suspiciously, while the newspaper man explains who I am. We shake hands, which is a bit awkward as I'm still holding the toy pirate.

'Nice to meet you,' he says. 'I have to go now. Thank you.' And with that he shuffles off.

*

My questions for the running monks of Mount Hiei have been gathering dust for some time. Eventually Max hears back from the woman at the temple in Kyoto. Her husband, the priest at the same temple, has decided he wants to meet me, too.

'That's how things work in Japan,' Max tells me. 'Especially in Kyoto. You have to grease the wheels if you want them to move.'

So a few days later we return to the same private Zen temple as before. I arrive there early and decide to visit the nearby Rioanji temple, just across the road. This is one of the most important temples in Japan, particularly famed for its rock garden.

I find myself entering the main building at the same time as a large group of teenage schoolgirls. By the time I've queued to stow away my shoes, and then weaved my way past the first wave of students, it's nearly time to leave. I stand looking at the garden from the veranda of the temple along with everyone else.

It's a gravel square with a few rocks sticking out of it. The gravel has been raked into neat swirls. The meaning of the garden, assuming there ever was one, was lost long ago in the slow churn of time. It is around five hundred years since it was built, although the exact origins are unknown. The leaflet I was given at the entrance speculates that it could be meant to visualise the peaks of mountains rising out of the mist, or perhaps baby tigers swimming in a river.

I'm sure I'm missing something. People have been coming to admire this garden for over five hundred years, but it feels a little like the Emperor's New Clothes. I can just imagine one of my children standing there and saying: 'But it's just a few old rocks.'

I move on my way before I'm pushed along by the school-girls swarming up onto the veranda behind me. The wooden floorboards are deliciously smooth under my socked feet. A smoothness worn down by millions of reverential, shuffling feet.

Back at the private temple, Max is waiting outside. We duck in under the low doorway, but Max bumps his head.

'Not humble enough,' he says, smiling.

In front of the temple a man in a tracksuit is tending to the garden. He looks up when he hears our feet crunching on the gravel path.

'Oh, you're early,' he says, in English, and walks off.

'That's him,' says Max. 'The priest.'

A few minutes later he's back in his priest outfit of simple brown robes. He leads us back into the same tatami-mat room, where we sit quietly as his wife serves us tea. The calmness of this empty room again fills me. I watch the sunlight on the garden, waiting for him to speak. There's no rush or awkwardness.

'How was your journey to Japan?' he asks me at last. I tell him about the train. We talk about my children, and Kenya. He tells me that he once did an exchange programme with some Catholic monks in France. A programme devised by Pope John Paul II.

He says that when the monks came here they went to the Rioanji rock garden across the road. When they saw it, he says, they sat down and wouldn't move. They were transfixed.

I tell him I went this morning.

'Did you get anything from it?' he asks with a wry smile, as though he knows it's a trick question. For a moment I'm about to gush effusively about it, but I know it will sound contrived, even to me, and this is a Zen Buddhist priest. Honesty, I decide, is the best option.

'Not really,' I say.

He doesn't seem surprised by the answer, but I can't help softening it with some excuses. There were too many people, and I was in a hurry. I'm sure it's something that needs to be given its time and space. Some of the other shrines were full of magic when I entered them in the spirit of reverence and ritual. In a rush, though, with a queue of tourists buzzing around, all that is missed. It's not the place, so much as your connection with it, that matters.

He nods, thoughtfully. Something about this place gets me talking too much. I ask him about the running monks. Can he put me in contact with them?

He tells me that one of the most famous of all the monks has just died. He was one of the very few ever to complete the thousand-day challenge twice. So right now is not a good time to contact them. We need to wait a few weeks, he says.

Switching to Japanese, he begins to tell me more about the monks. The idea behind the constant movement of the thousand-day challenge, he says, is to exhaust the mind, the ego, the body, everything, until nothing is left.

'When you are nothing, then something, pop, comes up to fill the space.'

He mimes a bubble popping.

This something, he tells me, is the vast consciousness that lies below the surface of our lives, beyond the limits of our usual, everyday experience. A sense of oneness with the universe.

We sit in silence for a moment. Perhaps sensing he has come to the end of his chat, the priest's wife glides silently into the room and crouches down to collect the tea cups. She smiles at us kindly as her husband stands up and thanks us for coming.

On the way out, in the entrance to the temple, we stop to look at a small, wooden statue of a god on display. It's the first thing you see when you come into the building.

'Do you know who this is?' he asks me, speaking in English again. I shake my head.

'Idetan,' he says. 'The god of running.' He claps his hands. 'In that time,' he says, clapping his hands again to be clear, 'in that time, he can go around the earth seven and a half times.' He smiles triumphantly.

'Faster than Usain Bolt,' he says.

11

The next time I return to Kenji's Blooming group, it's at one of their monthly training sessions in nearby Kyoto. It's now early October, but still a balmy 27°c. We meet outside a big baseball stadium, in the shade of some trees. Plastic sheets have been laid out on the ground to put our bags on. One of Kenji's schoolgirl prodigies is here to help with the timekeeping. She can't run because she's injured. She had to have an operation on her knees and won't be able to run for another year, she tells me, smiling resolutely. Kenji is also still not ready to resume training after his operation. Instead he's hobbling around like an old pirate and it's the shuffling army of jolly Blooming members, in their layers of lycra, who are doing the running. One of Kenji's assistants reads out the day's temperature and humidity levels, and they all note the information down neatly in their training logs.

After the data is recorded, we set off on a warm-up jog. Max is here again. He has been training on his own, he tells me. He says he wants to get revenge on some of the runners who beat him at the last session. 'I'm definitely on course,' he says. 'By the end of the six months, I want the ace running scared of me, too, not just you.' He has a plan. He says he ran a 10km in training in 50 minutes. Next month, he says, he will run it in 45 minutes. Then 40 minutes. Then 35.

'And then 30 minutes the month after that?' I ask him.

He grins at me. 'Who knows. Why set limits?'

As we jog, the woman running next to me tells us that Morita, the ace, is actually a bit upset that I beat him in the first session in Osaka. That was probably impolite, on my first night, I think, so I apologise.

'No, run harder and make him more upset,' she says, laughing. She seems to be building it up like some sort of face-off. Today's session is a 5km time trial. A time trial to the death.

'He isn't running today,' says someone else, jogging in front, turning her head. 'He's injured.'

Morita is there when we get back to the start, but it's hard to tell if he's annoyed or not. He looks at me sullenly from under his hair, but then that seems to be his normal look. He's just jogging today. It's only a small injury, he says.

I ask him if the ekiden he invited me to run in at Lake Biwa is still happening. 'Of course,' he says, bypassing Max and speaking in English. He has an American accent, which only makes him seem more like Charles Bronson. 'I will be OK by then, I'm sure.' It turns out he lived for five years in San Diego, California. They used to call him the Mexican, because, well, he looks Mexican. 'Your leg is 5km,' he tells me. 'So today is good practice.'

I must admit I was hoping for a tougher session than a 5km time trial, as I'm still trying to regain my full fitness after the journey to Japan. It's hard in this heat to judge how I'm running, but I don't think I've yet caught up with where I was before we set out on the train all those months ago.

Without Morita running, I decide to start off easy. I'll just sit with the leaders and then gradually wind it up, I tell myself. But halfway up the first incline, less than 20 seconds into the time trial, I take off.

All the polite shimmy-shammying at the start can be exhausting. In Japan it's even worse than in England. *You first. No, I insist, you first.* As we line up ready to go, none of the Blooming runners wants to stand at the front. It means everybody is 20 yards behind the start line in an embarrassed semi-circle. Don't be the nail that sticks out. Don't make any bold displays of self-importance like standing at the front at the beginning of a run. But someone has to. And so I go, racing off into the heat, into the crowds spilling out of the baseball stadium, the families taking a Sunday stroll around the park.

By the third lap, I'm wilting, the sun burning my eyes, turning my legs to goo. I struggle on, following the perimeter path, the sweat running down my temples. Up ahead I see Morita jogging towards me, composed, running laps slowly in the opposite direction. He gives me a tiny bow as we pass. I glance behind and see that one runner is closing on me. I think of Kenji's words, *in ekiden, you never let anyone pass*. I push on, running for my imaginary team, holding on to the end for the 'win' in 19 minutes 14 seconds. It's not exactly the course record, or anywhere near my best 5km time, but it's not too bad considering the heat. The Lake Biwa ekiden is in a few weeks. I want to be ready to do my bit.

Max finishes in 24 minutes. He's definitely improving, looking less like a football player, bobbing from side to side, and more like a runner. 'Yes,' he says, when I tell him this. 'That's what I'm working on. Alignment.'

After everyone has finished, we gather in the usual debriefing circle and Kenji imparts some advice about how important it is to rest after training. Kenji says that in twelve years as a serious runner, he only went out for a drink four times. He looks around, but they're only half listening. They want to present him with some gifts. It turns out that this is the two-hundredth Blooming training session. Someone has been counting them. In celebration of this landmark, they give Kenji a box of curry mixes and a personalised business-card holder.

'He's probably been to all two hundred sessions,' I say.

'He definitely has,' says Max. 'The other week they told me he was here on crutches and his foot in a bucket of ice.'

*

On the morning of the Lake Biwa ekiden, I meet Morita early at the train station in Kyoto. He's smiling, instead of his usual downbeat demeanour. The station is heaving even though it is still only seven o'clock on a Saturday morning. Lots of people are dressed in sports gear. People don't get much free time in Japan and when they do, rather than sleeping in, they tend to want to make the most of it. The station is busier early on a weekend morning than at any other time during the week.

As we head to the platform, Morita tells me his injury is better, but that he hasn't run properly for a month. Also, two of the team members have dropped out.

'They had to go to their jobs,' he tells me.

One of the replacements is Kono, an 800m runner, personal trainer and part-time model. However, he's also been injured and hasn't run for a month either. Almost everyone I meet, it seems, has some sort of injury problem. Kono has also been up since 4 a.m. seeing a client in Osaka, so he's tired. I begin to wonder if perhaps the lack of time dedicated to sleep in Japan has something to do with the high injury rate.

According to the US National Sleep Foundation's latest poll of sleeping habits around the world, Japanese workers get less sleep than workers in any other country. Whenever you get on a train in Japan, half the carriage will be sitting there with their eyes closed, their heads nodding like donkeys, trying to catch up on missed sleep. Even in their offices, it is common for exhausted workers to fall asleep at their desks. Rather than being frowned upon, the practice, known as *inemuri* – or 'sleeping while present' – is considered a sign of commitment to hard work.

One day I'm invited to give a talk to a lecture hall of over two hundred students at Ritsumeikan University about my experiences in Kenya. Before I begin, the usual lecturer sidles over to me and whispers in my ear: 'Lots of them will probably fall asleep while you're talking. Don't be offended, it's normal.'

And sure enough, ten minutes in, here and there eyes begin to close. By the end of my talk, around a third of the lecture hall is asleep. I'm glad I was warned.

The habit of skimping on a full night's sleep, however, can have a detrimental effect on people competing in sport.

Research in the US found that adolescent athletes who slept eight or more hours each night were sixty-eight per cent less likely to be injured than athletes who regularly slept less. That's a big difference. The US Sleep Foundation's poll found that on average Japanese workers kip for only six hours twenty-two minutes each night.

'Hi,' says our stand-in runner, Kono, with a yawn when we meet him at the station. He's unusually tall and looks more like a Pacific Island rugby player than a Japanese runner. 'So nice to meet you,' he says in good English, winking and shaking my hand, which people almost never do in Japan. It takes me slightly by surprise.

On the way to the race, our captain and ace, Morita, tells me he works in marketing, for a new health supplement. 'It's based on vinegar,' he tells me, when I ask him what type of supplement. He has actually only been running for a few years and his marathon PB is just 3:26, over half an hour slower than my best time. He used to be a mountain-bike rider, but when his friend suffered a bad accident he decided he wanted to find something he could do alone.

At first he started running with another club, but they were too slow, he tells me. So he joined Blooming.

'The first time I ran with them, I realised this was a better level,' he says.

I ask him if the chance to run with Kenji was part of the reason he joined.

'No,' he says. 'I didn't really know who he was. I wasn't a running fan then.'

*

We arrive at Lake Biwa an hour before the start of the race. One of the women in our team has brought a groundsheet which she lays on the ground near the start. We put our bags down on it. Then they all head off to begin their warm-up. It seems a bit early to me, so I decide to stay behind. I look around for somewhere to sit down. I wonder whether it would cause an outcry if I sat on the grass. It's dry, but if they won't even put their bags on it – what will they think if I sit on it? I look around at the other teams, but no one is sitting on the grass. Some of the other teams even have tents to sit in.

I try sitting on the roots of a tree but they're too knobbly so in the end I head off for a jog to pass the time.

I find a quiet spot and decide to stop and watch our first few runners go by, sitting up on a grass bank where no one can see me. The course heads along the road towards the lake, winding through a forest of autumn-tinged maple trees, before turning back to the start, where each change-over takes place under a big yellow arch of balloons. I'm running the sixth leg so I still have another hour to wait.

The teams in this particular ekiden are all made up of four men and three women. Our first-leg runner is the woman who told me Morita was mad I'd beaten him in training. Before the start, she shows me pictures of her cat on her phone, and jokes about the race, trying to provoke Morita. He doesn't rise to the bait, however, instead giving her his brooding Bronson look.

Despite setting off at a slow, tentative pace, she reappears at the end with her sweatshirt around her waist, her arms swinging like a boxer, making her way through the other runners as though the treacle she's running through isn't quite as sticky and debilitating as the one they all seem to be stuck in. It's a grind to the finish, but she gets there in about twenty-ninth position of the eighty or so teams.

A man of about sixty is our next runner. He's a teacher at a school in Kyoto and he tries to tell me about his school's ekiden team, but his English is as bad as my Japanese and we get no further than acknowledging the existence of the team. His wife is involved somehow, too, I think.

He sets off at a fairly steady pace, a couple of whizzy teenagers streaking straight past him in the first few hundred metres. I fear the worst, but by the end of his leg, as he comes rolling back down the hill to the finish, his mouth gaping for air, his legs moving in slow-motion, we're only a few places further back.

I'm trying to muster up some feeling for my team. I want to sense, when I grab the tasuki, that the spirit and toil of the team is depending on me. That every place I gain is crucial, that every place I lose is a stab in our collective hearts. This is what ekiden is all about, I'm told, doing it for the team. However, the fact I only met most of them this morning means my sense of team spirit is far from a burning fire in my soul, but more a half-hearted rubbing of sticks on a cold morning. I'm not sure it's enough to rouse me to any great feats of running. The fact that the rest of the team don't seem to care too much about the outcome of the race doesn't help either.

*

My turn has come. I'm standing in a pen with about forty other runners; all lean, serious athletes. Has everyone saved their best runners for the end? I'm the sixth leg of seven. I've got no idea how we've been doing as a team since I disappeared to do my warm-up. But I'm ready to go.

I need to concentrate. They're calling out the numbers of the runners coming in. I'm waiting to hear *yon-ju ni* (forty-two). Once they call your number, you need to step out onto the road to meet your incoming team-mate, and grab the tasuki from him, the symbolic ribbon that each team has to carry from start to finish.

One runner arrives in front of us and lets out a yell. His next runner was obviously daydreaming as he isn't there. Suddenly he leaps out from among us, grabs the tasuki and sprints off, leaving the first runner grumbling and shaking his head.

Another man comes in and stumbles over the line, going down in a slow-motion roll and lying there on the road for a few seconds until two stewards help him up.

'*Yon-ju ni*,' the voice on the microphone calls. That's me. I step out onto the road. The protocol seems to be to wave to the incoming runner, to let him know you're there. So I do that. It's Morita. He's the only person in sight, which is good. It means I won't have anyone breathing down my neck.

He doesn't say anything as he hands me the tasuki. I put it on as I practised it, slipping it over my head and tucking the loose end into my shorts. As I head out under the yellow arch my team-mates give me a cheer from the roadside. OK, team, here I go.

I'm running on my own, but I have people up ahead in the distance to chase. As I run, the people watching keep nudging each other and looking surprised as I go by. I like to think it's because I'm going so fast, but clearly they're just surprised to see a *gaijin*, or foreigner, in the race. I'm the only person running who isn't Japanese. But the fact I'm speeding by so fast must add to the effect, right?

Of course, I'm not running that fast. My 5km personal best dates back to 1991, when on a warm summer's evening my running club held a 5,000m track race instead of our usual training session. I was seventeen years old and had been playing football all day with my brothers. It was a cinder track and I'd never run a 5K before. So I didn't think too much about my time that night, which was 16 minutes 50 seconds. Twenty-two years and a good few attempts later and I've still never beaten it. After I came back from Kenya I ran 17:10, but I haven't run under 18 minutes in the last two years.

The course is all gradually uphill until halfway, with stewards along the route noting our numbers down every 500 metres. I imagine it's to plot a complicated graph of the race afterwards. In any case, I'm beginning to pass people. One, two, three. Some of them are running so slowly I'm worried they might topple over if I run too close.

The turning point comes surprisingly quickly. I feel as though I've barely started, and now it's just the long downhill back to the finish. I pick up my pace, and soon I'm streaking past runner after runner. I'm taking this team right up the leaderboard like some fabled Hakone runner. *He came from across the ocean, racing like the wind . . .*

Afterwards, I'm trying not to sound boastful when I tell the team back at our base that I overtook about ten runners on my leg.

'That's good,' says Morita smiling. 'Because I was over-taken by about ten.'

In the end, our team finishes twenty-sixth out of around eighty teams. Morita says it is an amazing result for Bloom-ing as most of the top teams were university teams. On my leg, I was the fourth fastest runner, finishing in 17:49, al-most a minute behind my seventeen-year-old self running on tired legs on a cinder track all those years ago. But over a minute quicker than the Blooming time trial in Kyoto just the week before. It's progress of sorts.

*

In truth, I'm not improving as quickly as I was hoping and all those PBs from a few years ago seem to be fading fur-ther and further into the past like hazy memories from a more sprightly age. One problem is that I can't seem to find anyone of my own level to run with. Whenever I run with the Blooming group, I feel like I'm flying. One night a few weeks after the Biwa ekiden, I find myself racing around Osaka Castle again, speeding past everyone, reveling in their gasps of astonishment as I go by. I feel like Wilson Kipsang, the new marathon world-record holder, my legs moving so smoothly, so easily across the ground.

The very next morning, however, I find myself back on the track with the Ritsumeikan runners. They're doing a 3,000m time trial, and the plan is for me to try to run with them for the first 1,000m. As soon as we start, I feel like a degenerate madman, sprinting for my life just to stay on their heels for two and a half laps. I run it in 2 minutes 50 seconds, falling off the pace by the end. This is pretty fast for me, I think, although as I usually work in miles I'm not entirely sure. In any case, I'm a long way behind the Ritsumeikan runners.

Everyone, it seems, is either much faster or much slower than me. There must be some people running at my pace, but they're hard to find. Perhaps I should start my own ekiden team, made up of the people closest to my level. We could all train together and race an ekiden.

While I mull over that possibility, Kenji gives me the details of another running club that meets once a month in Kyoto. They have some serious amateur runners, he says. However, when I set out on the train early one Saturday morning to find them, I end up, an hour later, back at the station where I started. I'm totally confused as to how it happened, which makes it difficult to explain to the woman guarding the ticket barrier, who wants to know why my pass is trying to exit at the same station it was used at to board the train.

I'll have to try again another day. But for now, until I set up my team, I'm stuck in the middle on my own, floundering away somewhere between Blooming and Ritsumeikan.

12

The first of the big three university ekidens takes place in the town of Izumo on the north coast of southern Honshu, not far from the port of Sakaiminato where we first arrived in Japan. Ritsumeikan have failed to qualify, but I manage to get an invite to hang out with an American Ivy League select team which has been coming over to Japan to run this race for almost fifteen years.

I arrive on the train and get a taxi to the finish area. I'm assuming the head coach, Jack Fultz, who was the winner of the Boston marathon in 1976, will be easy to spot, and sure enough, there he is, fair-skinned and baseball-capped as expected. I walk over.

'Oh, Finn, the writer,' he says. 'Welcome.' He gives me a firm handshake and starts telling me immediately about the history of the team's involvement in the race.

'This Ivy League programme started in 1990. It was the idea of Dr Vern Alden, an American businessman. He'll be here today. He set it up with his friend, Mr Kono, a highly respected politico in Japan. They happened to be associates from former business dealings, from what I understand.'

Initially the Ivy League team raced in the longer Nagoya ekiden, which is comprised of eight legs of nearly 20km each.

'But this proved to be far beyond the capabilities of our runners,' says Jack. 'They were just coming out of college and not accustomed to racing such long distances. Ergo, the team did not fare well, so the shorter distances at Izumo made more sense.'

The only runner around is the first-leg athlete, Joe Stilin, who sits brooding on a chair too small for him. He's switched off, not listening to Jack. Preparing himself for the race. The other runners are out in position on the course.

Joe is tall, fair-haired and handsome. A real American hero.

'He's got the lot,' Jack tells me, as we watch him warming up a bit later. 'Thirteen thirty-three for 5,000m. Grade A student at Princeton.' He hasn't worked out how to put his shorts on, though.

'They're on backwards,' Jack tells him.

'Oh,' he says. 'I thought they looked weird.'

The race starts under the stone entrance to the Taisha Grand Shrine and the place is packed with people cheering on the teams. These are the runners Ritsumeikan will be competing against at the national ekiden next month, and many of the teams who will bring Japan to a halt on 2 and 3 January in the Hakone ekiden.

I watch most of the race with Jack on a TV in a small room near the finish. I don't take much of it in as Jack is quite a talker, expounding on everything from whether the Kenyans are all on drugs, to the current state of running in the US, and his love of golf, which along with running and baseball is, he says, the biggest sport in Japan. As we talk, his Japanese fixer brings us updates from the race. Joe starts off well enough on the first leg, finishing in tenth place of the twenty-one runners, but after that the team starts going backwards. With each update it seems worse, with the team finally finishing in fourteenth place after a late rally.

One by one the runners appear after finishing their leg of the race, looking for something to eat, giving Jack their debriefing. Most of them are not happy. It was too hot, says one. 'I just didn't feel myself out there today.' 'I cramped up.' 'I gave it my best shot and that's all I can ask.' None of them mentions the team.

The truth is that the US runners are unprepared for the task. The Japanese teams have been building towards this race for six months. This is the first of the big three – the three races that matter most in their entire year. They know what to expect, and they're expected to perform. This is going out on national television across Japan, the streets are lined with supporters.

For the Americans, on the other hand, it's a curious jolly. A free week in Japan in the off-season. A chance to have some fun and run a relay race. The focus and intensity is simply not there.

'Also, ekiden racing is a novel format to American road-runners,' says Jack. 'It's very unique. And most of our guys are fairly new to any form of road running. In college it's all cross-country and track.'

Even at the closing ceremony afterwards, the difference between the Ivy League team and the others is marked. The Americans are the last team to arrive. The ceremony started at 3.40 p.m., with all the athletes lined up neatly in teams. Jack's Japanese fixer is in a flap, ushering the bemused Ivy League runners over to the hall where it's all taking place.

'Japanese ceremony, very punctual,' he says. It's 3.43 p.m., and there's a gaping hole in the ceremony where the Americans should be. They shuffle over, half-dressed, towels around their necks, bags sloping off their shoulders. They look around them, taking it all in, while the Japanese runners stand to attention, neatly turned out in their zipped-up team tracksuits, eyes fixed ahead.

One of the Americans still hasn't arrived.

'Quick, get out there,' says Jack, when the last runner appears. He's clearly a little embarrassed by the tardiness. 'And tell them to stand up straight,' he says. 'Not like they are.'

However, the Americans can seemingly do no wrong, even with their carefree ways and their long hair and beards. Rather than being annoyed, people keep coming up to me, assuming I'm part of the team, and telling me what an honour it is to have us in the race. They're also clearly pleased to see the American team finish well down the field. 'You tried hard, that is good to see,' they tell me.

A few years ago the Ivy League team drafted in some runners from other universities in the US. I'm not sure what the thinking was, but the organisers didn't like it when the Americans finished as high as eighth. So this year they were under strict instructions: genuine Ivy Leaguers only.

The race was won, meanwhile, by Komazawa University, in a course record. The star of the day was Kenta Murayama, one of Japan's brightest young runners, who broke the course record on the third stage by twelve seconds.

Behind Komazawa, in second, was Toyo University. These two teams will go on to meet again at the national ekiden the following month, where Ritsumeikan will also be on the start line, and again in Hakone in January, where their head-to-head battle for glory will enthral the nation.

*

That evening, after the race, there is a closing party. The Ivy League runners are in high spirits, laughing loudly at the idiosyncrasies of the Japanese, the lady with the flag leading us off the bus, the giggles from the women as we walk by, all the bowing. We're led into a room full of dozens of round tables with cooking pots on gas hobs in the middle. We're all given comedy hats to wear, and people keep shaking my hand and asking what song we will be doing tonight. I feel like a gatecrasher no one has noticed yet. Jack is off being introduced to everyone, and Joe is the only other person I've met properly. I sit down next to him. I don't have much choice but to tag along as Jack has got me a room at the same hotel, and I've no idea where it is.

A Japanese man who talks English is on our table. No one seems to know him and it's hard to tell if he's just being friendly, or whether the organisers have put him there to act as our host. He seems to know a lot about the ekiden teams. He has had a few drinks, so perhaps tells me more than he means to.

'One coach,' he says, 'today his team did not do so well. He tells me: "I need to talk with my president. I need more money."'

He says that the top university teams offer under-the-table payments to the parents of top high-school runners to encourage them to join. It's not allowed, but it happens all the time, he says. Of course, getting the best runners is crucial to becoming a top ekiden team.

The top runners, he says, don't even have to study at university. 'But it is a problem,' he says. 'Later in life they struggle.'

Someone is opening tins of meat and chucking it into the pot, which is now sizzling.

'You know what that is?' our English-speaking friend asks. 'Come on, guess.' We look at the tins. It's impossible to know, though I've got a good idea.

'Whale meat,' he yells, and starts pouring beers for everyone. The room is full of people now, and outside there are even more tables. People keep coming over to us and taking our picture. I'm not sure whether I'm supposed to be in or out of them. Nor is anyone else. It's all a bit awkward, so I get up to go for a look around.

'I think they're serving rice balls outside,' says Jack, who is back now, realising I can't eat the stewpot of whale meat.

Outside, music is blaring and people are queueing for food from under a large canopy. I join the queue. As I'm standing there, a Japanese runner comes up to me with his friend. He has short, spiky hair and a pockmarked face. He shakes my hand and leans in close to me.

'I have a small dick,' he says, in English, grinning inanely and pointing to his crotch to show he knows what he's saying. I'm not sure how to reply. His friend, in the same team tracksuit, is grinning as though I've fallen into some kind of trap. Or I am about to. He points to his crotch, too.

'I have small dick,' he says. I'm not getting the joke.

'That's great,' I say, wishing I'd stayed with my teammates.

'You?' they both ask, craning towards me like gaudy puppets in some nightmare fairground. The queue doesn't seem to be moving. I'm cornered.

'Medium,' I say. I don't know if they know that word, but they both cheer and give me a high five. The rest of the Americans saunter over from out of the dining room. The two Japanese runners disappear into the crowd, to my relief. Finally, I get some rice balls.

*

I end the night on a big stage with the rest of the Ivy League team miming to the song 'YMCA'. One of them has commandeered a huge inflatable arrow and everyone laughs drunkenly as we hash our way through the song. By the end it's painfully bad, but the crowd seems to love it, cheering, with many of them rushing up on the stage to join in.

All the teams have to do a performance, so after our song we clamber down and mingle back into the crowd. Everyone, of course, assumes I'm American. One man, standing next to me as we watch a troupe of cheerleaders from Juntendo University high-kicking and somersaulting, says: 'Japanese people like America. We try to catch up.'

When I tell Max about it all, days later, he tells me the Japanese have an inferiority complex when it comes to the west. 'They genuinely believe they have smaller penises,' he tells me. 'I think statistically they're a tiny bit smaller, but basically they're the same.'

I'm not sure where he got that particular bit of data, but it turns out that it's a widely held stereotype. And it's not just penis size. Max tells me the TV commentators are always talking about how short in stature the Japanese runners are, and constantly saying that, even though they have little legs, they manage to compete against the rest of the world because of their courage. That, they say, is the quality of the Japanese runners: courage, spirit, doggedness. Despite their size.

In this area of height, at least, there are many studies and it is indeed true that on average the Japanese have shorter legs relative to their height than other populations.

David Epstein, author of *The Sports Gene*, says that this is not an ideal ratio for running, and he believes it may have something to do with why the Japanese records from 10,000m downwards are surprisingly slow.

'It's still a surprise to me how poor Japanese track records are for a large running nation,' he tells me when I ask him about it. 'Even the Japanese road 10K record is above 28 minutes. Their national record wouldn't even win the minor Healthy Kidney 10K in Central Park.

'To me, the fact that, on average, they don't have the ideal body structure for speed [long legs relative to height] must be a factor.'

Yet the lack of prowess at 10,000m and below can at least partly be explained by the fact that these races are never taken seriously in Japan. The only races that matter are the ekidens and marathons. These are the only races shown on television, the only races the university and corporate team bosses are interested in. Everything else is just training. Middle-distance runners, such as Kasahara at Ritsumeikan University, are hustled into ekiden running from a young age.

In the Izumo ekiden, the winning team's fourth-stage run-ner was the national universities' 1500m champion, Ikuto

Yufu. At Hakone he will run the 21.5 km third leg. That's what he is training for, not the 1500m, even though he is clearly one of Japan's brightest middle-distance prospects.

Also, if it was genetics holding them back, surely a few outliers would come through a system as evolved as the Japanese running system to record some decent track times. The reason you don't find any great German rugby players, for example, is not because they don't have the right body type. The Germans are simply not interested in rugby.

British marathon runner Mara Yamauchi agrees: 'All the training in Japan is geared towards longer races. I imagine if some of these athletes and teams switched their focus to the shorter distances such as 5km and 10km they would do extremely well because the Japanese work very hard, they have huge depth in coaching, therapy etc. and the system is well organised and funded.'

In any case, short legs or not, the Japanese inferiority complex regarding size is in some ways misplaced, as being smaller can also be an advantage when it comes to distance running, and particularly in the longer events such as half-marathon and marathon where the Japanese do well. Yamauchi believes Japanese runners actually have a big advantage because of their body type.

'My ideal race weight,' she says, 'was forty-nine kilograms, but it was hard to get down to that. But most Japanese women runners are around forty to forty-three kilograms. That's a good starting point.'

Shorter runners are also better able to tolerate hot conditions, as a smaller frame can dissipate heat more efficiently. This was a big advantage for Mizuki Noguchi when she beat the much taller Paula Radcliffe to win the gold medal in the 2004 Olympic marathon in the baking summer heat in Athens. In the world championship marathon I watched in Moscow, two short Japanese women finished third and fourth in sweltering conditions.

In men's running, too, the greatest long-distance runners of them all are mostly tiny. The man usually regarded as the greatest of them all, Haile Gebrselassie, stands at five feet five inches (1.65m), while Kenenisa Bekele, the world record holder at 5,000m and 10,000m, is only a fraction taller at five foot six (1.67m).

Yamauchi says some male Japanese runners weigh as little as fifty kilograms even though they eat well. 'They're not this size through excessive weight loss,' she says, 'It's just their natural body type, but it's ideal for long-distance running.'

A French study found that the average height of the top hundred male marathon runners in the world in 2011 was five feet seven inches (1.70m). This just happens to be exactly the same height as the average Japanese man.

13

It's now November and the ekiden season is in full swing. The next stop on the schedule is the intriguing Chiba international ekiden. This is a relay of mixed teams of men and women from different countries. Without a British team competing, I somehow manage to find myself once again in the company of the Americans.

I travel to the race with Mr Ogushi, who meets me at Tokyo station. His plan is to hand me over to the US team once we get there. They have agreed to let me see what they get up to on race day.

For the last twenty-five years, the Chiba ekiden has invited the world to come and experience the thrills and spills of ekiden running. Chiba is unique among elite ekidens in having mixed-gender teams, with three men and three women running for each country. Also in Chiba the complete race distance comes out neatly at 42.195 km – exactly a full marathon. The year before, the competition featured some of the very best runners in the world, such as Galen Rupp (2012 Olympic medalist from the US) and Edwin Soi (2008 Olympic medalist from Kenya). Kenya won by just seconds ahead of Japan, with the USA third. It sounds like a thrilling race.

'It's just for fun. Not serious,' says Mr Ogushi dismissively.

I nod, not sure what to say. We're standing on a packed train rattling out through the eastern suburbs of Tokyo, a sea of tessellated roofs flickering outside the window. He pulls out his phone and starts scrolling the screen.

'Can Japan win it this year, do you think?' I ask, trying to stoke some national loyalty in him, to see if I can get him fired up about the race. But he's not listening.

The train pulls into a station and the doors beep open.

'Let's go,' he says, putting his phone back in his pocket.

When we arrive at the entrance to the sports stadium, I'm somehow recognised by a Japanese woman with perfect English, who takes me from Mr Ogushi and leads me over to the US team. The team manager, a woman called Patricia, has been expecting me. 'Oh, you're the writer,' she says.

All the teams are gathered in a bunker-like room under the main stand. Outside, the sun bathes an athletics track in bright, autumn light. But here in the bunker it's freezing. It's about an hour before the start of the race, so I stand around next to Patricia and ask her about the US team's chances.

'It's a young team,' she says. Fun as it is to get a trip to Japan to race an ekiden, not everyone wants to come, so the international team managers have to take the best runners they can find.

Suddenly a Japanese man is ushering me over somewhere. 'Quick, quick,' he says, taking my arm. I follow on, as I'm used to doing in Japan. 'Opening ceremony. Stand behind the flag,' he says, pointing to a person carrying a huge US flag.

'Oh. I think you want an athlete,' I say.

'Yes, an athlete.' He looks confused.

'Wait a minute.'

I suddenly realise the pass they've given me to wear says 'US team: official athlete' on it, so it's not really the man's fault. I'm also coincidentally wearing US team colours, although blue jeans and puffer jacket, and casual red shoes, are hardly the US running outfit. In any case, I take it as a compliment that I could even conceivably look like an international athlete.

Outside on the track, real athletes are warming up, bristling with grace and power. In some ways, it is in the moments before a race that these top runners are at their most impressive. They seem to grow taller in preparation for the race ahead, their eyes focused, striding along the track with complete ease, all long legs and sinewy muscle, like a separate species of super beings. Later, as they struggle across the finish line, or as they sink down on the ground afterwards, or drink beer and tell stories on the bus home, they seem normal again.

*

Despite Mr Ogushi's indifference, there's something about the colours and flags at an international event like this that make it exciting. You already have a complex and evolved set of affiliations and prejudices towards the teams, which is part of what gives sport its appeal. In any sport, if you don't know anything about the people or teams competing, and can't relate to them in any way, you won't be as engaged.

I often think sport is in some ways like a soap opera. Back in England, football is the country's favourite sport and I'm a big fan. It's thrilling to watch the top teams go head to head against each other in a crucial match. But is the game itself intrinsically exciting? Watch two teams you know nothing about, from the Norwegian league say, and it's hard to muster as much enthusiasm. Without the back-stories of the players and teams, it just isn't the same.

This is why newspaper sponsorship and coverage of the early ekidens was so crucial to the sport's popularity in Japan. The Chiba ekiden was a relative latecomer to the party, with the first race held in 1988.

The first-leg athletes are lining up on the track. The race starts at precisely 1.07 p.m. This is to give the TV company enough time to introduce the event and play an advertisement break before the race starts. As well as the national team, Japan has a universities team in the race, and Chiba prefecture also has a team. The first-leg runner for the US – my team for the day – is Will Leer, who stands at least six feet tall, with long hair and a big, bushy beard. Beside him is a sullen Russian in sunglasses, and at the far end is the former Olympic 1500m silver medallist from New Zealand, Nick Willis. But one vest seems to stand out, emanating a certain power over the field. In the black, green and red of Kenya is Joseph Ebuya, the 2010 world cross-country champion.

One insider tells me the organisers purposely ensure that Kenya doesn't pick its strongest available team, in order to give the Japanese a chance. I'm not sure if that's true, but it doesn't seem to matter who is on their team. Kenya have won the last two years. Everyone knows they will probably win again today.

Indeed, right from the start, as the runners loop twice around the track before heading off on their tour of Chiba, Ebuya runs purposefully at the front of the field.

Will Leer later tells me: 'We got out of the stadium and the Kenyan guy just slammed on it. The field split up real quick after that.'

I hear someone who is watching the race on the televisions in the bunker comment soon after the runners have left the stadium: 'It's just the Kenyan and a crazy Japanese dude at the front now.'

The crazy Japanese dude, the young Komazawa university runner Kenta Murayama, eventually drops off, and from then on there is no catching Kenya. They finish the race well ahead in yet another course record. The US team, after a poor start, work their way back to fifth. Japan claim second again.

I watch most of the race in the bunker. The team managers, coaches, physios, hangers-on (like me), and alternative athletes – the reserve runners who weren't needed – sit around watching it all play out on two small televisions. The Kenyans whoop and clap their hands whenever their athletes are shown on the screen. But they're soon away and gone at the front, and the TV cameras spend most of the time on the battle for second, which briefly features New Zealand, but eventually boils down to a tussle between Japan and Russia. The Russian team sit in the bunker watching in silence. Even when the athletes return to the bunker after finishing their stages, while the Kenyans hug and drape each other in their flag, the Russians simply shake hands without looking at each other.

At one point I spot the Komazawa university team coach. This is the team that just won the big Izumo university ekiden. I remember seeing him at the finish, basking in the glory of his team's victory, his permatan and slicked-back hair glistening in triumph. I sit down next to him. I want to ask him about his team. They must be doing something right. People are already talking them up as Hakone favourites.

'*Sumimasen. Aigo o hanashimasuka?*' It's the best I can do. *Excuse me, do you speak English?*

He stares at me for a second. 'No,' he says, turning away, his arms folded. I try to think of a way to carry on in Japanese, but it's no good, he has his back to me. The conversation is already over. I slide away sheepishly.

'Typical Japanese,' says Mr Ogushi, who was watching on from the back of the bunker.

*

After the race, as the sun begins to set, I leave the stadium with the rest of the US team. A small crowd of Japanese fans with little American flags has gathered to get autographs and wave us off. I avoid signing anyone's book, but I do find myself waving as I climb onto the team bus.

On the bus, the athletes are more relaxed. One starts passing around cans of beer, while another is playing hiphop on his phone as loud as it will let him.

'Man, we should do a race like this in the US,' says one. 'Do you think anyone would come and watch?'

'Maybe if you held it in Silicon Valley, and got corporate

teams to enter,' suggests another. 'You know, like Google. But just to watch elites like this? It would never work.'

One of the main differences between running in Japan and the rest of the world is the popularity of elite distance running as a spectator sport. One inside source who didn't want to be named told me that the reason the 2013 world championship marathons in Moscow were held in the middle of the afternoon, when the August sun was at its most ferocious, was because of Japanese television. Marathons are so popular in Japan that the TV companies leaned on the IAAF to start the races at 2 p.m., as this was peak evening viewing time in Japan.

Out in Chiba today, the streets were lined with hundreds of thousands of spectators, while the race was shown live on national television. A long-distance running race with no mass field of amateur runners, no charity runners, no one running in fancy dress. At each point along the course, people came out to wave and cheer as just thirteen athletes went by. As the Americans say, it would never happen anywhere else.

'They were going wild out there,' Will Leer tells me. 'I've no idea what they were saying, but they seemed pretty excited.'

It is this love of the sport that drives and underpins the entire professional and university ekiden system. Without it the Japanese simply would not be such good long-distance runners.

14

A few years before coming to Japan, I discovered barefoot running. I read the book *Born to Run*, and, like millions of others, I was convinced. It was brilliantly simple. To run faster, more efficiently and without injury, all you had to do was take off your shoes.

The debate that continues to rage in the wake of Christopher McDougall's bestselling tome is enough to fill a book ten times the size of this one. The key tranche of McDougall's book is a theory put forward by Harvard scientists that humans evolved to run long distances through persistence hunting – chasing animals down on foot until, exhausted, they collapsed and died. According to the theory, we are all, in effect, born to run, and we only struggle with running and get injured so much because we wear big, clunky shoes on our feet. This prevents them from working as they're designed to, landing lightly and carefully on the ground, feeding back information to the brain about how to run. The result is that instead of whipping across the earth like the Kenyans, who all grow up running barefoot, we plod along like badly designed robots, crashing into the tarmac in our heavy, brick-like footwear, sending seismic shocks up our legs, destroying our knees and other joints.

Of course, it's not quite as simple as that, but I'm a sucker for anything that tells us to take things back to their natural state, that simplicity is best, that over-thinking has ruined everything. So I went to visit a barefoot expert, Lee Saxby, who was working out of a boxing gym in north London and called himself the Che Guevara of running. He taught me how to run – head up, body leaning forward slightly, landing on my midfoot rather than on my heels, legs circling like I was riding a unicycle – and he put me in a pair of super-thin shoes. I still needed to wear shoes, as most people will, because after all these years in their boxes my feet are too soft and delicate to survive running actually barefoot. But these shoes were thin enough to mimic barefoot running. To avoid the obvious charge of having an oxymoronic name, they are often called minimalist shoes rather than barefoot shoes.

They felt great. Not only did they help me develop a faster, more efficient form, but they were super-light, which felt good. Suddenly I was lighter and faster, just by changing my shoes. I was buzzing around in them excitedly broadcasting the benefits of barefoot running to anyone who would listen. I ran three marathons in minimalist shoes, the fastest one in 2 hours 55 minutes. I was living proof that it worked.

Except I had a dirty secret. When I first started to run in my barefoot style, everything was fine. I ran some PBs, I felt great. I remember occasionally lapsing back into my old heel-first style on purpose, just to remember how bad it was. It was like slamming a car into second gear while cruising along at seventy miles per hour on the motorway. Everything came to a crunching halt.

But by my second marathon I had developed a sore achilles tendon. It wasn't too bad, and I ran through it. I was still convinced of the benefits of barefoot running. It was such a compelling idea that I put the achilles pain out of my mind. But by my third marathon, in London, both my achilles tendons were hurting. I couldn't understand why this was. Neither could I understand the pictures of me, taken either by my Dad or by race organisers, in the final throes of a marathon or half-marathon. In some of them, I appeared to be landing heel first. It didn't make sense. I put it down to an odd bad stride here and there. Also, it's notoriously hard to judge these things from a still frame, because it often looks as though you're about to land heel first until the last second, at which point your forward momentum means the foot actually lands midfoot or forefoot first. But in some of these pictures, my heel was clearly already touching the ground.

So before heading to Japan, I go back to see Lee Saxby. Since I first saw him, barefoot running has become a booming industry and he now has a high-tech lab in the Vivobarefoot offices in central London. I don't tell him about my achilles problems, but ask him to assess how I'm getting on.

He gets me to hop up on the treadmill and watches me running. I'm doing it fine, he says. No problems. But he has a new toy. A digital force plate which takes a picture of the pressure my foot is exerting on the floor. He gets me to stand on it. In the picture, I have no toes.

'Your running form is good,' says Saxby. 'That's what I call the software. Your brain has the right information and knows how to use it. But there's a clear problem here with the hardware, your feet.'

My toes, and particularly my big toe, are not doing anything. The big toe is supposed to be my anchor, providing stability as I run, pulling me through in a straight, forward momentum. But instead, I'm off balance, my weight still too far back in my heels.

'This means you'll get problems with your ankles and achilles,' he says. I nod, amazed. As well as Che Guevera, he's the Derren Brown of running. But what is the remedy?

Saxby says I am a typical 'zoo human', his rather delightful term for a person brought up in modern society, wearing shoes and spending most of the day sitting down on badly designed chairs. To prove his point he asks me to do a deep squat, keeping my feet flat on the ground. I attempt it, but it is fairly hopeless. All I can do is bend my knees, wobbling like a ninety-year-old man trying to find the chair behind him.

'You have no mobility around the ankles,' he says. 'This is why you'll have problems.'

In Kenya, everyone can squat – at least everyone in the rural communities where the great runners come from. If they couldn't, they wouldn't be able to use their pit latrines. That mobility and strength in the feet and ankles is one of the many advantages the Kenyans have when it comes to running, and according to Saxby it comes from walking and running around barefoot as children, and maintaining the ability to squat.

Everyone in Japan can squat, too. Here, again, the traditional toilets are holes in the ground that require you to squat unaided. In many places in Japan, such as in restaurants and train stations, there is often a choice of a squat-down 'Japanese toilet' or a 'Western toilet' with a seat.

Yet the Japanese don't generally have the same powerful 'barefoot' running style as the Kenyans. This is partly because in Japan people wear shoes outside at all times, and more importantly, children grow up running in shoes. Also, the more common shuffling running style is often dictated by coaches who believe it is more efficient to run with less bounce.

Kenji is convinced this is wrong and has begun a university study into why the Kenyan runners have such a strong, bouncy running form. He is intrigued by the idea of 'barefoot running', which is still on the margins of the running world in Japan, embraced mostly by less serious amateur runners. Those who do advocate it cite the traditional footwear of Japan's ancient runners, such as the marathon monks who wear simple straw sandals, and the original ekiden men, the couriers who used to run messages between Kyoto and Tokyo wearing only thin 'tabi' shoes, the sort still worn by rickshaw pullers who spend their whole day running. Tabi shoes have a separate big toe and look a bit like the modern Vibram Five Fingers minimalist running shoes. In 1951, nineteen-year-old Japanese runner Shigeki Tanaka famously won the Boston marathon wearing a pair of tabi shoes.

One of the sports science professors at Ritsumeikan University tells me that slowly more and more Japanese runners are changing their style 'as a result of all the "heel first is bad" information', and he points out that Toshinari Takaoka, who still holds the Japanese records at 10,000m and the marathon, had a forefoot-first running style.

But I already know about the benefits of forefoot running. What I need to do now, it seems, is learn how to squat.

In the loos in his lab in London, Saxby has a plastic platform, like a child's step, that fits around the edge of the toilet bowl. He shows it to me. 'For squatting,' he says. 'You can buy it on Amazon.'

Saxby tells me to practise squatting holding on to a door handle until I can do it unaided, and to walk around as much as possible barefoot.

'Sort your hardware out,' he says, 'and you'll be bullet-proof.' I liked the sound of that. I start squatting like mad.

*

Squatting is such a simple, natural movement that people the world over can do it without thought. Children can do it, and the younger they are, the better they do it. My children delight in watching me struggle to squat as they sit there hunched down like yogis, saying: 'What? What's hard about this?'

Kelly Starrett, author of the book *Ready to Run*, says the squat is a fairly low-level test, and the fact that I'm struggling so pitifully to do it means my body isn't functioning with its full range of motion.

A few weeks after visiting Saxby, one afternoon as I'm standing waiting for my children to come out of school, one of the other parents tells me he's a functional movement specialist. We get talking and once he hears my story, he tells me to come and see him. He says he has some techniques he thinks I might find interesting.

'The best way I can describe it,' he says, 'is that up to now, you've been running with the handbrake on. Once you take it off, you'll run faster.'

The parent, Joe Kelly, is well versed in the theories of barefoot running, and goes by the pseudonym BarefootAthlete online. He agrees with Saxby, though, that running efficiently is not just about taking your shoes off. To run well is a skill, and to do it well your whole body needs to be functioning properly, not just your feet. This is why many people who take up barefoot or minimal running end up injured. You can't just put on minimal shoes and start running unless your body, your hardware, is up to it. Is that what I've been doing, I wonder, with my malfunctioning body that can't even squat? Is that why my tendons hurt?

I decide to go to see Kelly, to see if he can get me running faster, without the handbrake on.

He tells me he has recently learnt a new treatment called muscle activation, which works on the premise that if parts of your body are not working properly, other parts will have to compensate for them, and soon nothing will be doing the job it was designed for, and the whole body will start to collapse in on itself.

The result, he says, is the hunched, shuffling running style many of us will be all too familiar with, and aches and pains in all sorts of places.

The particular technique Kelly uses on me is called 'Be Activated' and was devised by South African physiotherapist and kinesiologist Douglas Heel, but there are many other versions which all work along the same principles. Heel was a student under the eminent sports scientist Tim Noakes, author of running bible *The Lore of Running*. Noakes is famous for his central governor fatigue theory, which says that the brain controls the level of fatigue you feel in your body, shutting it down when it senses it is becoming overworked.

Over thousands of years, the brain learnt that it was best to overcompensate, shutting the body down early in order to keep something in reserve in case of an emergency. So, in theory, no matter how tired you are, no matter how exhausted you feel, if you were to spot a lion, you would suddenly find reserves of energy to run faster.

'However, in this modern world,' Heel explains when I track him down during one of his many trips to London to teach his technique, 'things outside running, things like stress at work, bad posture, or even a poor night's sleep, can cause the brain to register the body as overworked, and to start shutting it down, even though all you've been doing is sitting down all day. Any tension or stress in the body can cause this to happen.'

What the muscle activation treatment is doing, then, is sending a message back to the brain to say, it's OK, these muscles are not really fatigued, we haven't been running across the scorched earth for days, there are no lions around, everything is safe and well. Once the stressed muscles are switched back on, everything else can go back to doing its own job, and your body can return to its natural and fully functioning sequence again.

'It's like the trip switches in a household fusebox,' Heel says. 'The body also has override switches for when it gets overloaded. Muscle activation is like switching everything back on.'

Kelly gets me to lie down on his treatment table and starts pressing his finger into my malfunctioning stressball of a body. What follows is one of the most painful hours of my life.

'I've had women tell me the pain is as bad as childbirth,' he grins while digging his fingers into my hips. It feels like he is twisting a knife in at times, though he assures me he's really only pressing lightly. He's working on neurolymphatic reflex points, trigger points on my body that stimulate the muscles into action. And some of the results are unnervingly instant.

At one point he has me sitting on a chair and then standing up without using my hands. This is no problem, of course, although I can feel my legs straining when I do it. However, after some painful pressing, I try it again and I almost leap out of the chair as though I've been sitting on a compressed spring.

To demonstrate another activation point, he pulls my legs to the side and tells me to hold them there while he tries to push them back to the middle. I can't. Not even close. It's as though I have no muscles capable of carrying out the instruction. It's a blind spot in my muscle power. After a few minutes of torturous pressing, he tries again. 'OK, hold your legs out to the side.' He pushes, and suddenly muscles that didn't exist before kick into action and I'm holding him. He pushes some more, harder this time, but I'm holding firm. It's a miracle.

The next weekend, I take my newly activated legs out to race the Bideford half-marathon in north Devon. I'm not sure what to expect. As amazing as it was to see muscles materialising out of thin air to hold my legs out sideways, how useful is that for running?

Many of Heel's clients are sports stars from the worlds of rugby and golf, where extended mobility in different directions seems more important. In running the movement tends to be fairly unidirectional – just the same repetitive steps in the same forward motion. However, during my time in Kenya, training with some of the greatest long-distance runners on the planet, I realised that one of the biggest advantages they have over most western runners is their fluid movement and running form.

One of the most fascinating things about Kenyan runners is that the event they dominate more than any other is the steeplechase – they have won every single men's Olympic gold medal since 1968 in this event, except for the two Olympics Kenya boycotted. Yet there are almost no facilities for steeplechase training in the entire country. So why are they so good at it?

Kelly thinks it's all about their movement. 'If you watch the way a Kenyan runs,' he says, 'he is very upright. The back of his neck is straight. His body is functioning in sequence, so that when he comes across a barrier, such as in the steeplechase, it is no effort for him to leap over it and carry on running.'

With a more active lifestyle, and less time spent sitting slouched in cars, on sofas, or hunched over computer screens, Kenyans are accustomed to using their bodies in a more natural sequence.

'Most westerners, whether athletes or not, struggle to do a straight, unsupported squat,' says Kelly. 'This is a simple, basic action if your body is functioning correctly, but most of us can't do it.'

The squat again. While *Born to Run* railed against the evil of running shoes, Saxby tells me we should add another item to that list: chairs.

'The two big evils in the modern world, the things that break down our ability to function as we are designed to, are shoes and chairs,' he says.

Kelly Starrett agrees. 'Sitting on chairs is a disaster,' he says, before listing all the problems it causes. It's a long list.

If this is true, in Japan they are at least halfway there. As well as having squat loos everywhere, most people still eat kneeling on the floor around a small low table, both in their homes and in restaurants. When I go to interview people, or meet the teachers at my children's school, I often find myself being led to a room with cushions on the floor rather than sofas or chairs and tables.

Each time I amaze people with my inability to sit on my knees for more than a few seconds. It's as though every joint and muscle in my legs is being squeezed and twisted. I'm not alone. It's a rite many westerners go through when they visit Japan.

'It's OK, sit how you like,' people will say, looking at me kindly, with a touch of pity. But surely something is not right in my body for me to be struggling so much with a movement that seems so simple and natural to everyone else.

*

At the Bideford half-marathon it's a windy day, but the course is mostly flat. My best time, run shortly after I returned from my six months' training in Kenya, is 1 hour 23 minutes. I set my watch for 1:22 pace and head off.

Despite being hampered by a bad stitch, which forces me to stop twice, I run a big personal best of 1:19. A few weeks later, after some more prodding from Kelly, I run another half-marathon in 1:18. It's difficult to be sure how much of this improvement is down to Kelly's treatment, of course, but something is definitely working.

The key is not the specifics of the muscle activation technique, but the basic issue it is attempting to resolve: my malfunctioning body. Both Kelly and Saxby are making the same point, and giving me some techniques to address it, namely that if I want to run well, with good form, and to avoid injury, my body needs to start functioning as it was designed to. My whole body, not just my feet.

As well as his torture sessions, Kelly has me doing core workout sessions using kettle bells and he gets me skipping. He is also a big fan of climbing trees as a way to improve function. 'Form follows function,' he keeps telling me, as I clamber around on the wall bars in his warehouse gym in Devon.

All of this is about returning our bodies to their natural state. As Saxby's zoo humans, we're compromised by our environment, which is set up to make life ever easier, but less active. Many modern cars have now replaced the handbrake with a little switch operated by one finger. Even that tiny effort of pulling up a brake lever has been ironed out. Where will it end?

In rural Kenya, of course, life is much more active. When Saxby talks of zoo humans, I can't help recalling the words of Renato Canova, the coach in Kenya: 'To win a big city marathon, you need to be a little wild.' He meant you need to take risks, be wild at heart. But maybe, physically you need to be a little wild, too.

*

The problem is, after all this, my achilles tendons continue to hurt. I still have a long way to go in my rewilding process, of course. Perhaps, living in modern society, working in an office, driving a car, I'll never fully achieve it. At least I can now squat better than before, although it is far from the comfortable, relaxed way in which Ossian does it.

But on those few mornings when I get up at 5.30 a.m. to run with the teenagers from across the street in Kyotanabe, for the first few minutes of each run, it's like some gremlin is pinching my achilles tendons and whispering: 'Oh dear, oh dear, that still doesn't feel right.'

At the Ritsumeikan training camp up in the mountains, one evening in the lodge after supper, the trainer offers to give me a massage. I tell him I've been having problems with my achilles. I say it casually, like it's nothing. He gets to work, prodding and asking me where it hurts. Then he tells me: 'It's sore because you're landing on your heel when you run. It is better to try to land on your midfoot.'

He doesn't know what he's talking about, I think, although it does feel much better after his treatment. But I know I don't land on my heel. Or do I?

A few months later, Max calls me to say we're going to be on TV. He's excited. 'It could lead to me getting more work, translating for the TV company,' he says.

A Japanese television presenter is making a film about trying to run a sub-three-hour marathon, and as part of the programme he's come to learn from the Ritsumeikan team, and to run with them.

Kenji thinks I should come, too, to tell him about the Kenyans. They, after all, are pretty good at marathons.

We arrive at the Ritsumeikan track on a blustery afternoon. Some of the runners – the ones who could get out of classes – are lined up along the track as we approach, the TV lights making them glow against the grey sky. The presenter, a charming, smiley man with a headband, is asking them questions. We watch as they show him their muscles, lifting up their grey T-shirts to reveal their stomachs. They point at one of the younger students, who squirms bashfully under the lights.

'They're saying he has the best abs,' Max explains.

The plan is for the university runners to pace the presenter around the track for twenty-five laps. Ten kilometres in less than forty minutes. Kenji, hopping around in his suit, calls me over in a gap in the proceedings and introduces me to the presenter. He looks surprised to see me, and listens carefully as Kenji explains who I am, obviously for the first time.

The presenter makes a joke.

'He says, can you analyse his form, to see what he's doing wrong?' Max explains. Kenji has obviously been telling him about the form of the Kenyan runners, and how they have more bounce, and don't land on their heels.

'OK,' I say. 'Can I run too?' It takes two hours to get to the track from my house, I might as well get a run in too, if I can.

'Sure,' they say. I promise to stay at the back, out of the way. Ten kilometres in forty minutes. Now that I've fully regained my fitness, that should be reasonably comfortable.

*

The Ritsumeikan runners are wearing matching team T-shirts, which are as grey as the sky. The presenter is wearing a dark blue top. I feel a bit conspicuous in my bright yellow T-shirt. I'm also the tallest by some inches. I stand at the back, just behind the presenter, as the runners line up in single file, and when Nomura, the assistant team manager, gives the word, we set off on our way.

I've never actually run 10,000m on the track before. In the UK it would be considered far too monotonous for a training session. But in Japan I always seem to be running short repetitive loops of some kind, so it feels quite natural to be setting off on twenty-five laps of the track. It means, at least, we can get regular, accurately timed splits to make sure we're sticking to the right pace.

As we run, I watch the presenter. It's hard to tell from behind how his feet are landing, so as we run down the home straight on the fourth lap or so, I move out to lane three to run beside him. I make it obvious for the cameras that this is what I'm doing. I figure that will help them later when they come to edit it. As I'm talking through my analysis in a voiceover, I imagine, they can show the pictures of me running along beside him, observing his form. It's amazing the things that can be going through your head while you're running.

Stroking my beard for the camera, I analyse that he actually has pretty good form. Of course, I'm not really an expert on this, but they've asked me to do it, so I'll do what I can. They all seem to have relaxed shoulders, a slight forward lean, and feet landing midfoot first. Amazingly, not a single one of them is heel-striking.

As the laps go by, the pace seems to pick up. My brain becomes slowly more addled and I lose track of the Japanese numbers being called out as we pass each lap. About halfway through the twenty-five laps, I pull out again, to get another look at the presenter's form. His arms are more tense now, his shoulders slightly hunched – all the classic signs of a malfunctioning body. And interestingly, he's now clearly heel-striking. I'm quite pleased, as it gives me something to say afterwards. I begin practising how I'll say it, explaining the whole shebang about heel-striking being less efficient, more impact on the legs and the rest.

Along the back straight I pull out again to get another look, just to be sure. Yes, he's clearly heel-striking. And so are some of the Ritsumeikan runners. And then, to my horror, I realise, so am I.

I don't need to look down, I can feel it. My feet landing, crash, crash, crash, on the heel first each time. How is this happening?

And then it all makes sense. This is why my achilles are hurting. I'm wearing minimal shoes, but once I get tired, my body starts to lose its form, it starts to collapse in on itself. My core still isn't strong enough to hold my form. Trip switches are being blown all over the place. Muscles are shutting down, saving themselves in case of emergency.

But we're still running. Nomura holds up a board counting down the laps, but as soon as we pass it, I forget what it said, and begin trying to recalibrate. It seems endless. I'm straining now to keep up. Small gaps keep appearing between me and the group, and I have to keep working to close them. The wind blows ever stronger in my face. The presenter, with his heel-striking, is keeping up with the others, puffing hard, but keeping up. But me, I'm gone, drifting back, alone, a yellow buoy bobbing in a grey, stormy sea.

Finally we finish. I make it in just under 40 minutes as planned, but a good 100 metres behind the others. I cut a sorry figure crossing the line. I don't think I'll be getting signed up by any ekiden teams when that gets broadcast.

But I'm not really concerned so much with that. All I can think about is my revelation. I heel-strike. It may only happen when I'm tired, but that's probably midway through most runs. I need to squat more, I think. And climb trees. And stay focused on my form. Can I do it simply by remaining focused on it, I wonder. I decide to try it on my next run.

Before I leave, they film me telling the presenter that he heel-strikes. That the Kenyans don't do that. He nods, feigning a deep interest as television presenters are wont to do, grinning at me as I speak, as though what I'm saying is blowing his mind. Weeks later, when the show is broadcast, they cut out my interview. Rie, my neighbour, tells me she saw me running on TV.

'I thought, is that Finn-san?' she says, giggling. 'And it was.'

I ask her if they explained why there was a giant, yellow *gaijin* running around with the university team and the presenter.

'No,' she says. 'It was so strange.'

*

A few days later I take myself out for a six-mile run along the river in Kyotanabe. The pace is slow. I'm completely focused on my form, like never before. Every step. I focus on my backlift, kicking my legs out behind me as I run. That seems to help. Lee Saxby told me not to think about how my feet are landing, as it happens too quickly, but to concentrate on keeping my head up, neck straight, and making sure my stride is quick, rather than long. Three strides a second, he says. It sounds like a lot, but once you get into a rhythm it feels fine. When I first started forefoot running, Saxby gave me a metronome to listen to while I ran. I wish I still had it with me. Instead I count to myself, quickly, one-two-three, one-two-three. By the last mile I can barely run my calves are so sore. This is like when I first started 'barefoot' running.

My initial shock that I was still heel-striking is soon replaced first with relief – that it might explain my sore achilles, and those photos of me at the end of races – and then with excitement. For a long time now I've been struggling to find my top form, to chase down those ever more elusive best times. Doubts have been slipping in. Am I just getting too old? But here is another handbrake left on. How many more are there? All I need to do is release it, correct my form, and I'll be back up to full speed.

As the weeks go by, I begin to run faster again, concentrating always on holding my form. Quickly it becomes easier. My calves stop hurting. It feels different. In the same way as when I first started running 'barefoot style' a few years earlier, when I first began to feel like a runner, another transformation is now taking shape. From a runner, to a better runner. It doesn't sound like much, but it feels great, as I cruise through my runs, head up, heels kicking back, quick feet, pat, pat, pat. Amazingly, within just a few days, my achilles stop hurting.

15

Lila and Uma are lying on their futons. Their bedroom floor is slowly disappearing under piles of colourful origami birds and boxes. They sit up in the evenings folding paper until I make them stop. They and their friends all have little boxes full of origami paper. When they get home from school they sit out in the street, sometimes on the actual road, making pretty paper objects. This is their latest thing. Before that, it was drawing mazes on the road in chalk.

Every morning when I go in to wake them, they pull the duvets over their heads and say they don't want to go to school.

'Do we have to?' they say. But once they're up, the complaining usually stops, and they walk to school happily enough. It's touching to see them walking in through the gates together, into the swirl of their Japanese school, the bustling children, the bowing teachers, the excited laughter. Even to me, they stand out like two exotic swans with their pale skin and fair hair. People call out from the upper balconies, 'Lila', or 'Uma'. Friendly shouts. The other children are happy to see them.

But today Lila and Uma are particularly vociferous in their complaining.

'Nooooooo,' squeals Lila. 'It's Saturday. Why do we have to go today?'

They still haven't got used to going to school on Saturday. The classes are only until 11 a.m., and I have to admit, it does seem slightly pointless to make them go through all the rigmarole of getting ready for school, eating into any possible weekend excursions, just for two hours of class time. Especially when the morning welcome song takes up half that time on its own. But in Japan, Saturday is a school day. So they have to go. It's hard to explain.

It's now three months since they started school, and while they're able to play games and communicate with their friends using a mixture of pigeon English and Japanese, the actual lessons are still far too difficult for them to follow. I had hoped that they'd somehow just magically start speaking Japanese, but it isn't quite happening. 'Kids pick up languages so quickly,' everyone told me. But it clearly takes longer than that, especially in a language so different in structure from their own.

In the odd flashes, however, I'm left amazed by their ability to learn things, mostly without even trying. In England, before we left, we had some Japanese lessons as a family. It seemed like a good idea, all learning together at home, bonding over the preparation for our trip. But it was a disaster. Our poor teacher would battle on with her worksheets as the children lost interest and started fighting over the biscuits I'd put out as a bribe to keep them in the room. Although none of us knew any Japanese, it turned out we all had very different learning needs. Lila was most interested in the Japanese writing, while Uma was still only learning to read and write in English, and Ossian could barely write his name.

Marietta and I tried struggling on amid the chaos, but we seemed to get more confused with each lesson. I started getting flashbacks to the blind panic I'd felt learning languages at school. That feeling when you were asked to stand up and say something in front of the class and you would look at the words on the blackboard as though they were samba-dancing hieroglyphics.

'Come on,' the clearly exasperated teacher would say, unable to believe your stupidity. But nothing would make sense. It was as though your mind had shut down, throwing up a helpless error message. It was all flooding back.

Just when it felt as though we'd never learn anything, I remembered a documentary I'd watched years ago, when I was a student at university, about a teacher who taught a class of troublesome students in a London school to speak basic French in one week. It had made a big impression on me at the time. So I looked it up.

It was London in the mid-1990s. Michel Thomas was a language teacher to the stars in Hollywood. Woody Allen came on screen to say how Thomas had taught him French over a weekend. His secret was a belief that to learn properly you needed to be relaxed, not stressed.

Just like in running, in learning the mind will shut down and get defensive under stress. Joe Kelly loved talking to me about Usain Bolt, about how relaxed he always is before the start of a race, pulling faces for the cameras, shooting imaginary arrows into the sky. It's like he's just playing out there. Then he breaks the world record.

'It's his trick to stay relaxed,' says Kelly. If his mind is re-laxed, his muscles will function properly as they're not tensing up under stress. I remember watching the great Haile Gebrselassie on the start line of races, always smiling and grinning while the others were fretting and looking tense. He rarely lost either.

'No one can really learn,' said Thomas in his lovely thick French accent, standing in an empty classroom at the London school, 'unless anything that causes stress is removed from the experience.'

He was given a class of underachieving students – those expected to fail their exams. Some of them already had.

The first thing he did was remove all the desks and chairs from the classroom, replacing them with comfortable armchairs. He laid rugs on the floor and dimmed the lights. And then he told the students his most important ground rule.

'Never worry about remembering,' he told them. 'If at any point there's something you don't remember, that's not your problem. That will be up to me to know why, and what to do about it.' He was taking the pressure off them right there. You could see them looking at each other in disbelief, unable to hide their delight. It was as if someone had opened a door to them with that one sentence and invited them into another world.

Thomas also had a clever way of breaking down the language into building blocks, and then combining them to make sentences. But the key thing was how relaxed and comfortable the students felt in his class. At the end of the week they amazed the school's regular French teacher when she came in to see what they had learnt. I felt sorry for her as she reflected on her own lack of success at engaging the students.

'It was very impressive,' she said, emphasising the 'very' with an exaggerated nod of the head. 'They learnt in one week what they usually learn in five years.'

One of the students tried to put her finger on why the lessons were so different. 'He doesn't make you feel lost,' she said. 'If you're stuck on a word he'll just take you right back to the beginning, like as if you was a baby, and then, it's like click, and you know what you're saying.' Click. The knowledge, the understanding, the capacity was always there, but it couldn't come out until she was taken back to where she felt comfortable – safe and protected like a baby. When I found you could buy a Japanese language CD course based on the Michel Thomas method, I ordered it and we started straight away.

Marietta and I soon began to look forward to putting it on in the evening, sitting up in bed, the lights dimmed. It was like some kind of meditation technique. And it was exciting, finally, to be learning some Japanese.

The children, however, couldn't grasp it. It wasn't designed for such young minds, which obviously worked in a different way. They soon gave up trying completely. And so, by the time we got to Japan, while I was forming a basic understanding of the language, in its spoken form at least, they were still complete beginners.

However, spending day after day immersed in a chattering sea of Japanese does begin to have some effect. A few months after starting at the school, Uma's class puts on a play. We go along to watch on a baking hot day, arriving a few minutes late to find the whole school, and most of their parents, lined up along the balconies, waiting for us.

Uma stands among her classmates in the courtyard below, ready to begin. We hurry up the steps to the balcony, only for one mother to rush down and whisper to us to take off our shoes. Of course. We've forgotten. As we make our way back down the steps, shoes in hands, I catch sight of a few shocked faces, the children looking at each other, eyes wide. Did we really go upstairs in our shoes?

Finally, excruciatingly, we find a place to stand on the balcony, and the play can begin. It's still only five minutes past the time we were asked to arrive.

The play is *George and the Dragon*, and Uma is a baker. She's running around in the group of children, a huge grin on her face as they sing songs in their elfin, seven-year-old voices. And then suddenly she is talking. In Japanese. In front of the whole school. Her voice strong, unwavering. I've no idea what she is saying, but I'm welling up, looking at Marietta, looking at everyone. *Did you hear that? That's my daughter.*

Not only is she talking, but she's organising the other children who can't remember where they're supposed to stand. There she is, after only two months, whirling around in the thick of the action at school in Japan.

Another time they amaze me is when I go to buy them a rail pass at the train station. The ticket inspector gives me a form to fill out with their name and address. When I give it back to him, he shakes his head. The names have to be in Japanese script, not Roman script. The machine has to recognise the symbols to approve the pass. But there is no way I can do that. I've been working hard at my spoken Japanese, but I'm still clueless when it comes to writing the letters. The

Michel Thomas CDs don't cover writing. We're stuck. But then, what if . . .

'Can you write your names in Japanese?' I ask them both. They're collecting more tourist leaflets from the display. They have a big pile each.

'Of course,' says Lila.

'Really?'

And, of course, they can. Without hesitation. And the machine reads them, too, and approves them.

But these are occasional flashes of brilliance. Most of the time they spend their days sinking under a tumult of words and symbols, especially during class. Usually when I ask Lila what she has been studying, she will say: 'I dunno.'

'But what do you do in class? You must do something,' I say to her one day. Her school books are full of Japanese writing and beautiful pictures. One mother tells us that her son has been practising his Japanese script at home because he has been sitting next to Lila and has seen how neat her writing is.

'Today I practised my six times table,' she says. That wasn't the lesson. It was just what she did. While her teacher was telling a story she couldn't understand, rather than just gaze blankly at the walls, she was reciting multiplication tables in her head. If nothing else, the experience is teaching them to make constructive use of their down time.

Everyone keeps telling me it is a valuable experience for them to go to school in Japan. They will learn important life lessons. But I'm struggling to put my finger on quite what the benefits are. They are learning that other cultures exist where people do things differently, that what is normal in one place is not necessarily normal everywhere.

They're also learning what it feels like to be different from everyone else. I felt that if they could cope with this, they would be stronger, more resilient. That's why we had to push through the initial struggles. To overcome such a difficult start, and to arrive at the point where you were an integral, functioning part of such an alien group, was an achievement. It taught that perseverance worked. That even a seemingly insurmountable situation could be won over. If we had given up then, I felt, it would have taught them the opposite. To run and hide at the first sign of trouble.

So even though Lila is so bored she is reciting her times tables in class, the overriding lesson, I hope, is that the world is not a frightening, inhospitable place, but rather somewhere they can feel capable of engaging, climbing on-board and joining in.

*

It's not until they've been there almost three months that I find out that Lila and Uma's school has an ekiden team. Steiner schools are not renowned for their sporting prowess. Co-operation over competition is a key ethos underpinning Steiner education, and in the UK this extends to sport, at least until the children are of secondary-school age. But in Japan, even without a particular focus on competition, the Steiner children still spend hours practising after school every day. The two main sports the students seem to engage in are baseball and volleyball. But as winter begins to encroach, the attention switches to ekiden.

Around six weeks before the local Kyotanabe ekiden –
which pitches school teams against amateur teams – the
training ratchets up. Those students hoping to make the
team are given tight training schedules, with the students
meeting up almost every day. Ryohei, my fifteen-year-old
neighbour, is in his element. Most of the ekiden team are
also baseball players, using the running as a way to get in
shape for the baseball season. But for Ryohei, this is his
thing. One morning he knocks at our door and through
his mask manages to invite me to join the school team for a
training session.

'*Itsu desuka?*' I ask him. *When is it?*

'*Yon ji,*' he says. *Four o'clock.*

'*Kyo?*'

He nods. *Hi.* Yes, today.

I've already been running that morning, but I'm feeling
sharper all the time, particularly since I started focusing
more on my form. Now, if I'm going to break those PBs,
I need to start building up my training. Things always feel
like they've gone up a level when you start running twice a
day. You begin to feel like a serious runner. Of course, it requires lots of time, and I've never managed to keep it going
for long, but even one day here and there of 'doubling up'
always seems to give me a boost.

'OK,' I say, bowing. 'Thank you.'

*

Later, at 4 p.m. precisely, Ryohei rings the doorbell. It's
getting colder now. Everyone, it seems, is wearing masks.

Lila and Uma have become reluctant to go outside. The games in the street have changed and involve a lot of running around chasing each other. Lila has apparently fallen out with a neighbour over one of the games. But every day after school the doorbell still rings.

'Lila, Uma, outu?' they say. On the little screen they stand there hunched against the cold, still wearing sunhats, their faces sad when I tell them Lila and Uma don't want to go out.

'Ossian?' they ask.

'Ossian, do you want to go out?' I ask him.

He runs to the door and pokes his head out. '*Chotto mate,*' he says, closing the door and pulling on his boots as quickly as he can.

'Don't forget your coat,' I call out, but he has gone, the door clicking shut behind him.

But today the doorbell is for me. I pull on my trainers. Second run of the day. School ekiden training. Let's go.

*

At the school, Ryohei and one of his early-morning gang sit on the bank while in the gravel square outside the school the baseball team finishes its practice. They line up as the coach hits a ball at them one at a time, which they have to collect at speed and hurl to the catcher standing behind the coach. If they fluff their pick-up or throw, they have to go back and do it again. When they do it right, the rest of the team gives them a loud shout of encouragement.

Around and around they go. I've no idea how long they've been doing it, but they're focused. The more time I spend here, the more I realise just how sports-mad the Japanese are. And the top school and university teams are often more popular and closely followed than the senior, professional teams.

All this focus on junior sports, however, means athletes are getting pushed extremely hard at school to succeed, and this can have a detrimental affect on the careers of many of Japan's brightest young stars.

Earlier in the year, controversy raged around the sixteen-year-old baseball pitcher Tomohiro Anraku, who led his unfancied high-school team all the way to the final at Koshien, Japan's biggest baseball tournament. Over nine days, Anraku threw 772 pitches during five games. That's roughly what the average US major-league pitcher throws in six weeks.

But in the final game, Anraku fell apart. As millions watched in the stadium and on TV, his game disintegrated and his team lost the final 17–1. Baseball commentators in the US said it was insane to send him out to pitch so many times.

Speaking afterwards, Aranku said: 'I had a heavy feeling, like my body didn't belong to me. But as is particular for Japanese, I tried to use my mind to push through all of that.'

He certainly wasn't shy of hard work. According to an ESPN documentary on the controversy, his school team practises five hours a day, six days a week. Such an intense regime is not unusual in Japanese high-school sport, and is born out of the strongly held belief that success comes only through hard work. But Japanese sport is littered with young stars who failed to fulfil their potential. Kenji is convinced it was over-training that ended his career so early. Sometimes he is visibly angry, still, at those who pushed him to run so hard.

This is why he has taken three promising junior women runners under his wing. All three have been injured from over-training as youngsters and he wants to help them to train more intelligently. The eldest of the trio, Nagisa, who is eighteen, says at school she was running 125km a week. Then, if she did badly in a race, she was punished with two hundred sit-ups. She smiles when I look shocked.

'I didn't mind,' she says.

But Kenji is not impressed. He says this over-training is why she is still injured. He has even advised her to join a university without a serious ekiden team, so she won't be pushed into training too hard again.

A recent study by the American Academy of Pediatrics backs up Kenji's stance. It found that athletes between the ages of eight and eighteen who spent twice as much time in organised sports each week as in free play were more likely to be injured.

'I would have won the Olympics,' Kenji says. It's not a fanciful boast. At the 1994 world junior championships, Kenji took the silver medal behind the Kenyan Daniel Komen. His best time for the 10,000m at that time was faster than Komen's.

'I was the fourth fastest junior ever, at one point,' he says.

But two years later, while Daniel Komen was breaking the 5,000m world record in 12:45, Kenji was struggling to run under 14 minutes.

Of course, without training so hard, Kenji may never have been so good in the first place, but by 2001, at the age of twenty-six, he had had two operations to treat a persistent achilles tendon injury. 'By then,' he says, 'my career was over.'

*

One of the biggest ekidens on the calendar is the national high-school ekiden, which gets wall-to-wall TV coverage. It takes place in Kyoto, so I go along to watch.

The race starts in the stadium I ran around with the Kyoto Blooming group. Inside the stadium, teams of cheerleaders are defying the cold with short skirts and earmuffs. Squadrons of brass bands accompany them, battling each other along the stands, blaring out school anthems. Flags the size of billboards are held aloft by the school shot-putters.

I walk around trying to keep warm until the boys' race starts, a flurry of headband-wearing young men who whirl around the track a few times before disappearing out of the stadium and off on their way across the city.

As soon as they've gone the crowd starts making its way to the nearby train station. I join the flow, leaving the bands to play on, the cheerleaders shaking their pom-poms in gleeful unison.

The subway train is rammed with people carrying flags or wearing team colours. I'm not sure where I'm going, so I follow everyone else. At one station, they start to pile out, rushing excitedly up the stairs, teenagers in tracksuits, older men with rucksacks and trainers, families giggling and calling to each other over the rush. Those coming down the stairs move to one side, resigned to their city being taken over for the day by these hordes of ekiden fans. Although a sport that traverses an entire city over the course of a few hours is never going to be the easiest to follow live, clearly part of the fun is chasing around on the subway system in an attempt to beat the runners to the next viewing point. It's almost like we're in the race, too.

I find myself, a few minutes later, at one of the changeover points. Runners are getting ready on a side street, waiting for their team-mates to come along. I wander down among them. The atmosphere is charged. The runners all wear long coats, almost to the ground, to protect them from the cold. Their coats are in the team colours, and made of a shiny material that makes them look like the gowns boxers wear to enter the ring. In fact, these skinny kids with gaunt, pock-marked faces remind me more of boxers than runners. They have the intense, razor-wire look of people about to put their lives on the line. I skirt around with my camera, but they look right through me, battle-hardened soldiers with dead eyes, lost in the waves of adrenalin rushing through their bodies as they strap their headbands on in sweeping, ritualistic movements.

One by one they're called out to stand in the street and await their moment. We hear the cheers of the crowd first, and the whirl of the television helicopters. And then, the first two boys, racing along the wide, empty road, getting closer, hurling themselves over the line, the tasukis wrenched from them, flung over the shoulders of the two new men as they rush off at a sprint.

It's intensely dramatic. The pressure is hard to bear even for me just standing there watching, with no affiliations to anything. I can't imagine what these young men are experiencing. I ran what I thought were serious races at that age, but never anything like this, broadcast on television, in front of a city lined for miles in hundreds of thousands of spectators.

I think of Michel Thomas warning of how learning doesn't work under stress. Of Douglas Heel talking about the body shutting down under pressure. Of the Kenyan runner complaining about how the Japanese train too much when they're young. Of Kenji and his anger at the premature ending of his career. Standing here, it's easy to see how it happens.

*

Although Steiner schools are not known for their sports teams, and are unlikely to wreck anyone's career through over-training, this baseball practice session still seems pretty serious. I stand conspicuous on the grass bank, watching them, but nobody gives me a glance. Finally they stop and the coach comes over. He's a man in his sixties with a kindly face. Some of the baseball team disappear off into the school, but most of them gather in a group behind him. They're moving straight from baseball training to ekiden training.

'Welcome,' says the coach, shaking my hand and bowing. 'We are honoured that you will join us.' Then, without much ado, he makes his way out through the school gate and before I know it we're all running off up the hill behind him.

We wind our way through the neat streets of Lego houses and along a small river. It's the same route I've been taking on my own. The first time I ran here I saw an intriguing side road leading up into the forest. I decided to follow it. It seemed to head into the mountains. I was in search of running trails, away from the concrete sprawl, and this was my best lead yet. The deeper into the trees it went, the smaller the road became. But all along the way, the forest was fenced off with barbed wire and large signs that seemed to be warning of a danger of some sort. Rusting CCTV cameras chained to concrete posts pointed at me. I ran on, getting more and more nervous that I was about to arrive at the lair of some Bond villain, with huge dogs ready to attack me. But I came out in yet another suburban conglomeration. More grey box houses lined up in tight rows. There was no escape.

We jog behind the school coach at an easy pace, the students running mostly in silence. I linger near the back, not wanting to get competitive, skipping along happily, enjoying the scenery, the fenced-off, forest-covered mountains sticking up behind the buildings.

The coach doesn't follow any of the side roads, but keeps to the main path by the river. He never once looks behind to check that we're following him. Even when some of the runners begin to drop off the pace, he keeps shuffling on, further and further into the endless suburbia.

Eventually, still without speaking or checking who is keeping up, he turns around, and like a long flowing cloak we all turn around and carry on behind him. The runners who had dropped off have organised themselves into a second group, but they don't cut the route short, as I might have done, and rejoin the main group as we pass. Instead they persevere, running on to the point at which we turned around. It is clearly important not to cut any corners.

About halfway back to the school, the coach stops at a small shrine. He says there is an 800m loop here, and we're going to do two laps with a rest in between. He wants us to run as fast as we can. He gets his watch out. He is going to time us.

I run the first one relaxed, concentrating on my form, opening up after the easy running, racing off ahead of the group. I seem to be running on air, without any tiredness from the day's earlier run. He calls out my time as I stop, but I don't catch it.

'You have beautiful form,' he says, as Ryohei races in a few seconds after me. The others are strung out behind. Beautiful form? No one has ever said that to me before. It really is working. I'm excited that it's noticeable.

'I've been working on it,' I tell him. He nods, smiling, but I'm not sure he understands.

He talks to the students, telling them (I can just about work out) to watch my form as I run. To copy me.

I try to demonstrate the key elements. A slight forward lean, focusing on the backlift, quick steps. But my Japanese isn't up to it. He waves his hand. He wants me to stop talking. It's time for the second interval.

Later, back at the school, we stand in a circle as he explains things to the students. Then he asks me to say something that will help them in their running.

I decide against trying again to explain the fundamentals of good form to them. It's too complicated for my rickety Japanese. And in truth, I'm still not completely sure what I'm doing. It feels better when I run now, but what works for me may not work for everyone. Besides, without seeing myself I still can't be sure I'm doing it perfectly. I've already been fooled into thinking that once before.

Instead I tell them how important it is to breathe properly when they run, from deep down in the stomach. This is something else I learnt from Joe Kelly back in Devon. Good breathing and a strong diaphragm, he says, is the basis of core strength. I couldn't believe I'd never thought about my breathing before. When I tried it, breathing from my stomach, filling my lungs, rather than just taking shallow breaths from up in my chest, it was like getting a little turbo boost. Like pressing yet another go-faster button.

Ryohei, I noticed when I was running with him, was all shallow, gasping breaths, exactly how I used to be. It is information worth sharing.

'Your stomach should rise when you breathe in,' I say, putting my hand on it to show them.

It's not much, but the coach seems delighted with my input and he gets them all to clap me and invites me back to train with them again. In the end, though, the sessions are all at the wrong time for me, and the next time I see them in action is on race day, at the Kyotanabe ekiden.

*

I've been thinking more about my plan to form an ekiden team. The race at Lake Biwa was a taste, but being part of such an uncompetitive outfit, made up of runners some of whom I'd only met that morning, left me craving a more serious ekiden experience. Kenji keeps talking to me about the sense of responsibility you feel when you run ekiden, when the hopes of the team are on your shoulders. It pushes you to greater heights, he tells me. That's the power of the team. At least, in Japan it is. I didn't feel it in my race. Maybe that was just my individualistic, western mindset, but nobody in my team seemed to have any hopes to carry. I could have jogged the race and nobody would have complained. I want to feel the responsibility of carrying the tasuki (relay sash) when it actually matters. When every place we gain or lose counts. When we have a chance of doing well.

In my head I'll form an all-star team from my time in Japan. Morita, the Blooming ace, is on the list, and perhaps the next fastest Blooming member, a smiley, Asics sales executive in his fifties called Rogukawa. A few of the Ritsumeikan members, if they'll run. Maybe some of the first-years would do it. Max thinks they would. He wants to be on the team, too. He'll be running 35-minute 10Ks by the time I leave, he reminds me. Ryohei, my fifteen-year-old neighbour, might like to race, too. I ask Max if he can find me an ekiden to enter.

Max initially suggested I put my team together in time to take part in the Kyotanabe ekiden, but it turns out that all the team members would need to be from Kyotanabe, or at least live there. So we have to look for something else. In the meantime, I end up going along to the Kyotanabe ekiden as a spectator, riding my bike on a bitterly cold day to the first changeover point with Ryohei's parents and his two sisters.

Winter has fully set in now. It's hard to remember once sweltering in the muggy heat on these same streets as we stand shuffling from one foot to the other, our toes numb with the cold. Ryohei's two sisters are still wearing sunhats and they ride their bikes without gloves. Even through ski gloves my fingers are turning into brittle sticks of ice. I pull the woollen flaps of my hat down tighter over my ears.

At the changeover point, a team of officials sit at a table preparing for the runners to come through. They have clipboards and a megaphone, and are wearing identical yellow rain jackets. In a small car park behind them, the second-leg runners are warming up, jogging around on the spot, stretching. They seem tense. Only our local vegetable-delivery man, Gulliver, who is here to watch, seems to be in jovial spirits, laughing with anyone who will listen to him.

Just when I'm beginning to wonder how much longer I can stand here waiting in the cold, word goes out that the runners are getting close. It turns out we arrived over an hour early to make sure we didn't miss anything.

The runners come in one at a time, stumbling up to the line, handing over the tasuki. The reaction of those watching is muted, the cold sapping our enthusiasm. Some of the runners collapse dramatically after passing on the tasuki, falling to their hands and knees. Others, like Ryohei, sidle away into the car park as quickly as they can, merging silently into the crowd, their job done.

In the end, the Steiner school finishes third out of the twenty or so teams. They seem happy with that. It's the same position they finished in the year before. The first three teams are all school teams, with the first adult team coming in fourth.

The closing ceremony is at the Kyotanabe sports centre, in a big gymnasium. We all gather, runners and spectators, waiting for the procedures to begin. In the reception area are pictures of local sports teams and the trophies they've won in a large glass cabinet. In the centre is a grainy photograph of the Kyotanabe ekiden winners from a bygone era, and looking closely I think I recognise one young face. Beside the picture is another photograph of the same person, confirming my suspicion. In this one he is wearing the Japanese national kit, and is crossing a finishing line somewhere with his arms aloft, the local running hero: Kenji Takao.

16

Kenji has disappeared off the radar. Admittedly my radar works in another language and is barely functioning. I mostly rely on Max or Mr Ogushi to phone me with news of races, or training sessions, as these are the only two people with any link to the Japanese running world I can actually talk to directly. Of course, they each have their own lives to attend to, so occasionally I find myself drifting in a week of days spent taking the children to school and to the playground, and muddling through the aisles in the supermarket trying to work out which bottle is washing-up liquid and which is toilet cleaner. Before I realise it, the national university ekiden is upon me. This is the biggest race of the year for the Ritsumeikan team. All that training, all those time trials and preliminary races, everything for this one shot. For Kenji, it's his first big ekiden as a coach.

The day before the race, I take Ossian swimming. Splashing around in the learner pool, my mind is slightly distracted. Outside the blue sky has blackened and it is starting to pour with rain, the drops rattling against the huge windows. One woman, hand over mouth, runs for the changing room at the sight of the rain. She doesn't even stop to rinse her eyes with the eyewash taps beside the pool.

'Ossian, we have to go now,' I say. I realise I've no idea what the plan is for watching the race tomorrow. I'm assuming Kenji or Max is organising everything, finding me a hotel, checking the train times. I'm expecting to roll into action when they call me. But no one has called yet.

The problem with living in a country where you don't speak the language is that you start to sound like a child when you're speaking, and so people begin to treat you like a child. Then, to complete the circle, you begin to act like one.

The first time I stayed in Tokyo for the night, for the corporate track championships, Mr Ogushi booked me a hotel room. He then took me to the hotel, and even came upstairs to help me find my room. This was all very kind, I was thinking, as he pointed out the bathroom and the towels. I then noticed the room had two big sliding doors at one end.

'Oh, looks like I have a balcony,' I said.

'Yes, but be careful,' he told me. 'Don't fall off.'

I've asked Max if he can come to the national university ekiden as my translator and to ask Kenji whether we can shadow him for the day to get a real insight into how it all works. At the Kyushu ekiden the coaches drove behind the athletes in a car with a loudspeaker on the roof, for shouting instructions at the runners. I'm hoping the same will happen again and that we can get to ride in the car.

By the time Ossian and I get home, the rain has stopped and it's starting to get dark.

'Max called,' Marietta says after we take off our hats and coats.

'What did he say?'

'You'd better call him back.'

*

Two days before, Max moved house. He left his Kyoto town house and began a bid to make a new life in the countryside about an hour north of Kyoto. When I call him, he sounds much further away than that. The stillness of a deep, frosting valley seems to murmur in the background as he talks. Kenji has been too stressed preparing for the race to find me anywhere to stay, he says.

'It's his first time doing this, so he's not sure what will happen. He thinks the best thing is for you to take a train to the start of the race in the morning, and to just watch that. I don't think you need me for that.'

Max doesn't want to go. Kenji has other things to worry about. I'm left standing there with my thumb in my mouth.

'Can you try Kenji again?' I ask. I really want to see the race through his eyes. I can watch the start on television.

'I'll go to Nagoya tonight and stay in a hotel somewhere,' I say. 'I can find him first thing in the morning.'

Ten minutes later Max calls me back.

'OK, Kenji says to meet him at the Union hotel at 5 a.m. Don't be late. They'll be leaving from outside the lobby at 5.10 a.m. and won't have time to wait for you. All the hotels are fully booked, for some reason. There must be something going on in Nagoya this weekend. But you can stay in a capsule hotel I know. I'll email you the address.'

And so, after a quick supper, twenty minutes later, with my bag on my back, I'm bidding goodbye to Marietta and the children and heading off into the unruffled suburban night, down the hill to Kyotanabe train station. Somewhere in Nagoya the Ritsumeikan team are retiring to their rooms, bidding each other goodnight, the biggest race of the year awaiting them the next morning.

*

The capsule hotel is already full. It's past midnight by the time I find it, down a side street off a main road jittery with Pachinka parlours. Pachinka is a Japanese gambling game housed in huge, garish buildings covered in flashing lights. Nagoya is full of them.

Aside from the Pachinka parlours, the only other places still open in the streets nearby are the regulation convenience stores, and fast-food restaurants. I look helplessly at the man on the reception desk.

'You can sleep in the communal area,' he says. It sounds a bit daunting, but I don't have much alternative. I have to be up again in four hours, anyway.

I pay my money and they lead me into a changing area. The first thing you do when you enter a capsule hotel is take off all your clothes and put them in a locker with your other possessions. Then they give you a towel and a pair of pyjamas and you head into the onsen – the hot baths.

Inside a large, tiled room are about six pools of varying sizes. In the water lurk the heads of tired men. They slide in and out of the pools slowly, like giant seals rolling over to find a more comfortable spot.

In one pool, the water is pink. A little touch of pizzazz. I step into it – why not? – and sink down into the hot water. It makes my head spin, and for a moment it's hard to breathe; the water, the ceiling, men lumbering up the steps, switching pools, holding hand towels over their crotches, the plastic autumn leaves reaching down above my head.

Slowly, everything begins to settle, the sound of steam and running water washing through the air. I don't really enjoy languishing in hot baths and within a few minutes I'm ready to try another pool. Outside the fogged-up door it looks like there are more pools. I climb out of the water and slide the door open. The contrast with the fresher air is better. There are a couple of one-man tubs out here, like giant teacups. In one, a bald man is fast asleep, his head resting on the edge of the tub, his legs dangling over the other side, his face lost in the steam rising from the water.

In the sauna, my next stop, another man lies sleeping, while two men sit staring at a cookery programme on the television.

I skirt quickly through the rest of the pools before showering, drying myself and putting on my pyjamas. I feel incredibly clean and refreshed. I'm almost glowing with cleanliness. All I need now is somewhere to sleep.

Upstairs is a room full of reclining chairs, each one with a TV screen attached to it that doesn't seem to turn off. Most of the chairs are taken up with men sleeping. The place really is full to bursting. I try to fathom why all these single men need to be here on a Saturday night.

Down in the basement, things are quieter. It's almost two in the morning now. In the far recesses of the building I find the manga library. It's a small tatami-mat room with shelves full of comics. One man has laid out a futon and gone to sleep, while a couple of others sit reading. It feels calmer and quieter than the TV room, so I follow suit and lay out a futon and settle down to grab a couple of hours' sleep.

With the lights on, I wake up a few times, always to see different men sitting there reading comics. A few others have fallen asleep beside me.

At 4 a.m. my alarm goes. I get up, make my way to the entrance where I get dressed in my own clothes again, and head out of the door to my waiting taxi, the back passenger door already open in anticipation. At 5 a.m. I'm outside Kenji's hotel, ready to go.

*

Kenji comes bustling out, carrying bags. He grins, surprised, I think, to see me.

'OK, OK?' he asks. I nod. A few of the athletes are here. The others are at hotels dotted along the course. Kenji's job, he says, is to deliver them all to their starting positions on time, and then wait for them at the finish.

We board the team minibus and drive off slowly. In the street, women in short skirts and men with slicked-back hair wander home after being out in bars all night. The athletes stare out at them, two worlds passing momentarily.

Kenji is clearly not impressed, and makes a comment I don't catch. The others laugh only half-heartedly. Kenji's assistant, Nomura, sits in the front of the van alongside Kenji, navigating the way to the start of the race. We take a few wrong turns, with Kenji whizzing the car around sharply on the already busy roads. Of course, they've left in plenty of time, and it's still barely light when we drop off the first two runners. Kenji doesn't say anything special to them, other than the standard *gambare*, do your best. Perhaps he gave his team talk the night before.

As soon as the runners are out of the bus, we're off again, Nomura calling out the directions as the sat-nav gives them, and Kenji driving and chatting away. The week before, the Ritsumeikan women's team won their national ekiden yet again. I mention this to Kenji.

'*Hi*,' he says. 'Pressure, pressure.'

The last time I saw him, Kenji had been bristling with excitement at the upcoming races, making bold predictions. This year, he said, the team would finish in the top ten. Next year, the top five. After that, he was aiming for top three. It was an ambitious aim. With the Hakone universities taking all the best high-school talent on the men's side, it would be something of a miracle if Ritsumeikan or any other team from outside the Kanto region could ever manage to break into the top five.

Since the ace got injured, however, and all the other teams ran much faster than expected at the first of the three big university races, the Izumo ekiden, he has downgraded his expectations slightly.

He says the best he is hoping for today is tenth position, but that really he's expecting thirteenth. Such a precise prediction suggests he has been closely analysing the opposition. Last year, Ritsumeikan finished thirteenth, when they were in disarray and didn't even have a coach. Any worse than that, Kenji says, would be bad.

'Next year,' he grins, almost writing today off already, 'number five.'

We drive along the ekiden route a few hours ahead of the runners, collecting athletes and dropping them off at the different changeover points. The course runs in long straight lines through endless miles of nondescript flatlands scattered with car dealerships, ugly apartment buildings, golf-driving ranges covered in huge nets. Occasionally an old Japanese house pokes out through cracks in the ensemble.

While the race starts and finishes at picturesque shrines, the majority is run through this typical Japanese suburban landscape, broken up here and there by a few rice fields, with an old man tilling the earth by hand as though he hasn't yet noticed the modern world springing up around him.

Once the race starts, we get regular updates on the team's progress by phone. I'm not sure who's ringing us, presumably someone watching it on television. Kenji's car has a television in it, but try as they might, neither Kenji nor Nomura can get it to work. They keep flicking through the same few channels, then trying, again in vain, to find some commentary on the radio. So we're stuck with the phone updates.

Whenever Nomura gets a call, he reacts as though he has just heard that the whole of Tokyo has fallen off a cliff. 'No,' he says, his eyes spinning around at Kenji, his breath held. 'Uh!?' Kenji giggles, eager to hear what has happened now. They're like two excited schoolboys who have somehow got hold of the keys for the school bus.

The reality of the race doesn't match the excitement in the bus, as far as I can tell. The number two ace, Nagumo, runs a solid first leg. At one point he's in eighth place, but finally fades to finish his leg in twelfth. By the end of the second leg, the team have dropped to fifteenth position, and things seem to change very little after that. The fifth-leg runner, the team's 'secret weapon', does well to finish ninth overall on his leg, but things really fall apart when the captain, running his last race for Ritsumeikan, struggles home nineteenth out of the twenty-one runners on his leg. It leaves the team floundering as he passes the tasuki on to the injured ace, Yoshimura. Can his body hold out? Can he make up a few positions, and drag the team back at least to last year's thirteenth-place finish. It doesn't look hopeful.

After the first leg, the phone updates become less frequent, and as the team drops slowly back through the field, the mood in the car becomes quieter.

At the finish, by the famous Uji bridge at the Ise Grand Shrine in Mie prefecture, we find ourselves surrounded by thousands of people. The bridge is a popular tourist attraction and most of the people are here for that. But plenty are lining the streets to watch the race, too. On large screens we watch the battle at the front play out, with occasional glimpses of the runners further back. A squadron of Ritsumeikan supporters has come out carrying flags and wearing university-branded jackets. As the teams come in to finish, they wait quietly and patiently for the Ritsumeikan runner. It seems to take for ever, as we nervously count the runners coming across the line. Twelve, thirteen, fourteen. He hasn't made up any ground, it seems. Then the fifteenth runner appears. And still we wait. Finally, number sixteen is the ace, his face a pained grimace, his hand holding his side as he struggles across the finish line.

The mood in the Ritsumeikan camp has now fallen to funereal levels. From nowhere, men in suits, executives from the university, emerge and surround Kenji. They look like they're trying to hold back angry scowls, their jaws fixed, their arms folded. Kenji, too, is not good at hiding his feelings. He looks like a broken man.

One of the suited men makes a joke and laughs uneasily, as the Ritsumeikan supporters gather around. People from other teams watch as we form a huge circle, almost a hundred people in total. The supporters are other students and former students, some of whom look like they left the university forty years ago. In an act of defiance, they break out in song, singing the university anthem at the tops of their voices. It's a long way from the success of the women's team the week before. Pressure? Where will it come down, I wonder.

*

That night Kenji gives me a lift back to Kyotanabe in his car. It's a long drive, stuck in motorway traffic on a Sunday night, rain lashing the windows, Nomura peering out at the front as though seeking a sign among the red tail-lights. Kenji looks exhausted as we pull up outside my house. I'd invite them in, but it's late and all the lights are off. Since the cold weather set in, we have moved the futons downstairs and are sleeping in the sitting room, which is the only room in the house with heating.

Kenji's eager to get home, in any case. He has a lot to ponder. That top-five position in next year's national ekiden is looking more and more unlikely.

'Thank you for the lift,' I say, stepping out of the car.

'OK, OK,' he says, smiling. His mood has lifted since the end of the race. The team has the regional and the Kyoto ekidens to come. There is still time for some small redemption. He turns his car quietly and drives away.

Perhaps it's redemption of some kind that the marathon monks up on Mount Hiei are chasing, too. The next morning, I finally get the call from Max. We can go and meet them.

17

We collect the woman from the private temple, along with a young man in a baggy jumper she introduces as her friend, in Max's sports car and then drive out of Kyoto and up onto Mount Hiei. We've barely left the suburban outskirts of the city when we come to a stop among the trees outside some traditional buildings. This is where the running monk we're going to meet lives. I had imagined it being more of a pilgrimage, hiking up some steep mountain path to a temple high in the clouds.

We get out of the car beside a garage filled with pots of paint and planks of wood. A gentle drizzle is falling and the woman steps delicately under the garage awning to open her umbrella. Under a stone gateway we follow the path up to what looks like a traditional Japanese house. A dog sees us coming and stands up, stretching itself. For a moment it watches us calmly. Even the dogs of Zen monks are calm, I'm thinking, when suddenly it gets jumpy and starts barking at us.

I get to the door first with the man in the baggy jumper, who knocks on the wooden panel. A beefy man in a tracksuit opens it. He looks surprised to see us. They talk, the man in the jumper pointing and evidently explaining who we are, while the man in the tracksuit nods, and then suddenly looks pleasantly surprised. 'Ah, so,' he says, and slips on his flip-flops and heads out into the rain. We follow him across a small courtyard to another building, where he leaves us.

Inside it feels damp and cold. A scruffy, patchwork carpet covers half the room, while on the other side is a table and an altar filled with statues of Buddha, flowers and urns.

'First he will do the ceremony,' the man in the jumper explains. He shows me how I can get my own prayer included in the ritual. Along one wall is a list of all the prayers you can make, from success in exams, or a job promotion, to simply your dreams coming true. It doesn't seem particularly Buddhist, asking for the fulfilment of all these worldly desires, but I'm no expert. Still, I opt for the prayer of good health for my family. Marietta is still suffering from a severe skin irritation, which first came on during the heat of August but has refused to go away. If I have to pray for something, it should be that she gets better.

The man in the jumper writes it for me on a small piece of wood, I pay my 200 Yen, and it gets placed on a large pile of similar sticks on the table. Then we sit down and wait.

After a few minutes, the man in the tracksuit returns, except this time he's wearing the white robes of a priest. He comes in and looks at us sitting on the floor. 'You don't want a seat?' he asks. Behind us are some small seats. 'No, we're fine,' Max tells him. But the seats look nice. This could go on for some time. I reach over and grab one.

The priest climbs up and settles himself cross-legged on the table, and then starts chanting. It's a continuous, rhythmic chant that sounds like a didgeridoo. As he sits there, his voice echoing away, he arranges a collection of brass pots on the table in front of him, occasionally dipping a stick in a pot of water and flicking it. Then he starts piling the prayer sticks up in a large bowl in front of him, reading out the prayers as he does so as part of the same continuous chant. It's all in Japanese, of course, so to me it's just deep, guttural sounds, until I hear my own name as he lays one of the sticks on his ever-growing pile.

Then, using a candle, he lights the pile of sticks. The chant goes on as the fire crackles into life, and then he's throwing bits of sand and leaves and water, and more sticks onto it. Sparks start flying and I notice, as a few land on the floor just beside me, that the carpet is full of burn holes. So are his robes. A few times the sparks fly onto his lap. Without breaking his chant he quickly brushes them off. It goes on for about half an hour and by the end I'm ready to stretch out and lie down. The warmth of the fire and the soporific drone of the chant are making my eyes heavy. I'm hoping it looks like I'm closing them in thoughtful contemplation, rather than tiredness.

Then suddenly it's over. He stands up and says something matter-of-factly in Japanese, as though he has just come into the room to find us sitting there.

'He says we should chat somewhere else,' says Max, and so we put on our shoes and follow him across the courtyard back to his house. Inside, we sit down on the floor at a little table while he pours out four cups of green tea and carefully places one in front of each of us.

'So, what do you want to know?' he asks.

I may be misreading him, but something about his demeanour, suggests he is already getting impatient, as though he's expecting me to ask him something stupid. I need to fire a deep, perceptive question at him right from the start, to win him over with my understanding of running and the path to spiritual enlightenment.

'I'm interested in why people run,' I begin. Max starts translating and seems to talk for about five minutes before I can say anything else. The priest is nodding along, occasionally expressing interest at something, looking over at me. Then, in answer, he starts explaining the whole process of the thousand-day training. It's not just about running, he says. Along the way, each day you need to stop at over 250 shrines and temples. The running is really just a way to get from one to the other. And it is not even running. Much of the time you are walking.

'But why?' I ask. 'Why this thousand-day challenge?'

He ponders the question for a moment.

'All humans are asking the question, why are we alive,' he says. 'The constant movement for a thousand days gives you lots of time to think about this, to reflect on your life. It is a type of meditation through movement. That is why you shouldn't go too fast. In Zen Buddhism there are some people who burn themselves with incense to see how much pain they can take. But this, in my opinion, is not about that. It is a time to meditate on life, on how you should live.'

'And when you did it,' I say, 'did you find an answer to the question, why are we alive?' I may be pushing it here, but I'm waiting to hear about the nothingness, the sense of one-ness with the universe he experienced through his immense undertaking. I want to know what reaching enlightenment actually feels like.

'There is not this one point of understanding where everything else stops and you've made it,' he says calmly. 'Learning continues. Once you graduate from university, you don't stop learning. The thousand-day challenge is not an end point, but the challenge is to continue, enjoying life and learning new things.'

He is surprisingly prosaic about the experience, unlike those who had told me about it before, but who had never done it. Once they complete the thousand-day challenge, these priests are given the title of Daigyoman Ajari, or 'Saintly Master of the Highest Practice'. In imperial Japan, such monks were granted a special place at court, and were the only people allowed to wear shoes in the presence of the emperor. Today, those who complete the challenge become celebrities, with television cameras transmitting the final stages of their journey live to the nation. These are purportedly some of the wisest, most spiritual men on earth, with an insight gained through incredible feats of endurance that most other men can barely imagine. And yet here he was, this real-life Daigyoman Ajari, telling me that running for a thousand days was basically some good thinking time, and that really, afterwards, life went on as before.

'It's like Lady Di,' he says. *Lady Di?* 'Even though she was at the very top of English society, she found meaning in helping victims of landmines.' Now he has really thrown me.

'What do people think, was it really an accident?' he asks, leaning forward, watching me carefully. 'I saw a television programme about it, and it seemed to suggest some dark forces were in action, that she didn't die in a simple accident. What do you think?'

I'm not quite sure what to say. I shake my head. 'I don't know,' is all I can manage.

In some ways it's a relief to know that even the highest Zen Buddhists are sitting up in their temples in Mount Hiei watching television and gossiping about the death of Lady Diana. It seems to blow the whole idea of a higher spiritual existence out of the water. There is this idea, fostered by religion, that monks and priests are somehow different to us, more connected to God, to purity, free from the shackles of human desire, and whatever else they say. But really, deep down, they're just like the rest of us.

This can lead you in one of two directions. On one hand, you can despair. If the world's spiritual guardians, people like the Daigyoman Ajari, are sitting watching trashy TV, then we're all doomed, a hopeless species trapped in a futile headrush towards destruction. If they can't keep it together, what hope for the rest of us?

Or you can take solace from their everydayness. If the monks are like us, then it figures that we are like the monks. If they can gain a deeper understanding of life, yet still get distracted, still indulge their foibles, then perhaps we too can attain wisdom and fulfilment in our own lives. The search for enlightenment is not exclusive to Buddhist monks. The difference is that while they pursue it consciously and directly, the rest of us catch it only in fleeting, often unexpected, moments, when a vague sense of contentment can seem to descend upon us. Moments such as after a run.

I ask him what he thinks. Are there are similarities between what he found and the experience of athletes and recreational runners?

He says he saw a television programme about people training for the marathon and he was encouraged because he saw they often had slumps in their training when they didn't feel good or wanted to give up.

'This was the same,' he says. 'Sometimes I had slumps too, so it was good to see it wasn't just me.'

Now he is finding solace in the relatively minor trials of regular marathon runners. The thousand-day challenge is actually much harder than just running for a thousand days. At the end, after all that circumnavigating Mount Hiei, the monks enter a darkened room where they spend nine days without food, water or sleep. The idea is to bring the body as close as possible to death. It's such an extreme thing to do, and yet here is this man who has done it, and he still suffers the same doubts, has the same questions as anyone else.

'Look,' he says, as though he is reading my thoughts. 'Everyone needs to find something that suits them, that works with their body, with what they are doing in this life. I chose to undertake this challenge. But it is just one of many different paths to the same place.'

The idea of 'the path' or 'the way' is pervasive in Japan. Sport, too, is often seen as a way towards self-fulfilment, and the names many of Japan's most traditional sports, such as judo and kendo, end with the suffix -do, which actually means 'the path' or 'the way'.

Running, too, can be a way to self-fulfilment. It has a purity, a power, a way of clearing the mind, of putting you in touch with your essence, that few other activities possess. Sometimes it may seem unlikely, as we creak and struggle along, our legs heavy and tired, but then come those moments when we break through and our bodies begin to feel light, strong, at one with the earth. Sometimes it is only after a run that the feeling comes, when we tingle quietly with contentment.

But enlightenment, as the monk says, isn't a point where everything stops and you've made it, forever surrounded by a halo of bliss. No, it is something alive, something that pushes you on every day, that calls you to return, whether you are a Daigyoman Ajari on Mount Hiei or a data-management assistant in an office in Hounslow. Something deep inside us wants to know that place, to find it again, to return to it. And for some of us, it means lacing up our shoes and heading out for another run.

*

The Ajari tells us that there is one young monk currently undertaking the thousand-day challenge, but he can't take us to see him. The route is too secret, he says, too holy.

Max, however, says he knows where it is. Later, after we've left and are driving back through the trees into rain-soaked suburbia, he suggests that we go ourselves one day and run along it. If we're lucky, we may bump into the young monk on his challenge.

So, early one morning a few days later, we drive back up onto Mount Hiei in our running clothes, ready to complete one small section of the thousand-day challenge.

Fortunately, although winter is coming, the snow hasn't yet arrived. Not only would this make running in the mountain treacherous, but it would mean the monk would have stopped running. I had always assumed the thousand marathons in a thousand days meant a thousand *consecutive* days, but that's not actually the case. The monks stop in the winter, when it snows, and in the summer, when it gets too hot. In all, the challenge takes seven years to complete.

I've seen a number of television documentaries about the monks that deliberately gloss over this fact, even showing footage of the monks running in the snow. When I point this out to the Daigyoman Ajari, he laughs.

'Running in the snow? That was just for the cameras,' he says.

Max tells me the part of the route he knows is about 20km long. He's getting fitter all the time, now in the second-fastest group at Blooming and closing in, a month or two behind schedule, on a 45-minute 10K in training. His big issue, however, has been running on concrete, which he doesn't like. He's a man of the mountains. This is his terrain, and he's clearly pumped up to be here. With a little backpack he heads off into the woods, leading the way at a brisk pace.

The route follows around the mountain, rather than going up or down. But it is still a constant flow of steep inclines and descents. We pass shrines along the way, and temples where we have to walk. Shaven-headed monks, surprised to see us, stop and bow as we pass. And then we're on again.

We keep our eyes peeled for the white robes of the running monk, his narrow hat pointing the way forward. They wear special long, narrow hats that hit the branches if they attempt to turn their heads. It's a way of keeping them focused on the path, on the action of what they are doing, rather than getting distracted looking around at the forest. The real journey is internal, not on the mountain.

But we don't see him.

Although the pace is comfortable, and we get to walk for a while every time we arrive at another temple, the constant ups and downs makes it tiring, even over just 20km. And the monks average a marathon along this route day after day. In the seventh and final year of the challenge, the monks cover 50 miles (almost two marathons) each day along these trails.

Max keeps running strongly until almost the end, when suddenly he stops, complaining of a sore knee.

'It went coming down that last hill,' he winces, holding it. He carries on running, but unfortunately the injury turns out to be a bad one, and Max's plans to outrun me and the rest of the Blooming team are left up on the mountain that day – it is another two months before he can run again.

18

While Max recovers from his injury, and the aspiring Ajari continues to loop his way around Mount Hiei, the coach of the professional Nissin Foods ekiden team, Takashi Okamura, the man from Kyotanabe, has agreed a date for me to visit. I've been knocking at the corporate ekiden door for almost a year now. Finally someone has opened it.

The corporate system is the backbone of Japanese running. It allows thousands of runners to continue training full-time after university without the worry and pressure of having to find a job or make a living alongside their running. In the UK this is a luxury only a few top athletes enjoy.

Mara Yamauchi, who has experienced both systems, says many talented runners in the UK are lost to the sport because they can't afford not to work. In the US, too, even top Olympic athletes often struggle to make ends meet in a crowded sports market.

According to the USA Track and Field Foundation, fifty per cent of American athletes ranked in the national top ten in their event earn less than $15,000 (£8,800) a year from the sport.

Many of Japan's thriving company teams were first started to give hard-working employees something to cheer and get excited about, and to foster a spirit of company loyalty.

Many of the other top sports teams in Japan, such as the baseball teams, are also company teams.

But extensive media coverage means the ekiden teams are also good PR for the companies. The manager of one professional team, NTT, a telecoms company with 180,000 employees, told me that the firm's ekiden team exists for two reasons. 'One,' he said, 'is motivating company workers, to make them feel proud of the company. Two, advertising and PR.'

'Think about it,' says Mr Ogushi. 'A race that lasts for four or five hours, or two days even, with the television cameras on the runners the whole time, usually from the front. And they have the company logo on their vests, the newspaper logo on the race number. It's good advertising.'

If advertising is so important, you would think they'd be keen to have a journalist on board, telling their story to the world. Many of the corporate teams are owned by multinational companies who would surely appreciate a bit of free PR, firms such as Honda and Toyota. But the problem I was having was that the teams were too focused on their performance at the upcoming New Year ekiden. The pressure on the coaches to succeed was too great, that they couldn't countenance a foreign journalist turning up to training sessions. What good could it do? I was simply a distraction to the task at hand.

With only one big race a year, the coaches can't afford to mess it up. Today, the New Year ekiden is the sole reason for the existence of the men's corporate teams. It is a similar situation with the women's teams, who exist in similar numbers and at a similar level. Their big race is the women's national ekiden final held in mid-December each year. Both races are broadcast in full on primetime television.

While the runners themselves may have other targets, perhaps making the national team for a major championship, or running a fast marathon time, the companies are only interested in the ekidens. It is something of a tradition in Japan to get up early on New Year's Day to watch the men's corporate ekiden, and it regularly reaches TV audiences of well over ten per cent. While this is far below the figures for the Hakone ekiden, which takes place the following two days, on 2 and 3 January, it's still a sizable audience in a country of 120 million people.

When I put it to the team manager of NTT, who have won the New Year ekiden twice in their history, that surely one of their employees running well in, say, the Tokyo marathon, would be good for company morale too, he looked at me patiently, as though this was going to be hard to explain.

'Not really,' he said. 'The only thing that really matters for company spirit is the ekiden, passing the ribbon, doing it together. Even if the team does badly, it's OK. Everyone goes up and down with the team. We are all brought together in support of the team.'

The implication is that it's not so easy to support an individual as it is to support a team. The collective unit of the team is a more palatable representation of the company, a more powerful symbol of *wa*, than an individual.

Not that individuals are free from blame if it does go wrong. Kenji tells me that when he was running his team won the New Year ekiden six years in a row – (boy, he was good). Then, in the seventh year, they didn't win.

'Nobody ever said anything to me if I ran badly in an individual race,' he says. 'But when we lost the ekiden I got lots of mail, faxes from angry fans and from my bosses.' He laughs. 'Only ekiden matters,' he says.

By the time I get the OK from Nissin Foods, it's late November and the New Year ekiden is looming. I'm lucky that one of the corporate powerhouses has agreed to let me visit so close to the race. Mr Ogushi has pulled some important strings for me. The day before I'm due to join them, I pack up my running kit and take the bullet train to Tokyo.

*

The next morning, I'm in a taxi gliding through a tangled residential area somewhere in central Tokyo. It's 5.30. A solitary bicycle pedals by under the street-lights, the rider's face wrapped in a scarf. Otherwise it's quiet. The taxi driver is confused. His sat-nav seems to be contradicting Mr Ogushi's phone. They have a polite discussion, before the driver, apologising, does a U-turn.

'We'll walk from here,' Mr Ogushi says as the car pulls silently to a stop. The door automatically swings open.

We walk together through the narrow streets without talking. Houses and apartment blocks are packed tightly together with barely a few centimetres between them. It's hard to imagine one of Japan's top professional running teams being based somewhere around here.

Nissin Foods won the New Year ekiden the year before in 2012. Their roster includes the two-time national 10,000m champion Yuki Sato, who broke the record for the fourth stage of the ekiden in 2012.*

They've also just signed one of Japan's most promising young runners, Suguru Osako from Waseda University. Osako has been lined up to join Alberto Salazar and Mo Farah at the Oregon Project in America after he finishes university. He will only come back to Japan when he's needed to run ekidens. It's an unusual arrangement, but it will be fascinating to see how the attentions of the renowned US coach, and a completely different training environment, will affect his development in the coming years.**

For now, however, Nissin have more immediate concerns. In 2013, they could only manage ninth place in the New Year ekiden after some of their key runners got injured. The company's management was not happy. They weren't buying any excuses, this was a team built to win the race, not stumble across the line in ninth.

'If they do as badly again this year, the coach could be sacked,' says Mr Ogushi. The stakes are high.

*

We arrive at the Nissin 'clubhouse' a little early. It's a street like any other in the neighbourhood. Along one side is an

* Sato's record of 1:02:51 for the 22km fourth stage is equivalent to a 1:00:16 half-marathon, faster than the Japanese half-marathon record.
** On 7 September 2014, after less than six months training with Salazar in the US, Osako broke the Japanese national 3,000m record, running 7.40.09 in Rieti, Italy.

apartment block. This is where the athletes live, along with lots of other Nissin company employees.

Outside the building's main entrance, an elderly man is limbering up as though he's about to go for a run. Mr Ogushi, who is on the phone, doesn't notice him at first, but when he does, he springs into bowing mode, introducing me in the politest Japanese possible. This is the Nissin head coach, Teruoki Shirouzu. He's seventy-one years old and has been coaching ekiden teams for forty years. He shakes my hand and we then politely step back to let him get on with his stretching.

As we wait, runners gradually emerge from the building. They nod quietly, not showing any surprise at my presence. Among the group are three Kenyans, who come out together, all slow, sleepy movements. The Japanese runners are already stretching, despite the cold. As we wait, I'm introduced to the rest of the coaching team. Takashi Okamura, the coach from Kyotanabe who invited me here, Toshinari Suwa, who finished sixth in the marathon at the 2004 Olympics, and Kenjiro Jitsui, who ran the marathon in the 1996 Olympics. It's quite a stellar line-up.

Okamura asks me if I still want to run with the team, and laughs, as though it was always a silly idea. When I say I do, he looks concerned. The athletes are doing a one-hour 'light run'. They have a track session later in the morning, so presumably they won't be going too fast. Nothing I couldn't keep up with, I'm sure. The coach explains that they run alone, following whatever route they want around the streets. I think he's telling me that none of them particularly wants company, let alone from a pestering writer asking questions in broken Japanese.

'Bring your phone,' Mr Ogushi suggests, as though he suspects they may try to lose me if I attempt to run with them.

Then Okamura has another idea. 'You could run with the Kenyans. Is that OK?'

Sure. Are the Kenyans doing something different?

'Yes. Separate programme,' he says.

It turns out that the Kenyan and Japanese runners rarely train together. Initially, Okamura tells me this is because the Kenyans are too fast, but that doesn't make much sense. If I can attempt to run with them, surely the Japanese runners can too, especially on easy runs. Indeed, national champion Yuki Sato has run faster times than all three of the Kenyans.

Okamura later puts it down to the fact that the Kenyans have their own tailored training programme. This is because they run a shorter leg at the New Year ekiden, he says, and so between October and November they do more speed work than the others. It's also partly because they have different preferences when it comes to training. For example, today, while the Japanese head out for an hour along Tokyo's tangled streets, the Kenyans are taken in the team minibus to nearby Yoyogi park, where they can run on a dirt trail.

'The Japanese don't like this uneven ground,' Okamura tells me when we get there. 'They like firm ground. The Kenyans like soft ground.'

It's not the first time I've heard this. It makes me wonder why the Japanese runners don't look at the Kenyans and want to copy them. If they're so much faster, why don't they try running like the Kenyans? It seems a golden opportunity for the Japanese runners, as most teams have one or two Kenyans or Ethiopians in the team. But they're simply regarded as different. When I ask some of the other Nissin runners why they don't train with the Kenyans, they just laugh, as though I'm making a joke.

In the team minibus to the park, I ask the Kenyans if they'll be running fast or slow.

'Medium,' one says after a pause. I know from experience that any answer other than 'slow' is cause for concern. But the park is a 2.8 km loop, so I can drop out at any point without getting lost. The three Kenyans are doing six laps – almost 17km.

The youngest of the trio is nineteen-year-old Leonard Barsoton. He recently came second in the junior race at the world cross-country championships. He has been in Japan two years now and says he's enjoying it. In fact, he complains that his agent keeps trying to send him abroad to race. He tells me it interferes with his ekiden training. 'Nissin don't like it,' he says. 'I prefer to stay here and do well for the team.'

His main aim, however, is to be in the Kenyan marathon team come the Tokyo Olympics in 2020. I say it's his aim, but he presents it more as a certainty. 'I will run marathon here in 2020,' he says, calmly, when I ask him about it. It's not said with egotistical bravado, but simply with untainted confidence.

The park is quiet in the half-light of the morning, with just the occasional dog-walker or jogger shuffling along the trail. Unlike the Japanese runners, the Kenyans don't spend much time stretching before we're off, skirting along the narrow trail. We run in single file and after a few moments

I glance at my GPS watch, to see how fast we're running. A mere 3:30 minutes per kilometre. Oh boy, that's fast. I buckle up and hang on.

It's thrilling racing along behind the three Kenyans, leaping over the roots of trees, zipping around corners, up and down little mounds. It may be medium pace for them, but for me it's a charge, as though we're running for our lives. We pass other runners as though they're standing still, dashing past in a blur, the Kenyans hardly making a sound as their feet pat, pat gently on the dry earth.

I last for just under five kilometres. By the end of the second lap of the park, we're running at 3 minutes per kilometre pace, and they're getting faster. One of them takes off his jacket and throws it in the bushes. I'm beginning to drift away behind them, losing momentum without their methodical rhythm to follow.

I decide to stop. I watch them disappear into the trees, standing there alone, happy to have survived as long as I did. It was like tumbling down a hill, trying to keep my feet. It's only now that I notice it's daylight, a grey morning hanging quietly over the city. I walk back to the bus, to where Okamura is waiting. He is smiling. 'Good,' he says. 'They are very fast.' I pull on my tracksuit and head off for a little jog to warm down.

*

Back at the Nissin camp, the runners are quiet, focused. When they talk to each other, it is in lowered voices, a few muttered words only. The head coach gathers everyone around him. The ekiden is approaching, he says. As if they weren't serious enough already, he tells them it is now time to get serious. The runners listen intently as he talks, standing to attention with their hands behind their backs.

Mr Okamura tells me they only have six healthy runners right now. They need seven for the New Year ekiden. The race on which the head coach's job may well hang.

'He has a lot of experience, you should talk to him,' Mr Ogushi tells me. 'But after the ekiden. Until then he is . . .' He's not sure how to put it.

'Too nervous to talk?' I suggest.

'Yes,' he says.

New Year is still forty days away.

Later, I accompany the team to their mid-morning track session at one of the nearby Hakone universities. We travel in the team minibus in silence, and as soon as we arrive, the head coach walks off to the other end of the track and stands with his arms crossed. The runners spend over an hour warming up for their session, while the coach stands there in the distance the whole time, a brooding cloud on an already grey, chilly day. The scene is completed by the huge incinerator that towers like a smoking metaphor over the track.

The runners have different schedules and so some of them train alone, separate from the main group. The coaches split up, recording interval times and recovery periods on the multitude of stopwatches each one has around his neck. .

Whenever I try to engage one of the younger coaches in conversation, I'm met with a questioning look and they walk away from me. One of the runners, called Akinobu

Murasawa, has recently been training in the US. He seems friendly enough, and comes over to talk to me. 'Call me Aki,' he says, in good English. But he speaks in a hushed voice, and not too much.

Despite their reluctance to engage during training, afterwards the three younger coaches are more relaxed. Sitting in their small office in the 'clubhouse' apartment block, filling out the runners' times from the track session on pieces of paper, and discussing the upcoming training schedule, they jokingly tell me not to give away any of their secrets. Even though I can barely understand ten per cent of what they're saying, I promise not to. It's obviously the right answer, as when I come to leave, Okamura invites me to join them for a day at their training camp in Chiba the following week.

19

A week later, I find myself sitting in a hotel room with the same three coaches. It's the same hotel I stayed in with the American team for the Chiba ekiden. It's clearly the place to train in this corner of the world, the slice of country-side sandwiched between Tokyo and the Pacific coast in the south-eastern edge of Honshu. While the hotel hardly boasts the endless trails of Kenya, it does have an 800m woodchip running trail in the grounds: a tiny piece of regulated soft-ness in an otherwise concrete world.

On the low table in front of us are crisps, salted nuts, slithers of meat – food not for athletes, the coaches joke. They're also drinking beer. They offer me one. When I re-fuse, they're surprised.

'I have to be ready to run tomorrow,' I say, confusing my-self, in their eyes at least, with an athlete.

The Japanese group – everyone except the Kenyans – is doing a long run early the next morning, anything from 20km to 35km depending on each runner's schedule. They're going to run laps of a 5km loop, so I said I would join them – for one lap. It has provoked an amused response from the coaches.

'They will run the first 5km in 17:30,' one says to me, waiting for my reaction. In my 5km ekiden leg a few weeks ago, in which I raced flat out, I ran 17:49. My best time ever, though, is faster.

'My personal best is 17:10,' I reply, omitting the fact that it was on a flat course, in perfect conditions, and just after I'd returned from six months' training at altitude in Kenya. I've also had quite a busy training week, so tomorrow I'll be running on tired legs.

'Ah, but this is very hilly,' the coach says, popping another crisp in his mouth.

*

Of course, I don't have to keep up. But the more they egg me on, the more I want to. Even if they are just playing with me. These are men who've all run 5km in under 14 minutes in their day. They're amused at the fact I'm even bothering to try. But it's not every day you get to run with a crack Japanese ekiden team.

At breakfast the next morning, I sit with the Kenyans and tell them I'm planning to run 5km with the Japanese group.

'Ah, that will be so nice,' says the young Barsoton. He makes it sound like a stroll through a flowery meadow. I take heart from that.

The run is out along a fairly quiet country road, although not so quiet we don't have to watch out for the odd passing lorry. When I ask the coaches why they come to this place for their training camp, where there is no altitude or even running trails, the answer is simple: 'No traffic lights.'

Tokyo is so tangled with traffic that there is nowhere for them to run at a good pace without stopping now and then for the red man to turn green. It seems insane that they base themselves in the midst of this urban knot. The only reason is that the company already owned the apartment building and used it to house its unmarried workers. When the ekiden team was formed, the building had enough space in it for the runners, so they moved in.

I drive to the start of the training run in the team bus with the coaches, while the athletes jog there slowly. It's about 5km from the hotel. After some limbering up, and some last-minute sups on their energy drinks, we're ready to go. We line up on the desolate road, beside a small workman's hut and surrounded by rice fields. Okamura gives me one last questioning look – one last chance to drop out. But I'm good. OK, he says, and we're off.

I tuck into the group a few places from the back. They run in single file to avoid the traffic, with Aki taking the lead. None of them speaks. We're straight into it, knocking out a steady, regimented pace. I follow on, trying not to run too close to the man in front. I don't want to trip him up. I watch his feet, his heels flicking back and forth. Behind me is Sato, the team's ace. This keeps me on my toes, careful not to slow him down by letting even a small gap form in front.

After about 2km we head up the first hill. I dig in. I'm wondering how long I can keep it up, when already the road starts levelling out, and we're heading down the other side. At 3km, I realise I'm feeling comfortable.

At each kilometre point, the coaches, driving in the van behind us, call out the latest timesplit on a loudspeaker. I didn't realise they were behind us when we set off, so I got a bit of a shock the first time I heard the time being called out, as though the god of running had bellowed it from the clear blue sky.

At 4km, I'm still comfortable. We hit it bang on 14 minutes. These guys know how to run to a set pace. As I run, I concentrate on my form, trying to run like the Kenyan Barsoton. I know I'm not even close, of course, but I'm focusing on backlift, quick patter-patter strides, and on my breathing.

Of course, I'm only running 5km, but I reach the end still in my position in the line, in a time of 17:28. I resist giving the passing van of coaches a triumphant look. Of course, they don't really care, they have serious business to attend to, but I'm quietly nodding nonchalantly in my own world. I'm definitely getting stronger, that's for sure. I feel in my legs that I could have run that much faster.

*

To the coaches, it seems funny that someone as slow as me should take his running so seriously. I'm not going to win any marathons, or make any Olympic team. Once those goals are out of reach, for them running becomes simply a hobby. 'I want to keep my figure,' one of the coaches tells me when I ask him why he still runs. But he says he never races, or even times himself.

I admit, at times it can seem indulgent, selfish even, but I'm far from alone among runners in striving to beat my times, to improve, to run as hard as I can. Here, in this esteemed company, it seems futile to be pushing myself so hard. Like a man trying to catch fish with a stick and some string. Why *do* I bother?

For me, running slowly and running hard are two different things. Running slowly brings a certain meditative calm, a chance to take in your surroundings, and, as for the running monks, a chance to think, a space where the world is cleared of clutter and your thoughts are free to wander undisturbed. However, running as hard and fast as you can means entering another zone entirely.

It is here, in the racing of legs, the whirl of the trees rushing by, too fast to see or care, that your mind begins to empty. You enter a space where the outside world ceases to exist, except as a path to traverse. Beautiful scenery becomes irrelevant. You could be running through an abandoned industrial estate and it would make no difference. All that is left is you and the road. And it is here, in the push to run faster, that you can begin to surprise yourself.

When you really start to run, hard and fast, it can be like you've broken through something and come out the other side into a wide open space. It can sometimes feel like you've taken a drug. Something is always trying to drag you back – the pain, the hurt in your legs – but occasionally you can run so hard you want to laugh out loud. You look down at your legs. More? OK, let's do it.

It's all relative, but that's part of the beauty of it. You don't have to be a champion – though I often wonder what it must feel like to be able to run like Mo Farah or Wilson Kipsang. But to run as hard as you can, as fast as you can, that is the key. Then running changes from an exploration of your environment, a chance to drift like a leaf on the wind, to an exploration of the depths of your soul.

In Murakami's novel *The Wind-Up Bird Chronicle*, the

main protagonist discovers a dry well in the garden of an abandoned house. He takes to climbing down it to sit at the bottom for hours at a time. Days even. He begins to look forward to it. Down in the well, the world is gone. Without even light, he becomes a being of pure sensation. He revels in it.

It reminds me of the feeling of running hard. I often think to myself, just before a race, that I'm about to head down into my well. Down there it is dark, difficult, perhaps even a little bit scary, but it is pure sensation, brute simplicity. Down there, with everything else stripped away, life, the core of life, the breath itself, fills you entirely.

Beep, beep. The van has stopped further down the road. They're calling me. Waving me to hurry up. I sprint, still full of energy, to catch them up. They don't say anything as I clamber in, but speed off to catch up with the runners again. Just in time for the next kilometre split. Again, bang on 3 minutes 30 seconds.

*

'We don't exchange many words with him [the head coach],' Aki says with a smile.

We're sitting naked in a shallow pool of volcanic water. The rest of the team sit dotted around the other onsen pools, looking out over the surrounding forest, their tired legs soothed after their long run.

Aki is a recent recruit to the team and has not raced the New Year ekiden before. In 2011 he was a star of the Hakone ekiden, winning the coveted Most Valuable Player (MVP) award. It means he's one of the most recognised runners in Japan. Today he ran 30km and by the end he had left all the others in his wake.

When I suggest to him that he will surely be in the team for the New Year ekiden, however, rather than agree, he prefers to point out how good Yuki Sato, the team's ace, is. 'Mr Sato ran 35km,' he points out, almost apologetic for running off on him. Sato's training programme meant he ran further than the others today.

I ask Aki why he chose to join Nissin Foods after university. As a Hakone star he could have chosen almost any team.

'Nissin has some very strong athletes to train with,' he says. 'And good coaches. Also it is an unusual team. They give the runners a lot of freedom. I can choose my races and even where to train. That's why I went to the US. Later, next year, I'm hoping to train in Australia.'

'What about ekiden?' I ask him.

'Of course we must run ekiden. But that is the only obligation. And that is only two races a year [the New Year ekiden, and the qualifying race for the New Year ekiden].'

Although the head coach is in many ways a typical conservative Japanese coach, Nissin is a modern team. This tussle between the old, traditional ways and the modern world has been fought across Japanese life and culture for decades. When I first visited Japan in 2001, the modern world seemed to be winning. I was working for a computer magazine at the time, writing about technology, and I was excited to see what the computers in Japan could do. But when I arrived I was amazed to find nobody using computers. I had expected them to be everywhere. Instead, everyone was doing everything on their phones. This was mad. I had only just bought myself my first mobile phone in the UK. It was a phone. That was it. But in Japan you could listen to music on your phone, take pictures, even check your email.

Now, in the west, we have caught up. At every bus stop or queue for coffee in London and Tokyo, it's the same scene – people scrolling away on their phones. And while Japan may still have more robots, faster trains, and toilets that come with a remote control, my sense is less of a futuristic nation at the cutting edge of technology, but more an old-fashioned land resistant to change. It is often hard, for example, to pay for things in Japan with a bank card rather than cash. And when you meet people you are still expected to swap business cards, actual bits of card, always presented in the traditional manner, holding the two top corners and bowing. The offices are still principally full of men in suits, the only women usually being the PAs and secretaries. According to the World Economic Forum, Japan consistently ranks as one of the worst nations in the world for gender equality at work. Even the high-tech toilets seem somehow retro, like something out of a 1970s vision of the future.

In running, this tussle is playing out with a wave of young coaches trying different ideas. One of these is Kenji. He tells me he is often criticised for the way he approaches coaching, for questioning the traditional ways, but the more people I meet, the more I realise he is not as alone in his ideas as he thinks.

The traditional view of the coach in Japan is a person who knows everything and should not be questioned. In Japan the sense of hierarchy at work and in sport has always been strong. This is part of being in a team. To question the coach is to risk rocking the boat. But that is not the Japanese way. It is by fitting in and doing what you are told that harmony, or *wa*, is retained.

When I ask the Ritsumeikan ace, Yoshimura, how Kenji is different from the other coaches he has worked with, he says: 'There's more logic to our training now. Takao-san [Kenji] explains why we're doing things. He doesn't just tell us what to do.'

The other runners also talk about how training has become more fun since Kenji took over. This again, is not the traditional way. In Japan, the idea has always been that to succeed at anything you must work hard. In running this means training hard. Not having fun.

In Robert Whiting's *You Gotta Have Wa* he tells the story of how prior to the 1996 Atlanta Olympics, Japanese swimming sensation Suzu Chiba shocked her fellow countrymen when she announced: 'I just want to enjoy myself swimming there.'

While athletes from other nations are often heard voicing such sentiments, in Japan it caused a scandal.

'It was a departure from the "I'll win or die trying" martial arts school of thought,' wrote Whiting, 'that had so long characterised Japanese athletics, not to mention other facets of society.'

When, four years later, Chiba wasn't selected for the team for the 2000 Olympics, despite winning Japan's Olympic trials and posting the second-fastest time in the world that year, she claimed she had been penalised for her relaxed approach.

Aki slides out of the water and walks over to the showers. It's a row of small stools in front of mirrors along one wall, each with a shower-head and an arrangement of shampoos and other toiletries. I follow along, taking the stool next to him.

I ask Aki how the coaching was different in the US, compared to Japan.

'In America, the athlete has a bigger say in the training,' he says. 'Here in Japan, the coaches decide everything.'

I ask him if he prefers to have a say, like in America. He has already said he chose Nissin because it gave him more freedom.

'In Japan,' he says, 'the coach will spot if I'm tired, and tell me to rest. I don't know all these things. So for me it is good in Japan.'

After we're dry and dressed, it's time for me to head back to Tokyo. Aki kindly invites me to visit him again, to talk some more. I promise to do that.

'After the New Year ekiden,' he says.

'Of course,' I say, and head off down to the front of the hotel complex to wait for the bus.

20

While I was running with the Nissin Foods team in Chiba, Ritsumeikan were off seeking redemption for their disappointing performance in the national ekiden, competing in both the Kansai regional university ekiden and the Kyoto area university ekiden.

I arrange to meet Kenji to find out what happened. I haven't seen him since the national ekiden, when he stood looking like a condemned man at the finish.

I sit down at a small plastic table in a university cafe near the track. The wintery day blusters around outside the large window.

Kenji sits back in his seat, grinning from ear to ear. He's about to begin, when his assistant, Nomura, appears outside the window. He waves sheepishly and comes in. He's with his girlfriend, who just happens to be the assistant team manager of Ritsumeikan's all-conquering women's team. Of course, she can't tell him any of her team's secrets, they both joke. She sits down, too, at the far end of the table, and Kenji begins his story.

'I started as coach here in April,' he says. 'Just a few months ago. When I joined, the team was in a terrible condition. The atmosphere in the group was very bad.' In the national qualifiers in June, they finished third in the Kansai region and so missed out on a place at the Izimo ekiden, and almost missed out on the national ekiden completely.

'We had a meeting,' he says, 'I asked everyone to think about how they could improve to contribute to the team. It is important the team does well, but each individual is also important.'

They decided to run lots of track races to improve their times. He said this was an unusual strategy.

'The reason,' he says, holding up a finger as though he is about to reveal his masterstroke, 'is that I had a feeling we'd be behind at the national, so I wanted the team members to see their own progress.'

He says that in ekiden, when a team does badly, all the members' performances drop. So this was his way of stopping them from getting disheartened. It doesn't sound it, but it was a radical idea, putting the individual morale of the runners, their own personal aspirations, over team unity. Of course, the two are closely linked, but it was a big leap to put them the other way around like this. It was turning the concept of *wa* on its head.

It worked, says Kenji, pulling out files to show me the times of his runners over the last few months. Of the entire team of thirty, only three didn't run personal best times in that period.

'So after the national ekiden,' he says with a flurry of hands, marking the point at which his ingenious plan came together, 'the atmosphere in the team didn't drop, because of the track times. That was the plan.'

In their next race, the Kansai ekiden, they faced arch-rivals Kyoto Sangyo University, whom they hadn't beaten in over eleven years. At the national ekiden, Kyoto Sangyo had finished just ahead of them in fourteenth.

It was a hard-fought race, with the number-two ace running the last leg this time. He started at the changeover 30 seconds behind his rival, but managed to catch up with 4km to go. However, as they raced through the crowded streets of Miyazu city in northern Kansai, he lost out by one second in a dramatic sprint finish.

'Nomura cried,' Kenji says, giggling.

The final race of the season was just a week later, the Kyoto prefecture ekiden, and again they faced their old adversary, Kyoto Sangyo.

Kenji says he got everyone in the team to run a minor track race the day before the ekiden, to take the pressure off them.

'I also told them that the real goal was next year, to finish fifth in Izumo and the national. This gave them confidence.'

So, on a warm, clear day in Kyoto, their heads full of mind tricks and their legs tired from the day before, they ran their least important ekiden of the year. And, finally, they did it. They won. They beat Kyoto Sangyo for the first time in over a decade.

He looks at me triumphantly, waiting for my response to the story. 'You must be very happy,' I venture. I'm not sure if happy, or relieved, is the right word.

He nods, showing me the newspaper clipping with the report of the race. I've no idea what it says, but I look at it anyway. There's a small picture of Nagumo, the number-two ace, his face straining, his body twisted, running through the streets with the Ritsumeikan sash across his body.

'Thank god we beat them,' says Kenji, with a sigh.

*

Christmas in Japan is a funny time for westerners. The shops are full of tinsel, while in Kyoto Christmas music is pumped out over speakers lining the main streets. The commercial side is there, ratcheted up to almost the same levels you get in England. But nobody is doing anything special. Nobody asks you if you're 'ready' for Christmas – that delightful expression that always makes me think of Christmas as some kind of endurance event.

When it actually comes, despite the fanfare, it's just a normal day. People go to work. Go shopping. Do what they usually do. In lieu of any fixed traditions, it has become a custom for couples to go out on dates on Christmas Day, a bit like Valentine's Day.

My children, however, are demanding the full festive shebang, or as close to it as we can muster. I can't quite bring myself to buy the only Christmas tree I can find, an already collapsing, plastic, green stick tucked away in the back corner of the local hardware superstore. Marietta suggests sticking fairy lights to the wall in the shape of a tree. It's a suggestion that doesn't go down well with the children, who stomp around saying they want a real tree, but one day when they're outside playing I try it, and it looks great. They come in and dance around excitedly at the sight of it.

Later, Ossian and I decide to supplement our tree of lights with a piece of bamboo we find by the roadside. We stick it in a pot and hang things off its three tiny branches. So now we have two Christmas trees.

Amid all this festive cheer, I find myself running four

ekiden legs, all on the same day. Max has been trying to help me put together my all-star ekiden team, without much success. Morita, the Blooming ace, is interested in running, but is worried about his injury. Ryohei, my fifteen-year-old neighbour, was keen when I asked him, his mother coming to the door that evening, huddled under her umbrella at the foot of the steps, to profess her gratitude for the opportunity. I wasn't sure it was that much of an opportunity, but alas it turns out that in all the races the runners have to be aged sixteen or over. Max is still hoping to get involved, but his own injury means his training has ground to a halt.

It doesn't leave me with many options besides the Ritsumeikan runners, and I'm not sure they'll want to run anyway. I'm also worried I'll be out of my depth with them. I don't want to be the weak link in the team. That could be demoralising, both for me and everyone else. Why would they run so hard if I'm going to blow it all anyway? I didn't realise building a team would be so tricky.

Then I get a phone call from Max. Blooming are running another ekiden and would like me to run. It's in Kyoto that Sunday. While I ponder the make-up of my all-star team, I agree to run.

*

The race takes place in the grounds of the Kyoto aquatics centre, the same place some of the Blooming training sessions happen. In fact, there's a training session there that same afternoon. I arrive at the centre to find the Blooming runners standing inside the entrance in an excited huddle.

I recognise one of the runners – Rogukawa, the Asics sales executive whom I'm thinking of asking to run for my ekiden team. He's a 40-minute 10K runner. One of the quickest in the Blooming team. He also speaks a little bit of English.

'Finn-san,' he says, excited, when he sees me. He jokes in Japanese to the other runners, who all nod eagerly. He translates. 'How many legs will you run? Four? Five?' The race is ten laps of a 1km loop around the centre. The teams need to have at least five runners, but can divvy the legs up between them however they want.

'Why don't we do two each?' I suggest. I'd feel greedy running four legs. Besides, I've developed a small injury on the outside of my right knee. I've had it since the Nissin Foods training camp in Chiba. Right now I'm in the second stage of the injury process: denial. First you feel a twinge. Then you ignore it. You tell yourself it's nothing, that you're imagining it. That it will go away. It usually does. I'm right there, ignoring it. Except, I'm not really. Every day it bothers me. Every time I feel it walking down the stairs at home, or when I start off on a little trot down the street, it's like being reminded of a piece of bad news I've been trying to forget. I feel a little tightening of the stomach. I'm not supposed to be getting injured. I'm running with beautiful form now. I'm supposed to be bulletproof. So, irrationally, I tell myself that it's fine. I can still run. But more than two legs on the same ekiden, that may be pushing it.

'Yes, yes,' he says, as though it was the plan all along. 'Two each.'

It's a crisp, cold day, so we go for a team jog around the course to warm up. Halfway around the path goes up a steep rise, coming out at the top on a view over the city, a flat mosaic of rooftops stretching off to the hazy, almost translucent, snow-covered mountains in the distance.

Then the path swoops steeply down again, into a car park and back to the start. It's a short, sharp loop.

The team captain asks me to run the first leg, and so I'm given the tasuki to loop over my shoulder. It's nearly time, so I head straight out to the start.

If the Lake Biwa ekiden wasn't as competitive as I had hoped, it was a Diamond League race compared to this one. I stand back from the start, towering over the majority of my rivals, most of whom are children under the age of fourteen. Some are as young as eight. It feels faintly ridiculous. I've come here to Japan to run with some of the best runners in the world, not compete against schoolchildren. And these aren't even the serious, head-banded high-school ekiden children, who would leave me trailing in their dust. I try not to look like an idiot, with my huge arms and legs.

About a dozen other adults are also on the first leg, and a couple of them look quite serious. One wades through the children to the front, so I decide to join him. A man gives us some last-minute instructions, which hopefully aren't too important, and with a crack of a starting gun, we're off, tearing around the first corner, avoiding some bollards, and away.

The serious runner is fast. I follow him closely up the steep hill and down the other side, but can't quite manage to get past him, finishing my leg second in a fairly breezy 2 minutes 50 seconds. As I come into the changeover zone, I almost crash into my second-leg runner, a middle-aged lady in about twenty layers of running kit, who shuffles off as though she's not quite sure where to go.

By the time I get the tasuki again, on the sixth leg, we're way back among the children's teams, so I find myself flying through them, being careful not to knock them over, particularly as I let my huge frame tumble like a dislodged boulder down the steep descent. Even though the race seems a non-event, I can't help charging around. It feels at least as fast as the first leg, although I never get an official time, and I'm happy with my morning's work. The team gathers afterwards for a photograph, giving the regulation peace signs and thumbs-up as the low winter sun glares in our eyes. Then, a few hours later, we're all back for more.

*

That afternoon, Kenji decides to hold an ekiden as the Blooming club's end-of-year special training session. Around exactly the same course. Again teams of five, running two legs each. At least this time there are no small children running.

While the regular Blooming members might not be breaking any records, Kenji has enlisted the help of two young, aspiring coaches, who usually run pacing the slower groups, but who are both, I eventually realise, pretty good runners. One, Kanta, is usually one of those Blooming runners left flabbergasted by the times I post in training, while he jogs around with one of the slower groups. As he writes the times up on the whiteboard back in the meeting room in the Dawn Centre after the Osaka sessions, he shakes his head, as though my modest feats have left him stunned.

One evening, however, the final interval of our training session is 1km flat out, along the path stretching around Osaka castle. We are all of us, from the slowest to the fastest, to run it together, and Kenji says he wants us to break our PBs. It is only when we stand up to the line ready to start, that I realise I don't know where the finish is.

'How will I know where to stop?' Max isn't there that night, but Morita, the ace, steps in.

'Kanta will tell you,' he says. Kanta stands next to me. He nods and smiles. I don't know how to put this, but, er, how will he do that when he's still here now?

'Don't worry,' says Morita, sensing my confusion. 'He will get there first. He's faster than you.'

I've never seen him run fast. Maybe I've misunderstood. But it is too late, everyone is ready. Unsure how it will work out, as with many things here in Japan, I have no choice but to leap in and see what will happen. OK, let's go.

I start off at full pelt, Kanta running alongside me, the others drifting away behind. Perhaps I'm not running fast enough. It's only 1km. I pick up the pace. And again. Each time I do, Kanta accelerates beside me. I can feel my lungs bursting, when with surely hardly any distance left, he presses the turbo boost and accelerates away in time to reach the finish first, stop, pull out his watch, and calmly call the times out as first I and then everyone else races by.

He really is fast.

The other young Blooming coach is Kono, the part-time model who ran the Lake Biwa ekiden with me. He looks like an athlete, all long limbs and powerful, sinewy muscle. He says he is an 800m runner, so 1km is close to his distance.

[243]

All three of us line up together for the first leg of the Blooming ekiden. This isn't going to be easy.

We shoot off, sprinting. My legs feel fresh despite the two ekiden stages I've already run that morning. Before I know it we're up the hill and I'm dropping slightly back from my two younger rivals. But down the hill like a madman and through the car park, forcing an unsuspecting car to stop, I catch back up. I feel like whooping as we charge like three wild horses around the last corner. It's slightly uphill and we finish almost together, Kanta stealing the win by less than a second. The clock reads 2.49. With a big hill, that's a decent time for my third 1km interval of the day.

Of my four legs that day, it is the two where I start with everyone else, the two first legs, which are both in effect normal races, that I enjoy the most. It is the head-to-head challenge that really gets my blood pumping. That is exciting racing. Unlike the ekidens where, if I run a later leg, I feel like I'm drifting along alone, unconnected to my rivals or even my team, this is like being in the centre of the storm. This is hand-to-hand combat.

Ironically, by turning the race into a team event, a relay, you are more likely to find yourself running alone. After the first leg, ekidens inevitably become spread out, and most people find themselves starting alone and at best passing a few people along the way. In order to emulate this in training, the runners spend a lot of time running alone. At one Ritsumeikan training session I went to, Kenji set everyone off purposely at one-minute intervals around a 2.5 km loop. Kenji told me the idea was to get the team members used to running alone, because this was what was required in ekiden.

Alone, but part of the group. Ekiden, it seems, was a way of avoiding both confrontation and individual glory all at the same time.

After the Blooming end-of-year ekiden, I invite Kanta and Kono to be on my team. They both say they may be able to run. It just depends on the date of the race.

Max calls me later that week. He has found a race in February around the foot of Mount Fuji. Five athletes running around 7km each. A good level of competition. University B teams, top amateur teams from Tokyo, and high-school teams. It sounds perfect. I ask him to fill in the entry form for me, as the deadline has almost passed. I'll work out who can run later. I just hope my sore knee holds out long enough so I can be part of the team.

21

The biggest three days of the year in the Japanese running calendar begin on 1 January with the New Year ekiden. It may be the most prestigious race of the year for the professional teams, but for most fans it's merely a warm-up for the big one, the Hakone ekiden on 2 and 3 January.

For fans and writers, getting to see both races is a logistical challenge. Most people watch them on television, passing a rare few days spent with family dipping in and out of the proceedings in between feasting on New Year specialities such as *mochi* (rice cakes) and *osechi* (goody boxes crammed with fish, pickled vegetables, black beans and the like). Watching the ekidens at home has become a tradition for many people, but I may only be in Japan this once, so I want to experience both races live if I can.

It means an early train on New Year's Day up to Gunma, a region to the north of Tokyo. It's a long way from Kyoto and I get there too late for the start. I arrive in a taxi to find the start and finish area largely deserted. Around a small square they've set up a small seating area with a big screen showing the race. It's a chilly day, but the sky is a deep blue and the morning sun is warm out of the wind, so I take a seat and try to work out what is going on.

Everyone in Japan talks about how brilliant the television coverage of the two races is, with lots of background stories and details of how the teams further down the field are faring. To me, though, it's a challenge just to work out who is in the lead. When I arrive, the second leg is just beginning. This is the leg all the Kenyans and Ethiopians run. They race off, one by one, with the young Leonard Barsoton from Nissin Foods in third or fourth place.

A few of the teams have opted to do without foreign runners, and I can't help feeling sorry for the few Japanese runners lining up among the Kenyans on the second leg. They look petrified as they stand there, waiting for their men to come in. The Kenyans start so fast that the Japanese runners seem caught in a whirlwind, running with their heads down as though into a terrifying gale.

Up at the front, Barsoton holds his position well against some of the best east African runners in the world, handing over to former Hakone darling Akinobu Murasawa in second place. Aki wastes no time in racing to the lead and opening up a big gap. He has an unusual, high-stepping style for a Japanese runner, which he tells me is because he loves to run cross-country. Interestingly, Nissin's three biggest stars, Aki, Yuki Sato and Osako Suguru, who is yet to join from Wasaeda University, all come from the same high school, which is famous for getting its runners to train on cross-country trails. It seems the benefits of running off-road are not completely unknown in Japan.

'At school we trained mostly cross-country,' Aki later tells me. 'This is why I run like this. Otherwise I would have a style like other Japanese runners, less bouncy.'

Aki bounds along on the screen, reaching the changeover with a big lead, handing the tasuki on to the team ace, Sato.

This is the star man, and he starts off like a train, running at an even faster pace than his own course record, extending the team's lead with every stride. Far behind him all sorts of battles are raging, but he seems to plough on serenely, untroubled. Until, that is, about 16km in to his run, when disaster strikes. The commentators are yelling wildly as the camera zooms in on Sato stopped by the side of the road holding his leg. Surely not? He starts jogging and then running again, but not with the same flow as before. He has a pained expression on his face.

The injured Sato still manages to hand over the tasuki in the lead, but not by much. By the end of the next leg, Nissin are back in third place, and that's how it stays until the end.

By the time the runners finish, the area where I'm sitting is crammed to bursting with fans. Most of them are waving team flags and wearing team jackets. People are climbing up lamp-posts or trees to get a view over the heads of the crowd.

Third place is a decent result for Nissin considering their injury problems, both before the race and for Sato while he was running. Sato's reputation is only enhanced by the fact that he carried on running, putting the good of the team before himself. It's the sort of spirit that goes down well in Japan.

*

After the race, the teams gather in large groups to greet their supporters, who are mostly company employees. Some gather on the grass beside the finish, but Nissin seem to have their own spot in the entrance to a nearby skyscraper. Inside the door is a small marble lobby area and a huge staircase leading away into the dark recesses of the building. When I find them, the runners are giving speeches and posing for photographs. Aki is being mobbed by young women looking for his autograph.

'He's popular,' I say to Barsoton, who is standing around quietly, not getting as much attention.

'He was a good university runner,' the Kenyan replies. As well as being a great runner, with a handsome face, the main reason Aki is so popular is because he is a recent Hakone star. It lasts a little while, the glory of Hakone, until the next batch of stars begin to emerge.

The head coach, Shirouzu, is smiling, at least. I assume his job is secure for another year. He still doesn't say much and his closing speech is barely audible, even though he gives it through a megaphone. And then they all line up, the athletes, the coaches, managers and supporters, in their matching red Nissin Foods jackets and tracksuits, up along the staircase for one giant group photo. It's a huge wave of uniform red. Nobody stands out.

*

The final act of the day is an excruciatingly slow awards ceremony. I sit at the back next to a small group of east African runners, and in a lull in their conversation I introduce myself. Two of them are from Ethiopia and have only recently arrived in Japan, while the third is a Kenyan who has been here for nine years.

I ask them how they find the running in Japan, and the

two Ethiopians shake their heads as though it's not good.

'What wrong with it?' I ask, and they both answer together, without hesitation: 'No forest.'

'In Japan,' says one, 'it is all road.' They lift up the legs of their tracksuits to show me the injuries they've been getting since they arrived in Japan.

The Kenyan runner is also full of complaints. He says he has to train alone because the Japanese runners are too slow.

'Sometimes I get my training programme from my coach in Kenya,' he says. 'Or I make it myself. The Japanese schedule is no good.'

Again I ask him what's wrong with it.

'Too many long runs,' he says. 'Not enough speedwork. Even if they go on the track, it is only ever 2:58-pace [per kilometre]. Too slow.'

Running on hard surfaces, running too many miles and not enough speedwork – these are recurring themes, at least when I talk to the east African runners.

The Kenyan athlete runs for a team where, unlike at Nissin, the runners have to work in the company offices every day. A few weeks later I visit the NTT corporate team, who are based in Osaka and finished twenty-seventh out of the thirty-eight teams in the New Year ekiden. After their morning run the athletes all have to rush off to be at the office for 9 a.m. They work in various departments in the company until about 2 p.m., at which point they're let off to go for afternoon training. I'd always imagined the Kenyan runners were excused this office work, but that's not the case. For the sake of team harmony, everyone must do their share. I ask the Kenyan runner how he finds it.

'Fine,' he says. He tells me, quite proudly, that he wears a suit and has his own desk. He says he helps his company deal with foreign clients, writing things for them in English and making phone calls.

I ask him if he'll stay in Japan after he finishes running.

'I have no dream to stay in Japan,' he says. 'After one more year, I'm going to Canada.'

*

The next morning, I'm off again, too. This time to central Tokyo, to the start of the Hakone ekiden.

The race starts by the office of the Yomiuri Shimbun newspaper, the main sponsor of the event. I get there early, in time for the 7 a.m. start. Already the streets along the course are lined ten people deep, while in every space between the buildings teams of cheerleaders have set up and are singing and dancing to their university's anthem, backed by full brass bands and drummers. As well as female cheerleaders, male cheerleaders join the fray, performing a mad war dance that looks like they're trying to direct aeroplanes using a form of exaggerated semaphore.

The excitement is contagious, bouncing off the lower tiers and arches of the skyscrapers that reach and sway high above us, all polished steel and glass glinting in the morning light. Overhead, in the patches of sky, helicopters churn, while down here on the streets police and stewards walk slowly along the course, keeping people back behind the barriers. In the midst of it all, I find the runners down a sidestreet, striding back and forth in their long, boxer coats. Twenty-three of them in total. Their young faces are calm, like experienced competitors, focused on the job at hand, ready for their moment, to play their part in the great show. They know their team-mates are waiting somewhere, out on the course, for this race of races to begin.

Teams of marshals in matching jackets call the runners to the start. I spot Nissin's new recruit, Osaka Suguru, among the melee. The runners make their way forward, splashes of brightly coloured singlets among the black and beige jackets of the crowd.

Freed from the side-street holding pen and out onto the empty course, they stride back and forth, lunging into deep, last-minute stretches. People are calling out instructions. Behind the start is a squad of cars each with a megaphone on the roof. These are for the coaches to drive in behind their runners, using the megaphones to blare out instructions. To make sure there is no slacking. I spot the coach of Komazawa University, the pre-race favourites, winners of both Izimo and the national ekiden, standing by his car. He is the one who refused to talk to me at the Chiba ekiden. His hair seems extra slicked-back today, and his tan deeper than ever. He has, I'm told, a fierce reputation for screaming at his runners along the way.

'He is one of the old-style coaches,' Kenji tells me. It seems to be working for his team so far this year.

The marshals are calling the runners to the start. They form two quick lines. Presumably the faster teams get to stand at the front, not that it matters in a race that traverses over 200km. And then the gun goes and they streak off, along the road. Almost immediately they disappear around a corner. And that's it. They're gone. It's really not much of a spectator sport.

*

Of course, the best way to follow the action is on TV. I've managed to get a press pass for the race and so I clamber into the media bus where the race is being shown on an on-board television. I settle down for the ride to the lakeside town of Hakone, where the race finishes at the end of the first day.

On the screen the runners are bunched up in a big group. The commentators are mistakenly complaining that it is a slow pace, but in fact they're running at under 60-minute half-marathon pace, for a 21.4 km leg (almost exactly a half-marathon). Incredibly, all twenty-three runners are going at this pace, which is well inside the national half-marathon record.

The fact that all the runners have gone with the pace is what has thrown the commentators. This isn't slow, this is insanely fast. As we make our way to Hakone on a parallel road, I try to keep up with what's going on using the TV, Twitter and by asking the other journalists on the bus.

The leaders reach 10km in 28 minutes 36 seconds, which is a 10km personal best time for most of the ten runners still in the group.* And they're still not even halfway through. Leading them the whole way, half a stride ahead, is Suguru Osako, Nissin's new signing. He doesn't falter in his smooth,

* In the whole of 2013, the fastest 10k time by a British man was 29.12.

methodical running style, never looking around to see who is with him, running like a gang leader in a West End musical, his head up, the morning sun lighting him, the star of the show. He knows millions of people across the country are watching.

The pace inevitably drops by the end, and Osako is passed. With about a mile to go, the runner from Komazawa University makes an impetuous surge, sprinting away at the front of the race. Off such a fast pace, it's an incredible effort, but ultimately a mistake, as before the finish he starts to wobble and slow, allowing the runner from Nittai University, the reigning champions, to cross the line first.

It may have been a wild surge, but it is moments like this that make Hakone so exciting and different to the more controlled world of the professional runners.

The first leg is so fast, even with the uneven pacing, that the first three complete the course in a time equivalent to a sub-61-minute half-marathon. Only four Japanese men in history have managed that in a half-marathon, yet here in Hakone three students have done it on the first leg. And they haven't even broken the stage record. And most of the teams' best runners are still out on the course waiting to run.

The gauntlet is well and truly hurled down and as the second-leg men head off on their way, they have a lot to live up to. But this is how ekiden, and in particular Hakone, works. Each performance inspires the next athlete to run harder again. They thrive off each other. This is it, the race of their lives. There's no holding back. For many of these runners, even making the Olympic team later in their careers will not match the high of running in Hakone. They are prepared to within an inch of their lives, they have the hopes and efforts of their team-mates on their shoulders, and they have the nation watching. They run like they will never run again.

This is what makes this race so special. Kenji often says ekiden brings out the best in Japanese runners, but it can be hard to understand how. Once you're out there running, it's just you and your own legs, your own power, the team can't make any difference. The Kenyan ekiden runner in Kyushu said as much to me. 'The team doesn't matter,' he said. 'When you run, you're on your own.' These are sentiments that would shock many Japanese ekiden runners, but it was also how I felt. When I ran my ekiden at Lake Biwa, I felt more alone than usual, unsure how to pace myself as I set off without any other runners around me. If anything, being in the team seemed to take the pressure off. We were doing so badly, it didn't really matter how I ran. Even when I think about running with my all-star team at the Fuji ekiden, I know I'll only be part of the equation. It won't all rely on me. And this seems to make it somehow less important.

But for the Japanese, I now see, when they pull on the tasuki, it's like a switch is flipped. Times that almost never get run in normal races are obliterated. Like Sato's course record at the New Year ekiden over 22km, in which he passed the half-marathon mark faster than the Japanese record. Here in Hakone, these guys are only students, aged twenty and twenty-one, yet three in the first leg run under 61 minutes for a half-marathon.

In fact, all of the race's ten stages are close to a half-marathon in distance, and over the two days an incredible thirty students run a half-marathon equivalent time of under 63 minutes – and that's excluding the times on the race's fastest sixth stage, which is mostly downhill.

For comparison, among British runners, only one man ran a half-marathon in under 63 minutes in the whole of 2013, and that was the double Olympic champion Mo Farah.

At every changeover, the effort and passion for this race is etched across the contorted faces of the runners. They seem to run with their eyes closed, their mouths gnashing. Even their hair seems to be getting in on the act, straining from the tops of their heads. As they pass on the tasuki, they tumble to the ground and are helped up by comforting team-mates, who wrap jackets and towels around their broken bodies, their faces twisted, sometimes openly weeping with the effort. It usually takes two people to hold them up. A marshal, too, is usually on hand, giving them air from a handheld canister, fixed over their mouths, though they hardly even seem to notice it through their tears.

I've seen this falling across the line in other ekidens and always thought it was at least partly an act. Even in the amateur ekidens, people were doing it, presumably copying their idols. It reminds me of the dramatics of footballers looking for free kicks. Except, rather than trying to show the referee how hurt they are, here the runners are trying to show their team-mates, and the spectators, how much effort, or *doryoku*, they're putting in to bring the tasuki home.

It is noticeable, in every ekiden, how the teams in the lead are less dramatic at the changeovers. When, at the end of day one here at Hakone, the Toyo University runner crosses the line in first place, he is all smiles as he gets mobbed by his team-mates. He doesn't even wait for the customary towel, which his friends have ready to drape around him.

By winning the stage, he doesn't need to show how much he has tried. But every runner after him puts on a bigger and bigger display of pained effort. The further back they are in the field, the worse the dramatics become, with the last few runners collapsing as though they've run their legs into a useless pulp, refusing to be dragged back to their feet, pleading to be left to die at the side of the road.

But even knowing it is partly an act, it is moving to witness it, particularly at the end when I manage to get a spot right by the finish. Normally Japanese people baulk at even shaking hands with each other, preferring the restrained dignity of a little bow. Expressions of emotion are rarely on public display. But here, the waiting team-mates are clearly concerned, and do their best to comfort and help their companions, with loving arms around their shoulders, and kind words whispered in their ears. As the man at NTT said, in ekiden you win and you lose together. Seeing this spirit at the end of such genuinely incredible performances, with the whole country watching, feels like stealing a tiny glimpse into the collective soul of Japan. The raw emotions, the companionship, the drama. I feel almost uncomfortable standing there watching, taking pictures with my camera, as though I've gatecrashed an intimate family occasion.

At the end, I see many of the fans, who are mostly young women, crying. When I ask one woman why she likes Hakone so much, she can barely speak. 'It is so moving,' is all she can say, biting her lip.

Another man, waiting by the finish with a small portable radio, answers the same question with one word: '*Bushido*.'

This is a complex term that can be loosely translated as 'the way of the samurai'. In a bestselling book published in 1900, called *Bushido: the Soul of Japan*, the writer Inazo Nitobe laid out the key tenets that he said were most admired by the people of Japan, and were followed as an unwritten code of honour by the samurai. Foremost among them were loyalty, courage and honour.

All three of these traits are clearly embodied by the young runners in Hakone.

*

Our media bus gets to the finish of day one before the runners, but only just. We wind up and up into the mountains, following a parallel road to the last-leg runners, inching along in slow-moving traffic, beyond the snow line.

The ekiden course follows a section of the famous Tokaido road – one of the oldest roads in Japan – from Tokyo into the mountains to Hakone, and then back again the next day. It was along this same road that couriers used to run messages between Tokyo and Kyoto in the Edo period, the original ekiden from which the races were born.

Across the lake from the finish at Hakone rises Mount Fuji. It's the postcard image of Japan. It also has particular significance to the Japanese on this very day, 2 January. This is traditionally the morning after the first dream of the year, known as Hatsuyume.*

For Hatsuyume, it is considered a good omen to dream of

---

* The reason Hatsuyume occurs on 2 January and not 1 January is because you're not supposed to sleep on New Year's Eve.

Mount Fuji, along with an eagle and an aubergine. I'm not sure where those last two come in, but right here, in its full glory, across the lake, is Mount Fuji. It brings a dreamlike quality to the finish of the race, imbuing everything with an almost overwhelming sense of symbolism, as though the very essence of Japan had been distilled into this one moment. It's no wonder people are crying.

'The Hakone ekiden perfectly captures the mood of New Year,' one of the other journalists tells me later, in the media room in a nearby hotel. I'm shifting through the remains of the packets of food on a table, trying to work out if any of them are vegetarian. 'The Tokaido road, Mount Fuji, the teamwork, passing the tasuki, the effort of the runners. It has everything. This is why it is such good TV.'

*

I spend the night in a nearby lodge owned by a friend of my brother. He's not here so I have the place to myself. From the bedroom window, Fuji rises pink in the dusk. Standing watching it, I feel somehow touched with the spirit of something greater than a running race. I don't even know most of the runners, but the atmosphere of the day has been quite extraordinary. It feels as though every other race I've ever watched was like a football match played out in front of a half-empty stadium. Here, though, the stadium was full, the noise was deafening. This was long-distance running as a blood-and-thunder sport, where every last competitor was willing to break himself to keep up. It was fantastically epic.

The next morning I get up early and head to the start for day two. The first-leg runners are ready to begin the journey back to Tokyo. Teams of marshals, mostly old men, also full of adrenalin, check the runners' numbers and tell them when to come to the start line. It's a smaller crowd at the start today. Hakone is a small town with few places to stay.

The teams start in the order they finished the day before, with the same time gaps in between. The first two runners are from Toyo and Komazawa universities. They prowl up and down the road behind the line waiting to start, avoiding looking at each other.

Komazawa have already won the two other big university ekidens this year, the Izumo ekiden and the All-Japan national ekiden. But they've been pushed into second place so far in Hakone by Toyo. The rest of the teams are far behind. It's a battle between these two now for victory.

After they start, I head off to the finish in Tokyo in the media bus, again following the action on the on-board television. As the day goes on, and the two teams battle each other for supremacy, the story of the race begins to centre around the contrasting styles of the two team coaches.

The Toyo coach, Toshiyuki Sakai, is one of this new breed, like Kenji, who believe the traditional Japanese approach to coaching is outdated. Rather than acting as an all-knowing dictator, ruling his team with feudal authority, he is softly spoken, and talks about how his runners are 'nice guys'. Along the course he can be heard encouraging them, telling them they are doing well, that they look good.

In the interviews after the race, the Toyo runners repeatedly talk about how the coach gets them to enjoy their running. They say that this is part of their strength as a team. 'It is fun to be in this team,' one says. 'This is the secret of our success.'

In contrast, the Komazawa coach, Hiroaki Oyagi, is around thirty years older and the very embodiment of everything Kenji is trying to get away from. I've experienced his bark first-hand, but here, on the biggest day of the year, he is fully unhinged. I can't understand anything he says, but I can hear from the tone of his voice, from his wild screaming over the megaphone on the roof of his car, that he is angry. And the further behind his team drop, the more rabid his instructions become.

The other journalists laugh when they hear him shouting on the TV, but when I ask them what he is actually saying, they can't bring themselves to tell me. 'Not nice things,' they say, chuckling.

'Like what?' I insist. But they won't repeat them.

On his website, 'Japan Running News', one English-speaking blogger writes: 'Throughout the race, head coach Hiroaki Oyagi shouted and screamed things at his runners from a loudspeaker in his chase car that would get a coach in the NCAA [the US college running system] fired.'

In the end Toyo hold on to win the race. This could be seen as a condemnation of the old ways, but Mr Ogushi later points out to me that the Komazawa coach has made a big difference to the team. He has been coach for sixteen years and has had a lot of success, he tells me, including six Hakone victories.

'When he first arrived as coach,' Mr Ogushi tells me, 'he found a slot machine in the team dormitory. There was lots of gambling. He cleaned the place up and instilled discipline. The team is much better now.'

Coaching is an inexact science and in every sport there is room for different styles. But in Japan, the modern coach, who is friendly with the runners, explains the training to them, and asks them how they feel, is still, according to Kenji, in a much-criticised minority.

He says he takes encouragement from Toyo's win at Hakone.

'There's a shift happening in coaching style,' he says. 'The bullying style is being criticised a lot in the newspapers recently. People are beginning to change their view.'

A number of scandals involving coaches beating and abusing athletes has also lead to some navel-gazing in Japan in recent years about the overbearing style of some coaches.

In January 2013, the head coach of Japan's women's judo team, Ruuji Sonoda, was forced to resign after he admitted beating athletes with bamboo swords. Initially the national judo federation decided simply to reprimand Sonoda but to retain him as head coach, and it was only the public outcry that followed that forced his resignation.

Speaking in the aftermath of the incident, the executive director of the Japanese Olympic Committee said abuse in sports in Japan was not limited to judo, and that the incident was just the tip of the iceberg.

Indeed, in 2007, a sumo coach was sentenced to six years in prison after ordering three senior wrestlers to beat a teenage sumo apprentice. The beating was so severe that the seventeen-year-old wrestler died.

More recently, in December 2012, a high-school student

in Osaka killed himself after being repeatedly beaten by his basketball coach.

In the ekiden world, cases of beatings were uncovered at the top high-school team in January 2013. The team's coach had led the school to fourteen straight national high-school ekiden titles and was considered one of the greatest ever high-school coaches, when it emerged that two of his students had left the school because of the severity of the beatings they had received. One of the students needed two weeks of treatment after his eardrum was damaged.

Amazingly, the unrepentant coach's public response to the story was to say: 'The student's awareness of things was pretty dim, so I was making reality clear to him.'

The school responded by asking the other members of the team whether they had experienced any abuse from the coach, and ten of them said they had been slapped in the face, kicked, or received other physical punishment. Many of the students said they had been beaten on multiple occasions.

Fearful of losing their top coach as a result of the crisis, the other adult members of the coaching staff closed ranks and stood by him. 'If the ekiden team is going to make the National Championships then we need our coach and his strength,' one said.

The school cowed to their wishes and allowed him to keep his job, urging him, as though it was some sort of resolution to the problem, to exert more self-control.

Just to fully show how deep-rooted and accepted this type of behaviour still is, in April 2014, the same coach was signed up as head coach at another high school in Tokyo.

Eight members of his star ekiden team transferred school with him.

Of course, being strict and disciplined is not the same as beatings and abuse, but the idea that runners, particularly at high school, need to be forced to train is so ingrained in Japan that even Kenji agrees with it.

'The bullying style has been criticised recently,' he says, 'But sometimes it is needed, especially at high school, otherwise the runners get lazy.'

Kenji was formerly a high-school coach, but looking back he thinks he was too permissive. And now, even though he is a notably relaxed coach by Japanese standards, so much so that he often gets criticised for it, he still has Nomura, his assistant team manager, get up at six every morning to make sure the team members don't bunk off their morning run.

It makes me think of Kenya and the hundreds – thousands even – of runners who get up at six every morning to run. Most of them don't even have a coach, and those that do will only check in with him once or twice a week. Certainly, for a steady morning run, the coaches don't need to be there.

The difference is stark. Why is this?

The Kenyan runners are, almost without exception, from poor backgrounds. Running can change lives, not only for the runners, but for their families and communities – many successful runners end up setting up schools and even hospitals. The stakes are much higher. They know that if they don't get up to train, they cannot hope to win. The incredible level of competition in Kenya for races and places on teams also spurs them on. Surrounded by so many great athletes – most of the Kenyan runners live in clusters around certain towns and are very visible to each other – they are both inspired and driven to succeed.

Being self-motivated has another advantage: it makes you more self-reliant in a race. When the crunch comes, when the pain inevitably kicks in, the drive to push on needs to come from deep within. As Gandhi said: 'Strength does not come from physical capacity. It comes from an indomitable will.' If you're not used to digging down to find this will, you're unlikely to suddenly unearth it at the end of a race. Instead, unless your coach is driving behind you in a car with a megaphone blaring abuse at you, you're likely to falter.

When the football player Cristiano Ronaldo, recently voted the best player in the world, first started scoring ridiculously brilliant free kicks for Manchester United, the columnists and pundits began debating how he did it. Was it some kind of trick? Did he have a unique way of striking the ball?

His manager, Sir Alex Ferguson, found it amusing. 'All that stuff about hitting the ball in a certain spot in a certain way,' he said, laughing. 'There's no secret. The important thing is practice. It makes perfect, as I was taught in school. The boy practises every day, that's the reason he's so good. We go for a cup of tea and leave him to it.'

He goes for a cup of tea, he says. He doesn't stand there hovering over Ronaldo in case he bunks off.

The problem for Japanese high-school coaches is that they don't have time to sit back and wait for their star runners to feel inspired to practise. Self-motivation can ebb and flow, particularly in younger people. As a coach, sometimes you need to be patient and give it time and space. But Japanese high-school coaches are not in the business of patiently honing the stars of the future, they are trying to win now. With the high-school ekidens almost as important as the university and professional competitions, the coaches themselves are under immense pressure to succeed. Their jobs and reputations are dependent on it.

This pressure-cooker environment begins in high school and continues until an athlete retires. It's not conducive to developing an athlete over time to fulfil his true potential. Instead, everyone wants to wring as much as they can out of the runners at every stage of their careers.

To try in some small way to counteract this problem, Kenji has set up a new team, one that will oversee the careers of athletes from high school to professional level, with a focus on their long-term interests. It's a radical idea, which he plans to run as an NGO with financial support from companies looking to invest in athletes of the future. He says it will be called Smile Blooming.

Whatever happens with Kenji's team, with Toyo winning Hakone the new breed of coaches have been given a big boost. The upcoming Olympics in Tokyo in 2020 is also giving the authorities an impetus to try new things. After Hakone I speak to the coach of Waseda, who finished fourth in the race, and he too, like Kenji, feels that things need to change.

'If nothing changes, there is no chance of Japan winning a medal in the marathon [in 2020],' he tells me. 'There are lots of talented young coaches in Japan, but they are not involved in the national federation, which is still ruled by old-style coaches.'

*

The Toyo coach finishes the final post-Hakone press conference by saying: 'We won today not just through running, but because we grew up as people.'

He is tapping into a belief in Japan that sport is not only about winning. To be truly accepted and celebrated, you have not only to win, but to win in the right way.

Shige Yamauchi, the coach and husband of British marathon runner Mara Yamauchi, who has experience of both sporting cultures, says: 'In Japan, there is more emphasis on personal development through sport.'

He says that in the UK, everything is more competitive and the attitude is to try to win at all costs.

'Your culture respects winners,' he says to me. 'But in Japan, not only winning, but being a good team member is important. How you harmonise with the team.'

He says the contrast can be clearly seen in the way the two cultures play football. 'In England, everyone wants to score. Nobody wants to pass. But in Japan, it's the other way around. Nobody wants to score, they prefer to pass.'

This idea is cultivated in Japan, he says, through the ubiquitous manga comics. Many of the stories are about sport, but the storylines are very different from a typical western narrative. In the west, the most popular and repeated sports stories are those of the underdog, such as Rocky Balboa, or Harold Abrahams and Eric Liddell in *Chariots of Fire*, who has to prove himself, who has to overcome all the odds, to succeed.

The typical story in Japanese manga, he says, is about team spirit.

'Usually it starts with an individualistic person who wants to do everything his own way. But this causes trouble. Finally, he is brought into the group, into harmony with the team, and then the team starts to win.'

Manga stories like this are a big influence on young people to take up sport, he tells me. But they do it in the spirit of *bushido* – the way of the warrior.

There's that word again. It shares that same ending character, *-do*, 'the path' or 'the way', as judo, kendo, sado (the art of tea ceremony) and kado (the art of flower arranging). All these pastimes are primarily seen in Japan as a way to develop yourself. 'A way to refine yourself as a harmonised person,' says Yamauchi.

Legendary Japanese baseball coach Suishu Tobita, known as the god of Japanese baseball, often compared sport to *bushido*, once writing: 'The purpose of training is not health, but the forging of the soul.'

Although it doesn't include the word *-do*, as I witnessed at Hakone, ekiden also pushes those who take part in it towards this lofty goal. It is, you might say, the way of the runner.

22

I leave Hakone feeling as though I've just witnessed one of the greatest races on earth. The next day, as I board the train back to Kyoto, it feels like the morning after a great adventure, the first day back at work after the holidays, when the excitement from the events that went before still lingers and you can't quite adjust to normal life again.

But as I sit on the train, watching the winter landscape fly by, patches of melting snow on fields and rooftops, I recall all the people who have criticised Hakone, and I can see their point. It is dangerous when one race engulfs an entire sport. Particularly when that race takes place before most of the runners have even begun their careers.

Hakone and the other ekidens are widely blamed for a perceived decline in Japanese running. Although one of the great running nations, and certainly more obsessed with long-distance running than any other country on earth, Japan's men have not won an Olympic medal in the marathon since Koichi Morishita won silver in Barcelona in 1992, over twenty years ago. In that time, runners from Morocco, Uganda, Italy, USA, Brazil, South Africa, South Korea, and, of course, Kenya and Ethiopia, have all won medals.

'Ekiden is much more popular now than when I was running,' Kenji says one day in a talk he gives to professors at an event at Ritsumeikan University. It's actually a miniconference convened by the university to examine why the top Japanese runners can't compete with the Kenyans on the international stage. Kenji is one of the guest speakers.

'But ekiden is destroying our athletes,' he says, his voice trembling with the weight of his statement. He goes on to repeat his story about how he was once the second-fastest junior runner in the world, but was forced to over-train. He says coaches don't think about the long-term prospects of the athlete, particularly at high-school and university level. The pressure to win the ekidens is too great, he says, so they push the athletes too hard.

He is particularly critical of Hakone. He says the preparation for Hakone requires regular 30km runs from student runners. 'It's too long, too hard,' he says.

If you compared the Toyo team that won Hakone to the top professional teams, Kenji says, Toyo would be one of the best. 'Most of the professional teams would lose Hakone,' he says. Yet very few of the Hakone runners will have running careers after university. The Waseda coach told me that only one or two of his runners graduating each year, out of around ten, would go on to have any type of professional running career. He, too, was critical of Hakone.

'It is too big,' he says. 'The guys get big-headed, they think they're big stars, but after graduation, reality hits. They nose-dive. Their motivation drops, they stop training.'

One journalist tells me that many people believe that it is because they don't have the pressure of Hakone that the Japanese women do better internationally. Indeed, Japanese women have won two of the last four Olympic marathon gold medals.

However, it could be argued that although there is clearly a perceived decline in the level of marathon running in Japan, in reality the standard has remained fairly constant even as the popularity of Hakone has grown. At any rate, it is nothing close to the decline seen in many other countries, particularly the UK.

In 1984, the year a Welshman, Steve Jones, broke the world record, eleven different British men ran a marathon in under 2 hours 14 minutes. In the same year, seventeen Japanese men achieved the same time.

Fast forward to 2013, however, and the picture is very different: while not one single British man broke 2:14, in Japan they're now doing even better, with twenty-five men breaking the 2:14 barrier.

In the context of the decline seen in much of the rest of the developed world, Japanese running could be held up as a success story. And a large part of this is down to the highly developed ekiden system. Without ekiden, of course the runners would be free to focus on marathon running and competing with the Kenyans, but the national fervour for running, fed by the excitement and spectacle of ekidens such as Hakone, would be diminished. This would in turn lead to the professional teams being scaled down or disbanded, and many of those thousands of runners would be left with hard choices about quitting work, or quitting running.

It's a conundrum, but while ekiden may be a distraction, and a force for over-training, it is also firmly at the driving wheel of Japanese elite running. Without it, the system would be at risk of collapsing.

*

Making a life as a top athlete outside the system in Japan is almost unthinkable for most runners. But one man has done it. He is self-coached, self-motivated, and he has a full-time job. In Japan he is known as the Citizen Runner. His name is Yuki Kawauchi.

Kawauchi is a phenomenon. Rather than join one of the top corporate teams after university, he chose instead to combine his training with a full-time job in the office of a high school to the north of Tokyo. Despite this, he is one of Japan's best marathon runners and was selected for the national team to run in the 2013 world championships.

Not only does he break the rules by having a job, but he takes a wildly unorthodox approach to racing. The rationale for most marathon runners across the world is that you should only race two, or at most three, marathons a year. In 2013, Kawauchi ran eleven marathons. Six of them he ran in under 2 hours 12 minutes. On top of that he also ran a 50km ultramarathon as well as lots of half-marathons and other shorter races. The other Japanese runners think he's mad.

But the fans love him. He's known for his intense commitment to every race, running it with incredible *doryoku* (effort), gritting his teeth like a man racing for his life, pushing himself through wall after wall, never giving up. He makes the corporate runners with their cushy paychecks and teams of coaches look like pampered autotrons.

I first see Kawauchi running in the Fukuoka marathon, where he repeatedly surges into the lead, racing ahead of the Kenyans. They keep reeling him back, only to see him surge again. In the end, he doesn't quite make it, finishing in third place, less than two minutes behind the winner, Martin Mathathi of Kenya. But as always he leaves his indelible mark on the race.

Afterwards, at the awards ceremony, I see him being interviewed for Japanese TV. He is wearing the tracksuit of his regional education body. His office team. His shoes, a pair of unbranded black trainers, are scuffed at the toes. The citizen runner to the last.

Because he has a full-time job and no agent, he's a hard man to track down, but I want to ask him about why he chose to follow this amateur route when he could have opted for an easier life as a professional athlete.

I finally get through to his local education board who pass a message on to him in his office. He gets back to say he is running his local ekiden in February. I can come and talk to him after the race.

*

So, on a chilly February morning I find myself again standing beside a school wall waiting for an ekiden to come by. But this time it's not my brother I'm waiting for, but Japan's most famous runner, Yuki Kawauchi.

I'm in a narrow valley in Saitama prefecture, watching as high-school runners race by one at a time, straining to get to the line, the tasuki already in their hand. People clap, and call out 'Gambare', as more and more of them roll in. Among the high-school teams are university runners, both men and women, and other runners, mostly amateur teams, or teams from the local fire department or tax office.

This is a community event, like the ekiden my brother ran in all those years ago. At the changeover point a man in a huge inflatable sumo outfit is bouncing around in front of a group of children.

Kawauchi is supposed to be running on this stage, but he hasn't appeared yet.

Standing next to me is an old man waving a Hakone ekiden flag. He says he brought it because they don't have flags at this race, but he's clearly proud of it. 'I went to Hakone,' he says. 'I have ten of them at home.'

I ask him why he likes coming to watch ekidens. He sucks his teeth, unsure how to answer.

'It's not an easy sport to watch,' he says finally. 'Because the runners go by in a few seconds. But I like to see the great effort of the runners.'

Right on cue, puffing like a steam train, Kawauchi appears around the corner. He's motoring past the other runners like they're training bollards left out in the road. His face is as contorted as ever. It may be a local fun run by his standards, but he's not taking it easy.

And then he's gone. I squeeze back on the train, along with everyone else, back to the finish and the closing ceremony, and hopefully a few words with the citizen runner himself.

*

In the end his team finishes in about eightieth position, but Kawauchi breaks the record for his leg of the race. So he has to sit among the other stage winners at the closing ceremony, in the car park of the local town hall, to collect his prize.

A biting wind blows across the tarmac as we listen to the speeches of the dignitaries. Kawauchi sits listening attentively, his hands placed humbly on his knees. He's wearing the same scuffed shoes and office-team tracksuit he had on in Fukuoka. He's sporting a gawky, adolescent moustache and looks like someone who still lives with his mum. But all eyes are on him.

Among the crowd, I find myself standing next to two other journalists, both from national newspapers. They're here solely because of Kawauchi. They say they follow him around everywhere, like a pair of royal reporters chasing Prince William to every function, no matter how insignificant.

They know everything there is to know about him. Why doesn't he join a corporate team, I ask them.

'Kawauchi likes to do what he wants,' one of the reporters tells me. 'If you're in a corporate team, you get a salary, but you have to do what you're told. You can't run a race every weekend.'

'Also,' says the other one, 'he got injured a lot when he was at high school and university. That's why at first he didn't get picked up by a corporate team. Now they would love him, of course, but he says no. He says he is worried he would get injured from over-training. He prefers to be free to train however he wants, which is just once a day.'

After the ceremony, I follow the two reporters, who chase after Kawauchi as he is whisked away into the building and up some stairs. I'm not sure if he knows or remembers that he invited me to talk to him, but nobody stops me as we enter a small office. Against one wall hangs a plastic sheet decorated in sponsors' logos, with a chair in front of it. Kawauchi sits down. There are about eight reporters in all and a few photographers and immediately they start firing questions at him. They're asking him about his upcoming races, his plans for the year, his fitness.

I've come with a friend who has offered to translate, but he's not a journalist, so he's struggling to get my questions in among the barrage. But then Kawauchi turns to me and nods. The others all look at me.

The message I got from Kawauchi about joining this press conference was conditional. I was only to ask him about the race. Nothing about his views on the corporate ekiden system. I had thought I'd circumvent that somehow, but his eyes are watching me so intently that I'm too scared to try anything clever. I ask instead about why he chose to run this race today.

I'd been warned that he talks as quickly as he runs, and my poor translator has a hard time keeping up.

'I have to do this race for my work colleagues,' he says. 'It is one of my obligations. But it is good to run ekiden and marathon at the same time if you are training for marathon. Ekiden is good speed training.'

This was the original purpose of ekiden racing, before it took over the world of Japanese running.

'Actually,' he says, 'most of my races are part of my training. There are many advantages from being in a race rather than running on my own, such as traffic control, good time-keeping, water stations, and even people cheering me on.

'I believe marathon running is all about experiences. Without running real marathon races, runners can't acquire a proper sense of tactics and timing in races, such as when to speed up or down.'

He tells me he runs a race every three or four weeks – usually a marathon, but sometimes an even longer race. He has a set pattern of running at half-pace for two to three weeks, and then doing speed work in the week before the race.

My translator misses much of the detail of his answer, but what is clear is that this is a man with a plan. He doesn't just run lots of races because he's naive or crazy. He has a clearly thought-out method, and it seems to work. He says his aim for the year is to run 2:07 in the marathon.* Then, he says, he will aim to break the Japanese record.

And with that, he is gone. He signs a few autographs for those who have waited outside in the cold for him. School-children and old ladies, mostly. The old ladies shake his hand warmly, looking at him with loving, motherly eyes. He waves as he gets into a car, driven by his chaperone, and away he goes.

I, too, take my leave, though without waving to anyone, making my way back through the quiet Sunday streets to the train station.

*

* Kawauchi's best marathon time is 2:08:14.

Many weeks later, back in England, I get a letter from Kawauchi. Although he didn't want to answer all my questions after the Saitama ekiden, he asked me to email them to him. He has since taken time to think about them, and sent me his considered answers in long form. What he writes confirms many of the things I've heard, and many of my own thoughts, about running in Japan.

The first question I asked him was why he chose to remain outside the corporate system. Life would surely be easier for him if he joined a top ekiden team.

'I think I'm a bit against the elite system in Japan,' he writes. 'I've never been an elite runner. I felt inferior after not joining elite teams at university or at a company. But I want to prove that a runner who had a severe injury and was frustrated can come back. I want to beat elite runners without joining the corporate teams.

'Actually, in my last year at college, only one corporate team asked me to join. No other team. By then I already knew how to train myself. That was why I was chosen for the Kanto Select Team to run the sixth leg of Hakone twice. So I didn't think I particularly needed to join a corporate team.

'Also, I felt like running freely without coaches or any corporate burden. Unlike a lot of professional runners here, I'm not running for the Olympics or ekidens. Unlike the African or other professional runners, I'm not running for prize-money or sponsors. I'm running to satisfy my own interest and my own challenge. So I don't want to lose my free will by joining a corporate team. Running for me is completely different from running for corporate runners.

'Also, I want to show promising junior runners how fun it is to run freely without coaches.'

Fun can be a rare commodity in Japanese running, from the stressed high-school runners, to the tyranny of many of the coaches and the serious professionalism of the corporate teams. But often where you find fun, you find success. Look at Usain Bolt, Haile Gebrselassie. In Kenya, most of the runners I met were having fun training. They enjoyed it. The coach of Toyo, the Hakone winners, and Kenji, both encourage their runners to have fun. In my own running, too, despite the cold, rain and tired legs, it is a deep sense of enjoyment that gets me out training. Fun can sound like a trivial word, but it lies at the core of the way of the runner. As the enlightened Daigyoman Ajari told me: 'The challenge is to continue enjoying life.'

Kawauchi continues the theme in his answer to my next question, which is why are Japanese runners posting such fast times at junior and under-23 level, but not at senior level? Although he is only twenty-six, Kawauchi is a relatively late bloomer by Japanese standards.

'Junior and U23 runners aren't enjoying their training,' he writes. 'That's why they can't improve their times when they become senior. There is always an issue of over-training and too much pressure on their minds and bodies.

'Now the coaches teach these student runners with the method of corporate team training. For this training the junior runners are overgrown for their ages and there will be no room left for improvement when they become seniors.

'I think that is the reason that the level of junior and U23 runners are much higher than that of ten years ago, and that the level of senior runners is not high enough.'

He also blames the old-style coaches for much of the problems.

'There is an issue of coaches,' he writes. 'A lot of coaches in Japan believe in the need for severe, perpetual hard training for long-distance runners. But runners are not machines. Runners are inevitably destroyed by over-training. Most student runners here normally run about 800km per month. I usually run 550km per month. Even in the month of hardest training I run less than 800km.

'Japanese training is still about strong mentality. A lot of coaches still believe that only over-training can make the strong mentality necessary for winning. It's very Japanese. I don't think it's scientific or effective or logical. Over-training causes injury and mental burnout. It can be the reason that students lose their interest in running.

'Because of the repetition of over-training, junior or student runners get injured even before they run the races. Their injury gets chronic and their time never improves.'

Finally, I asked Kawauchi for a breakdown of an average day, to get some idea of how he managed to fit the training of a 2:08 marathon runner into the day of a full-time office worker.

'On normal weekdays I get up at around 7 a.m.,' he writes, 'and do training for about 90–120 minutes. Then I go to my office at 12.45 and work until 21.30. During summer or winter vacation at school, I get up at 5.30, do training for about 90–120 minutes, and then work from 8.25 to 16.55.

'I work 465 minutes per day (the rest time is not counted) if there is no overtime.'

While few of us will ever reach his times or levels of commitment, Kawauchi is an inspiration for all those who have to fit running in around work and other responsibilities. If I can muster even a fragment of his steely focus, surely I can run faster again. I have entered another race, a 10K road race in Osaka, the week before the Fuji ekiden. I was thinking perhaps it was too much to do two races in a week, but now after talking to Kawauchi I'm fired up to run both.

23

Kawauchi may shun the corporate system, but for the majority of senior Japanese runners it is the bread and butter, or buckwheat noodles, of their existence. And it is among the walls of the corporate teams that most of those talented young Hakone stars end up. People such as Akinobu Murasawa.

As promised, I return to see him after the New Year ekiden to experience a normal day in the life of a corporate runner.

I'm only at the Nissin Foods clubhouse for the day, but they've given me my own room, down one of the building's dim, strip-lit corridors, with worn carpets and piles of running shoes outside each room. The next month's training schedules have been slipped quietly under each door.

My room is exactly like the athletes' rooms, though empty except for a single bed and a few weights. Before I get a chance to settle in, Aki takes me out on an early-morning jog through the empty city. We run to the national stadium, past skyscrapers and under railway bridges. A group of elderly people are doing star jumps in a square. Someone shouts something to us and Aki waves back.

After we get back I take a quick shower, get dressed, hanging my sweaty running clothes on a rail, and sit on the bed to wait for Aki. He says he prefers to go out for breakfast.

There's a knock at the door.

'OK, I'm ready.'

A few of the other runners are joining us, including Keigo Yano, who has just run the Hakone ekiden for Nittai University. He is one of four new recruits to the Nissin Foods team this year. After their injury problems over the last two years, it seems they are building a bigger squad of runners.

We make our way through the streets of the local neighbourhood, the morning fully awake now, people in suits heading to work, children in yellow hats walking to school. I'm imagining a small restaurant down a quiet side street, with a little old lady who knows them by name and serves them their favourite food without needing to ask, but after about five minutes we come to a busy crossroads. Aki points to a brightly lit outlet on the corner. The sign in the window says 'Denny's'.

'That's it,' he says.

Inside it's full of elderly people sitting alone, fiddling with the salt-shakers or just staring ahead. The waiter comes over with a pile of laminated menus full of pictures of ice cream. Despite the temptations of cream-filled waffles and other American dishes, the runners all opt for Japanese food. It's surprisingly healthy considering it's a fast-food restaurant. Noodles with tofu and seaweed, and miso soup. One of the runners can't resist, and also orders an ice cream, which arrives in a tall glass.

I ask Yano, the new recruit, whether life as a runner was more serious at high school or university. He looks at Aki, who translates the question.

They both laugh. 'High school,' they say. They almost seem relieved, like two executives who have finally made it after years of scurrying around, working late into the night to scramble their way up the corporate ladder. Now they can sit back and enjoy the easy life. After breakfast, when they're ready, they'll go back to the apartment for a sleep.

'But now, the result is very important,' Aki says, perhaps sensing the impression I'm getting, and worried it doesn't look good. 'There is more pressure now, even though we get more free time. This training programme is the most serious.'

He says that when he first joined Nissin, he was shocked to see how hard the team ace, Yuki Sato, was training. Shocked, but also encouraged. 'It made me realise that he was human, and that if I trained hard, maybe I could be as good as him one day.'

But he admits that motivation can be an issue for the runners after the highs of Hakone.

'Hakone is a problem in Japan,' he says, 'because after graduation there is no race as big, so runners lose their motivation. The New Year ekiden is not so popular.'

'But what about the Olympics or world championships?' I ask Aki. 'Surely they're big races?'

'Yes, but only a few get to experience that,' he says, 'while Hakone is open to many runners.'

He sounds deflated, in contrast to the optimism of his Kenyan training partner Leonard Barsoton, when he told me he would be running the marathon in the 2020 Olympics. For Aki, there is no real sense of progression when the likelihood is that his career highlight has already happened. Like scorched moths who have flown too close to the light, after Hakone the professional runners are left struggling to find their way again.

*

It turns out that today, unusually, the Nissin runners won't be going to sleep after breakfast.

Instead, like the athletes on most other corporate teams, they have to go in to the company offices. I asked the manager from another corporate team how important it was, when he signed up new runners, for them to have relevant office skills too.

'Their running ability is the most important,' he told me. 'But they need to be employable. No long hair or ear-rings.'

This is the traditional model for a corporate ekiden team. Usually, after their running careers are over, the athletes simply continue in their jobs within the company. Nissin Foods, however, is a more modern team. The runners don't have a set job in the office, and they rarely have to do anything other than train, rest and race in the New Year ekiden. Except occasionally, such as today.

So after breakfast, Aki dons his suit and we set off for the office on the train. We meet two of the other runners there, who have both arrived by bicycle. They're waiting in the large reception area of the Nissin Foods head office, larking around on some comfy chairs like two boys on a school trip. Once we arrive, an employee comes to meet us. She is all demure giggles as Aki tells her who I am. I get the impression her job is to keep the runners occupied. Their task for the morning is to replace all the old magazines in the reception area with new ones. They also have to get their photographs taken with some new ekiden merchandise – toy fluffy birds dressed in Nissin Foods running vests.

After a few hours in the office, we head back to the 'clubhouse'. Aki's afternoon schedule is a sleep followed by a run. Worried about my sore knee, which hasn't gone away, I decide to skip the second run, so I spend the afternoon lazily dozing in my bed and writing notes. At one point I venture into the coaches' office, where two of the coaches are discussing training schedules and races with one of the runners. They welcome me in and I sit on a swivel chair like a student on a work-experience placement as they carry on with their business. Eventually, after another snooze, it's time for supper.

It's dark outside now, and this time it is only Aki and I who head out to eat. Rather than go back to Denny's, he takes me to the little restaurant I had conjured in my mind, with the small, homely dining room and the old lady taking the orders, her hair dressed up, her make-up immaculate. In the kitchen her husband, in a dirty white apron, works away preparing the food. She pulls a curtain aside to call in the next order to him.

After eating, we walk back through the quiet streets. Although we're in the middle of Tokyo, it feels more like a small, sleepy town somewhere. Aki tells me he used to have a girlfriend, but it ended recently. He doesn't seem too upset. He says she lived in Hiroshima and he only saw her once a month.

'After training,' he says, 'I'm too tired. I like to go to sleep, or to the onsen. I usually go alone.'

We walk in silence for a few moments. I feel like I've been plying him with questions all day and I need to leave him alone now. I tell him I'll get my things when we get back and head home.

'I'm lucky,' he says. 'I love to run, and now it is my job.'
He looks surprised, as though he hasn't thought of it like
that before.

I ask him if it was always his dream to be a runner.

'At high school, I couldn't think beyond university,' he
says. 'But now . . . now my dream is to win the Olympic
marathon in Tokyo.' It seems he isn't so different, after all,
from his Kenyan team-mate.

*

A couple of days later I finally make it to the other running
club in Kyoto, the one Kenji told me about months ago.

In many respects it's just like an English running club.
The first people there, laying out the membership forms on
a table, staking out a spot beside the track to put the kit, are
the oldest members. They wear faded running kit and walk
bow-legged. One man gives me a big, squinting grin as I'm
shown over to him. He grabs me by the arm, to keep me in
sight perhaps, and asks me if I speak Japanese.

The older members are slightly older in Japan than in
England. At least ten of the forty or so runners who turn up
appear to be over seventy. Most of the rest are past fifty. Dotted here and there, if you look for them, are a few younger faces. These must be the serious amateur runners Kenji
talked of. They're not as friendly as the older guys. They're
here to train, not socialise, and they stand stretching, this
way and that, as we wait to begin.

The track itself is in some industrial wasteland. Big, grey
factories on three sides trail white smoke into the clouded

sky, while a high wire fence keeps the runners in. It's the type of place modern-day fairytales begin. Once upon a grey day . . . but it's too late for that. I haven't got the heart to tell the old men I'm only here for one session and that in a few weeks I'll be heading back to the UK. They're too excited by this tall, exotic stranger in their midsts. They keep prodding each other, daring each other to talk to me, laughing.

One man asks me where I live. 'Kyotanabe,' I say. It's only four stops on the local train but they look at me bewildered as though I've said I live in Zimbabwe. 'Eh?! Kyotanabe? Eee.'

We warm up for an hour. Then it's time to run. A young man of about nineteen is also here for the first time. He looks a bit lost, wondering why everyone is so old, I suspect. The next youngest person is about thirty-five. The teenager tells them his best time for 10km is 35 minutes and they all suck in their breath and nod, impressed. He smiles bashfully.

Meanwhile, I'm told to stick with one particular runner for the session. 'Coach,' one of the old men tells me, pleased to use an English word. Coach looks unimpressed but he gives me a small nod to show he's OK about me running with him. 'Your target,' says the old man again in English. He's on a roll now.

I've picked up conflicting messages about what the session actually is. One man told me it is continuous running of anything between 10km and 16km, and that I can stop when I'm tired. This seems to be the usual session they do most weeks. Before I came to Japan, I'd never run 10km on a track before, but here I am, ready to do it again.

Mara Yamauchi says that the reason the Japanese do all their running back and forth along short loops, either on the track or elsewhere, is because of the lack of available space for long runs.

But it's also because it's tougher mentally. It fits with the idea that only through repetition and struggle can success be achieved. At the Nissin training camp in Chiba, the Kenyan Leonard Barsoton ran his first-ever 15km on the track. It was only a training run, but he told me after that he was surprised by how tough it was.

'When you run 15km on the road,' he said, 'it is easy, but on the track it is very hard.' For the Japanese, it is usually the hard option that is considered most worthwhile.

The other session the running club may be doing is still a continuous 10km on the track, but with alternating kilometres a bit faster. In either case, I'm ready to run 10km, and to just follow the pace set. I'm anticipating, looking around, that I'll be able to keep up. Even with my sore knee. I've been training with the famous Ritsumeikan ekiden team. This is nothing.

Right from the start a group of eight runners heads off at the front. My 'target' man is running much slower further back, so I'm stuck for a moment. Will he be insulted if I overtake him and chase after the front-runners? Will I look like an idiot if I do that and they turn out to be way too fast for me? I take my chance before they get too far ahead, racing up to the tail end of the group. The teenager is with them, and his 10km best time is the same as mine, so I figure I should be OK.

Gradually we settle into a steady rhythm, skipping

through the kilometres in around 3 minutes 50 seconds. I can handle this, I think, hanging at the back of the group. The laps tick by and we reach 5km in 18:20, at which point the teenager does a dramatic ekiden-style wobble and stops. The rest of us cruise on. I keep tucked in. So far, so good, until around 6km the repetitiveness of the laps starts to play on my mind. I've been counting off the kilometres every two and a half laps, but I'm suddenly confused. Was that two laps or one since the last kilometre? I try to work it out by the time, but my brain is too addled. Also the other runners seem to be speeding up, and I'm beginning to cling on.

At around 9km a fatal gap appears. When you run in a group, it's like there's a magic string tying you together, helping to pull you along. Lap after lap, the motion and movement of the other runners seem to pull you closer, making it feel easy. But then the string snaps, and suddenly you're drifting, every movement your own, the ground now like a choppy sea, the wind blowing in your face.

But I'm nearly there. Two of the other runners, who are all about 50 metres ahead of me now, stop at the end of the next lap. Have we done 10km already? My watch says 35:30. Faster than my PB. We can't have run it that quickly. My frazzled mind makes it two more laps to go. And so I trundle on.

I'm the only one of those still running to stop at the end of what I calculate is 10km. I stand in the warm winter sun, confused. My watch says 39:50, which is slower than I was expecting. Maybe I ran twenty-six laps?

I walk around the track as the remaining four men run on. They must be doing 16km, I guess. One of them is pulling away from the others. Lapping quicker and quicker. He's about forty-five years old. He has a strange running style, his legs and arms barely moving. He looks like a mannequin on wheels being driven around the track by remote control. His expression is steely and unchanging, his neck bolt upright. The others sweat and flounder as the laps go on and on, but the man at the front doesn't flinch. At the end he crosses the line, checks his watch, and quietly heads off on his warm-down.

Afterwards, none of the runners speaks to me. They're off warming down in twos or alone. It's all very serious. The old men are still out lapping the track. I decide to slip away before they ask me when I'm coming back.

On the walk back to the station, I feel a strange tinge of sadness come over me. I couldn't keep up with these runners. It's fine not keeping up with the Ritsumeikan team, but this is an unremarkable group from a nondescript Japanese suburb. Yet here are six runners who have never been to Kenya, have never been coached by anyone famous, who just run laps around this industrial track, and they leave me floundering. In every town in Japan there's probably another six just like them. It suddenly feels hopeless, my quest to get faster, to keep improving. All my core exercises, my hill repeats, my work on my running form, yet essentially I'm still in the same place.

But I'm not just sad for myself. After he finished, the fastest man, who destroyed everyone else with his steely face and barely moving legs, sat down, pulled on his tracksuit and stared into space for a few moments, before heading off to warm down. Nobody came over to slap him on the back and tell him what a star he was. That brief moment of self-reflection was all he got.

I know running can bring joy and a sense of well-being, but for these men, pushing themselves to run always faster, harder, to beat their times, to win minor races, a chilling sense of futility can blow across the track. I feel it this morning, touching me.

And yet, on I go, planning my next race, the 10K road race in Osaka. And then the big ekiden in Fuji. It all has a point, I'm sure. I just can't remember what it is right now. In any case, I need to get this sore knee looked at first.

24

It's getting worse. I'm feeling it on every run, and going up and down the steep stairs in our shoebox house. So much for my latest change of form being the perfect solution, the final bulletproofing piece of the machine. In an effort to find out what's wrong with my knee, I go to visit a sports injury clinic in Osaka.

Inside the clinic I point at my leg and tell them it's sore. Rie, our next-door neighbour, has written down my symptoms in Japanese on a piece of paper, which I hand over to the woman in the reception. She asks me to wait. The room feels more like a GP's surgery than a sports injury clinic, and I wonder if I've come to the right place, particularly when I get to see the doctor and the first thing he wants to do is take an X-ray of my knee.

I try to tell him it's not *that* sore, just a dull pain, but he simply smiles and sends me into the X-ray room. Of course, this gets me worried. What if I have done something more serious? This could be the end. My knee could be shattered.

Luckily, after studying the X-ray carefully, he tells me everything is fine. I've just got tightness around my ankles and in my feet and calves. He massages my foot and sends me on my way.

'Too much running on asphalt,' he says. I nod. If only I had another option.

Virtually everyone I've run with in Japan has been injured at some point. Of course, there are many reasons why people get injured, but in Japan most runners have good core strength from all their squatting and sitting on the floor, while most people have a fairly light frame, which is good for running. The big problem seems to be the concrete.

In an article in *Outside* magazine in the US entitled 'Alberto Salazar's 10 Golden Running Rules', the great coach's rule no. 4 is: 'Stay on the trails.' He says: 'Pavement damages joints, tendons, ligaments and muscles. The more you can run on grass, woodchips or dirt, the better off you are. My athletes run 90 per cent of their workouts on soft surfaces.'

When Kenji, who loves Salazar, sees this, he is finally convinced. He begins to tell the Blooming group in his pre-run talks how much better it is to run on soft surfaces.

'The Kenyans never train on asphalt,' he tells them as they sit there only half listening. Half listening, because then we go out and run on concrete. At the Osaka sessions, there is a dirt trail beside the tarmac road. It is the same length and width as the road, with only the odd bump. But none of us ever uses it. Even when Kenji starts returning from injury himself, with his crooked knee, he doesn't run on the trail. Not even for the warm-up. The pattern of running along nice, smooth, marked-out stretches of road is too ingrained, it's like they don't even notice they're doing it.

When I suggest to Kenji that he take his Ritsumeikan team out into the mountains that surround Kyoto to run, up where the monks carry out their thousand-day challenge, he only laughs. When I press him, telling him it's just like the mountains outside Addis Ababa where all the great Ethiopians train, he tells me the university would sack him if he took the team there to run. The worry, he says, is that they may fall over a tree stump, or off the edge of the mountain.

Near our house in Kyotanabe, unfortunately, there are no trails. And so it is with a crooked knee and very little training in the previous six weeks that I catch the train the next weekend for my final run before the big Fuji ekiden: the 10K race around Osaka's Daisen park.

So that I don't get lost, one of the Blooming runners, the Asics sales executive Rokugawa, has come along to race with me. He is in training for an ultramarathon, he tells me. But he, too, has bad knees. They're both strapped up in blue Kinesio tape. 'OK, OK,' he says when I ask him about it, giving me a big thumbs-up. Injured knees are business as usual for runners in Japan.

It's a damp day. The winter chill has been replaced by an almost cloying warmth. When Rogukawa sees I'm planning to race in a singlet he looks surprised, but delighted. 'Oh, serious runner,' he says. It's 16°C according to the park thermometer. Lots of the other runners have their race numbers pinned onto the outside of their tracksuits and running jackets. They're going to boil. Rogukawa is wearing a light long-sleeved running top and shorts. Sensible, but nothing as presumptuous and showy as a vest.

It's a sea of deference as we wait on the start line. Nobody wants to stand at the front. Most people shuffle apologetically in their layers of tights and thermal tops as we watch the clock tick around to the 10 a.m. start time. The morning's drizzle has now lifted and the sun is starting to push through the thinning clouds, making it even warmer.

[295]

We're saved from our awkward waiting by the hooter sounding the start of the race. Within a few hundred metres, I find myself at the front with three other runners, the rest of the four hundred or so competitors already disappearing behind us. My initial thought is that finishing in the first four is pretty good – which is hardly the mindset of a hardened champion, but then, it's not often I find myself at the front of a race. However, my legs are feeling sprightly today. Somehow the soreness in my knee has disappeared. I'm feeling strong, light on my feet, my legs kicking back. This is the way I felt that day I ran with the Nissin Foods team in Chiba. Before my knee started hurting.

Without planning to, I keep surging, picking up the pace, testing the three runners around me. It's like my legs are getting carried away, sprinting off like excitable whippets. I have to keep reining them back in. But by the end of the first of two laps, two of the runners have dropped off and we're down to just two of us at the front. We weave our way side by side through people out walking in the park, and then through backmarkers still struggling around on their first lap.

It's thrilling to be at the front, leading the charge. We're putting on a good show, the two of us, as first one, then the other, edges a little ahead. It's a real battle.

Of course, no one is watching, except two old ladies on a bench who give us a smile each time we pass. But my imagination is running almost as fast as my legs. I keep thinking the other runner is just waiting for his chance to sprint away from me. I don't win races, I think, I'm always second, I hate sprint finishes, I'll let him have it at the end. These are actual thoughts I'm having, even though I never finish second in races – why am I thinking that? But then my skittish legs take over for a few minutes and I'm forging ahead, pushing the pace, trying to drop him, actually trying to win. In these moments, my head goes: 'OK, why not, let's give it a go.' But each time he sticks with me. With 1.5 km to go, I make a big push and get a five-metre gap on him. But I can't sustain it, and with a kilometre to go he bursts past me and starts to open up a lead. The part of me expecting this is almost righteous. 'See,' I say, to myself. 'I knew this would happen. He's just been waiting. Like I said.' I've fully accepted second place as we cruise into the final straight. But I'm still pushing myself to run a good time. My legs still feel strong.

Suddenly I realise he's not getting any further ahead. He's there, in front of me, and there's the finish line. My brain is making quick calculations, dividing distance left by energy, multiplied by the gap to runner. But my legs have already made their move. Come on, you old goon, we're not done yet. I'm sprinting, catching him. I whizz past and charge like a madman for the line. He's just behind me, but it's too late, I've got it, I've won.

After I want to shake hands and slap his back. What a battle! But he's already disappearing sheepishly into the throng of people in the park.

*

I'm not quite sure where that came from. In the end I ran the 10km in 36 minutes 6 seconds, which is only 16 seconds off my best ever time. But I've been injured and I hardly ran in the weeks leading up to the race. Even before that I was only just getting up to top speed after our overland journey to Japan. Yet here I am, being presented with the winner's trophy by some famous Osaka comedian, the local press taking my picture. The only thing I can put it down to is the further improvements in my running form. I'm now, hopefully, running with good form for the entire race, not just the first half.

As long as my knee can hold out, it bodes well for the climax of my trip: the Fuji ekiden. Unfortunately, my all-star team never quite materialised. Injuries, age restrictions and work commitments have left me with just Kono (the Blooming coach and part-time model) and the Ritsumei-kan University runners. I decide to ask some of the first-year runners to join me. The Professor, and his friend, the English-speaking Kasahara.

I tell Kenji my plan at one of the Ritsumeikan training sessions. 'OK,' he says, calling me to follow him. As we stand in a wide circle at the beginning of the session, I re-alise that he is telling them about the ekiden, and telling them that I have chosen the Professor and Kasahara to be on my team. They all look surprised, particularly the Professor, who looks as though he has just had a blinding spotlight turned on him.

Kenji tells him he must do his best and he nods, squirm-ing under the glare. The others are confused. Why didn't I pick the fastest runners? The ace, and number two. I want to tell them that I thought my race, my team, was a little beneath them, that I didn't want to feel out of my depth in a team of superstars, but my Japanese is not up to it, so I just bow, to show my humble thanks to them all.

*

Two days before the race, our Kyotanabe cul-de-sac is covered in a thick, wet blanket of snow that quickly turns to slush. It's rare to see snow here, we're told, as the children in the street slide down the hill on plastic bags and trays. By the end of the day, it's all gone.

My children are now finished with school. After all they've been through, travelling to Japan and dealing with months of lessons in Japanese, we've taken them out of class for the last few weeks to give them a rest before we return to England. It's a bit of down time, and a chance to do some home schooling to catch up on what they've missed in England.

This doesn't go exactly to plan. My knee has started feeling better, so I'm squeezing in some last-minute training runs, and chasing a few last meetings with Japanese runners, while Marietta is still suffering terribly from her itching skin. She tries ordering every remedy from every corner of the globe, but nothing works. She drinks Max's home-made microorganisms, bathes in herbal concoctions sent over by the neighbours and douses herself in strange potions, but nothing has any effect. Eventually, Rie, our neighbour, goes with her to the hospital, where they carry out a series of allergy tests. The results reveal a strong reaction to Japanese dust mites. So we heat the futons with Rie's special futon heater, vacuum everything, and throw out the sofa we bought from the local recycling shop, while Marietta stocks up on antihistamine tablets. The itching subsides and she finally begins to re-emerge into the world. With weeks to go, rather than start teaching maths to the children, she takes them to the temples and mountains she has missed. The sums they can catch up on later.

*

As well as our brief snowfall, I hear mentions here and there about snow falling in other parts of the country. Little snippets of maps on television screens and conversations on the trains. Nevertheless, it seems like a fairly mild February morning when I set off early a few days later to our race at Mount Fuji. The plan is to catch the train to Kyoto, where I'm meeting the rest of the team. As well as Kono, the Professor and Kasahara, Kenji's assistant coach at Ritsumeikan, Normua, has agreed to run. He has been training, Kenji tells me, and is in good enough shape to run 5km in under 16 minutes, which is significantly faster than me. He has also agreed to help me organise the trip.

Between the five of us we are a decent team, capable, I hope, of challenging for a high finishing position in the ekiden. I'm down to run the third leg. Kenji tells us to put the two first-year students, our two strongest runners, on the first two legs. This way we will hopefully get a lead, which will stress the opposition and make them panic and run too fast too early. Also, if the team starts well, it somehow sets a pattern and the rest of us will be inspired to run above and beyond ourselves to hold the team's position. This is the theory. So I'm likely to get the tasuki in a strong position, possibly in the lead, with the team's hopes resting squarely on my shoulders. Then I will finally experience what it's like to be an ekiden runner, to feel my energy raised by the greater good, to find myself fighting, racing for something bigger than my own glory.

I get a call on my mobile phone. I'm on the train so I don't answer it; instead I quickly switch my phone to silent. Even letting your phone ring on a Japanese train is a faux pas. I look to see who it is. It's Kono. He is in Tokyo that day and the plan is for him to meet the rest of us at our hotel near Mount Fuji that evening. I really hope he's not dropping out. It's too late to find a replacement. My phone buzzes quietly. A text. I open it.

'Finn-san. Have you spoken to Kenji? Please call me.'

Even at a time like this, it feels wrong to make a phone call on the train, so I wait until we arrive at the station in Kyoto.

'Hello, Kono? It's Finn.'

'Have you heard? It has snowed in Fuji. Do you think we should cancel the trip?'

He obviously doesn't realise how important this is. I'm not going to cancel the trip because of some snow. The hotel has assured us that even if it does snow, the roads will be clear.

'No,' I say. 'I think we should still go.'

'Oh,' he says. 'I don't think the others are coming. They thought you would cancel.'

I'm not sure what to say. I have a rental car booked. I'm leaving for England in a few days. This is my last chance to run an ekiden. I'll race the whole thing by myself if I have to. Just then, through the criss-crossing crowds on the concourse in Kyoto station, ambling slowly towards me, smartly dressed and pulling small suitcases on wheels, come the rest of the team.

'They're here,' I say to Kono. 'We're going to run. We'll see you later?'

'Oh,' he says. 'OK. See you later.'

They grin when they see me. I feel scruffy standing there in my sports gear and rucksack, like I've badly misjudged the dress code at a party. They don't say anything.

'*Ikimashoka*,' I say. *Shall we go?*

Nomura leads the way to the car-hire garage.

*

We drive out of Kyoto through fine drizzle and along the highway, gradually rising up into the mountains, where the hills are covered in a light dusting of snow. Mist moves between the hills, covering the forested peaks. Kasahara has plugged in his iPod and it's playing the haunting music from one of the fantasy Ghibli animations. For a moment I'm flipped back to the magical world I experienced in those first few days in Japan, when everything seemed sketched by some cartoon artist. Here we are, a team of young warriors, each with his own character and set of powers: the speedy Professor, with his jet-powered sandals; Kasahara, the linguist; our leader, Nomura; and me, Finn-san, the long-legged *gaijin*. Waiting for us at the hotel will be our own strongman, Kono. Even his name sounds heroic. Together we are known as The Ekiden Men.

Nomura is driving with one hand on the wheel, his cap tipped back on his head. His phone rings. He answers it.

'Eh?' He's making those big exaggerated gestures again. The others are pitching in, saying things I don't understand, looking concerned. He puts the phone down and looks ahead without saying anything.

'Is everything all right?' I ask.

He doesn't answer at first. They all look at him.

'The race has been cancelled,' he says. 'Too much snow.'

*

A few minutes later we pull into a service area off the motorway. We have no choice as far as anyone can see but to turn around and head back to Kyoto. It turns out the biggest snowfall in twenty years was dumped on the race course during the night. In the sixty-year history of the race, it is only the second time it has been cancelled. The others are all as disappointed as I am.

'Maybe we can run a different race?' I suggest. They look at each other, weighing it up. Kasahara, taking the lead, nods. 'It's possible,' he says. I know there is an ekiden in Kobe the next day, and a few days later there is even one at Ritsumeikan University. It's lunchtime, so we decide to get some food and make a plan. Once we're sitting down, they get out their phones to look for other races. Kasahara has found the one in Kobe and is calling the organisers. I'm crossing my fingers.

He talks quietly, politely. '*Ah, so desune,*' he says. *Of course, I agree.*

He puts the phone down and shakes his head.

'The deadline to enter has passed,' he says. Most races in

Japan have entry deadlines months in advance, and there is little chance of getting around them. The freak snow in eastern Japan hasn't led to any softening of the strict rules. They try ringing a few other races, but the response is the same. I suggest telling the organisers it is for a British journalist who wants to write about the race, but I can tell they're uncomfortable with this. Instead, each time they simply ask if the deadline has passed, which of course it has, and then apologise for calling so late.

Kasahara tries ringing Kenji about the Ritsumeikan race. Surely we can do that one, at least. I'll have to run it on our way to the airport as it's on the day we're due to fly back to England. But it should be just about possible. A dramatic last-ditch ekiden as the last few hours of our visas count down.

'Takao-san will ask the organisers,' he tells me after he puts the phone down.

If the university coach can't get us a race in his own university ekiden, then we don't have any chance. We decide to get some soba noodles while we wait for Kenji to call back. On the television screens dotted around the echoing dining hall, the rolling news reports are full of pictures of blizzards and children making snowmen in the street. Maps with arrows show the snow blowing down from across Siberia, right onto our ekiden course. I curse Siberia again, with its endless wilderness and slow, rickety trains.

When a freak snowstorm cancels everything, there's no one to blame. You can't get angry at anyone. How many more people are turning back, I wonder. This is the worst part, to have come so far, across so many lands, through so many training sessions, unintelligible meetings, train

journeys, days in our quiet cul-de-sac feeling discombobu-
lated, reaching out into the fuzzy, unknown world of Japanese running, sliding into hot baths, climbing onto buses,
to have done so much and to be turning around on a road
only half travelled, the final act, the ekiden, buried in the
Siberian snow.

Then, for some reason, I'm reminded of a cartoon I once
saw about a Zen mechanic. When the customer turns up to
collect his car, the mechanic looks at him calmly, his hands
in prayer, and says: 'There is no car.'

There is no race. It's very Zen. Why do we need the
worldly construct of a race? What purpose does it fulfil? It is
the completion of a goal, sure, but wasn't that goal only ever
a mechanism to get us out running? Those days of training
are not wasted If we don't run the race. If you miss your
exam at the end of a course, it doesn't mean you haven't
learnt anything. If anything, perhaps the race is what stops
us from ever seeing this essential truth. Perhaps our focus
on completing the race distracts us, so we never see or understand why we run. When the race is taken away at the
last moment, however, we're left hanging in this empty,
charged space where the questions begin to arise. Why *do* I
run? And in the quiet pause, we know the answer. In every
training run, we fill ourselves with the experience of life, the
air rushing through our lungs, our hearts pounding. Maybe
the thought of the race gets us out the door, but it is only
ever the carrot dangled before us. Sometimes we don't get to
eat the carrot, we already know that. And even when we do,
it is only ever a fleeting moment of satisfaction. Even if we
break our best times, or win the race, a few days later we're

lacing up again. Like the Daigyoman Ajari who said enlightenment wasn't an end, but just another step on a lifelong journey, the race is not the end we hold it up to be. Whatever happens, the next day, we need to start all over again.

Yet, while deep down I know the race is not important, at the same time I can't quite banish my sense of disappointment. I never run in training quite like I do in a race. Something happens to me in that mass charge after the starting gun is fired. In the 1960s, Hungarian psychology professor Mihaly Csikszentmihalyi, working at the University of Chicago, came up with the concept of flow: a state of perfect concentration in which your awareness and movements merge, in which you have no ego, just complete absorption with the task at hand. The time I get closest to this is almost always in a race. This is partly because in a race all the external factors are taken care of – the roads are closed, people are kept off the course, the route is planned and marked out – and I can concentrate purely and simply on running. In a race, miles can whizz by unnoticed. Speeds that would seem manic in training feel smooth and easy. Not in every race, but sometimes. And not for the entire race, but for spells here and there I'm gone, lost in the wilds of my own existence.

Kasahara's phone rings. It's Kenji. *So desune. So desune.*

He shakes his head. 'They said the deadline has passed.' Of course it has. Deadlines are moved for no man. If no one will cross an empty road at six in the morning without a green light, they're hardly going to break the rules on entering an ekiden.

'Takao-san suggests we run a 10K on the track together, to help you beat your time. We could do that tomorrow?'

It's a kind offer, but it was the spirit of ekiden I wanted to experience. This wasn't just any race to validate my training, or to give me a fix of flow, this race, of all races, was different. I wanted to know what it was like to run for a team. This has somehow eluded me through everything. Yes, I have run ekidens, but not with the deep sense of responsibility I've heard so much about. I wanted to see if I could be driven to push beyond my limits when the fate of my team was relying on me. Although even that, perhaps, was a selfish desire. Perhaps the best way to play my part, the most Japanese response to my situation, is not to ruffle the feathers of race organisers by trying to get them to break the rules, putting my team, and Kenji, in a awkward position by asking them to try to find another race. Perhaps, for the sake of harmony, the best thing to do is to accept and return to Kyoto. In the end, we have no choice.

On the way back we sit in silence listening to Kasahara's music. The excitement of the outward journey, only a few hours earlier, has gone. We're no longer a team of running superheroes, but just a group of people returning from a wasted journey. We're already thinking of other things we need to do that weekend. No doubt they have studies to do, and training, other ekidens to prepare for, while I need to start packing up the house ready to return home to England.

On his iPod, Kasahara is now playing his favourite band Coldplay. A band from near my home in Devon in England. It seems appropriate.

'*Nobody said it would be easy*,' warbles the singer, full of pained emotion. '*It's such a shame for us to part . . . Take me back to the start.*'

25

A few days later, I'm back in the UK. After Japan, every-thing in England feels unruly and fraying at the edges. The first train I board is delayed, the seat cover is torn, the man sitting behind me is shouting into his mobile phone, broad-casting the intricacies of a night of heavy drinking. Another man is refusing to pay for his ticket, standing in the gap between the carriages, being jolted threateningly from side to side as the conductor tells him she'll call the police.

Even stepping off the plane I'm immediately hit by the contrast with Japan. After a fourteen-hour flight, my chil-dren are exhausted, so I'm carrying all five bags. Right out-side the plane, there in the corridor, is a luggage trolley. Re-lieved, I dump my bags on it.

'Nah, mate, that's there for a reason,' says an airport work-er appearing behind me, his words laced with weary sarcasm.

'Not for passengers with bags?' I retort.

'Nah, mate.'

He makes me remove my bags and carry them. In Japan, this just wouldn't happen. If the trolley was for someone else, they would find you another one, or at least they would be apologetic. I see all the Japanese people, being led in large tottering groups towards the arrivals gate by airline staff waving little flags in the air, and I fear for them. Be careful, I want to tell them, it's a jungle out there.

The other notable difference, however, as we make our slow way home on the train back to Devon, is the endless miles of English countryside. Everywhere there are fields, crisscrossed with pathways and quiet lanes perfect for running. As soon as I get home, I set off at a trot across the trails, enjoying the mud and uneven ground, skipping over trees that have fallen down since I was last here.

As I run, I reflect on what I learnt during my time in Japan. I went, in part, to find out why the Japanese are so good at long-distance running. In some ways this was easy. They love running as a sport, they take it seriously and, just like the Kenyans, they train in large, dedicated groups, spurring each other on, inspiring each other. The other similarity with Kenya was the way in which distance running is a celebrated pursuit in Japan. Unlike most of the world, in Japan, as in Kenya, running is a viable career option and a culture and system exists to support the needs and ambitions of the athletes.

A few weeks after I return from Japan, the British half-marathon trials take place in Reading, featuring what the organisers call the best ever line-up of British elite runners. The winner, Scott Overall, runs a time of 64 minutes 44 seconds. On the very same day, in Japan, the national *university* half-marathon championships take place. The student in that race finishing way back in 100th position runs almost exactly the same time as Overall, the British champion, finishing in a time of 64:47.

So yes, they are good. But in the end, the more interesting question was why are they not better? Why, with a highly developed running system unrivalled anywhere in the world, was the winner of the university championships that day, a full hundred places further ahead, only running 62:09? While this is quick, it's hardly a time to cause even a ripple on the international stage.

The question begs two possible answers. Either more Japanese runners are running at the limits of their potential, or they are doing something wrong.

The high level of support and opportunity certainly means fewer talented runners are lost to the sport in Japan compared with other nations. But with so many reaching a high level, you would expect at least a few of them to be coming out at the other end with times capable of challenging the top Kenyans and Ethiopians. But it is just not happening.

David Epstein, the author of *The Sports Gene*, tells me this expectation is assuming too much.

'You would only expect that if everything else about the populations was standardised,' he says. 'And, of course, it isn't.'

Of course, there are lots of differences between Japan and east Africa, and few of them are in Japan's favour when it comes to producing long-distance runners. For a start there is the lack of trails and high-altitude areas in which to train. Spending time at altitude, it is widely accepted, increases your blood's ability to carry oxygen and most top athletes from all nations will include at least part of their year at altitude. But nothing can replicate the huge benefits of being born and raised at altitude, as all the great Kenyan and Ethiopian runners were.

The lack of trails in Japan, too, is a clear disadvantage. By the end of my stay, Kenji is so convinced of the need to train on trails rather than on concrete that he keeps repeating the story of the day he met former marathon world-record holder Kalid Kannouchi. It was just before a marathon in Japan. When Kannouchi saw Kenji, he stopped him and said: 'I know you. I remember you as a junior. I thought you'd be my rival, but then I observed you and I knew you'd lose it.'

Kenji asked him: 'How did you know?'

Kenji pauses at this point in the story, for dramatic effect. 'He said one thing to me,' Kenji says. 'He said: "You ran on asphalt. It's too hard."'

It is only a matter of time before Kenji has his team out training on Mount Hiei with the monks.

But it is more than altitude and running on soft ground that divides the two nations. Another difference is the motivation of the runners. In Kenya, there is nothing to gain from being a 'good' runner. The competition is so fierce and the opportunities so scarce that to succeed you have to be a great runner. In Japan, it is easy for runners to get too comfortable with a paid salary on an average team.

'The protection and support of a corporate team can have downsides,' says Mara Yamauchi. 'When you need to succeed just to put food on the table, your motivation is higher. In Japan, sometimes a place on a corporate ekiden team can be too easy.'

The athletes also struggle to stay motivated after the highs of Hakone. When, by the age of twenty-two, your career highlight has already happened, as it has for most professional Japanese runners, staying motivated to train hard, to push yourself to new levels, can be difficult.

The Nissin Foods coach, Okamura, told me that his biggest challenge as a coach was to keep his runners motivated.

'The five key points to being a top runner,' he told me, 'One, eat well. Two, sleep enough. Three, look after your body. Four, training. And five, motivation. As a coach, the most important thing is to communicate with the athletes to make sure this fifth point is OK.'

As well as potentially making life too easy for the runners, the team system can also lead to a risk-averse, safety-first approach to racing. Nobody wants to risk blowing the team's chances, or looking like an idiot, by tearing off at the front of a race at an unsustainable pace. Kenji told me that when he did this at a big ekiden once, even though it worked and he gained a big lead over his nearest rival, his coach was angry with him afterwards. The Japanese way, as I was often told, is to run even pace.

Yet it is the go-for-broke approach of the Kenyans, the wild surges, that leads to the stellar performances. Often, of course, it backfires, but to win big races, as Renato Canova says, 'you need to be a little wild'.

This wildness is born out of a sense of freedom and abandon the Kenyans seem to bring to their running. Despite the huge stakes, where success can transform lives, somehow they remain remarkably laid back and carefree in their approach. If they fail in a race, they don't dwell on it. 'I will do it next time,' they're fond of saying, usually with a big smile. Like Usain Bolt prancing around before the Olympic 100m final, the theory is that the more relaxed you are, the better you are likely to perform.

Contrast this with the immense pressure the Japanese heap on themselves. The start line of an elite race in Japan is a study in tension. Failure is not taken lightly. After

Yuki Kawauchi finished fourteenth in the Tokyo marathon in 2012, he called his own performance disgraceful, and shaved his head in penance for disappointing his fans. In an even more extreme example, Kōkichi Tsuburaya was so distraught at finishing 'only' third in the 1964 Olympic marathon in Tokyo that a few weeks after the race he took his own life.

Of course, intensity can be a driver of success, but too much pressure and stress can also shut the body down, limiting performance.

On top of all this, in Japan you have the many problems associated with over-training at an early age, brought on by overbearing coaches only interested in the short-term results. This leads to a high rate of injuries and burnout. Indeed, it is the university runners who are most impressive in Japan, running times that would rival even the Kenyans at that age for depth of long-distance talent. But by the age of twenty-five, the numbers of top athletes in Japan have dwindled and the times of the fastest runners are much less impressive.*

Yet it is another factor that is most cited by the Japanese themselves, when they consider why they are failing to win global medals in long-distance running. The Nissin Foods coach explains to me: 'Kenyans have greater physical capacity than the Japanese. They have bigger lungs, they are stronger.'

* Compare this with Dennis Kimetto, the Kenyan athlete who six months after I return from Japan breaks the world marathon record in Berlin running a mind-blowing 2:02:57. Kimetto only began training seriously at the age of twenty-six.

It's a commonly held view in Japan. Despite being the ideal height for marathon running, the Japanese prefer to talk about their short legs, which they say stop them from winning.

Scientists have been digging away at this for years and the more they discover, the more difficult they realise it is to attribute genetic advantages to certain populations. One day Kenji invited me to a conference at Ritsumeikan University where a team of scientists were reporting back from an extensive research trip to Kenya where they were attempting to uncover whether the Kenyans had a natural advantage over the Japanese when it came to distance running.

The results were inconclusive. The scientists found, for example, that the muscles of Japanese runners were on average more tense before hitting the ground, which meant they lost more energy. But this, they said, was because the Japanese runners were anticipating a heel-first impact, which is harder to bear, while the Kenyans were more likely to land forefoot or mid-foot first when they ran.

This led to Japanese runners suffering from overworked muscles and tendons at a young age, which the researchers said, combined with over-training, meant many had lost their bounce by the time they reached the senior ranks.

They also found that the Kenyan runners had longer achilles tendons, which made them sixteen per cent more efficient, they said. However, they pointed out that tendon length is not fixed and can change with environment and training. They studied two twins who competed in different sports and found they had different-length tendons.

At the end of the talk, the professor in charge of the study held up his hands and said simply: 'In truth, we still don't know. We can't find a significant difference. Perhaps there isn't one.'

The final factor limiting the prowess of Japanese runners on the international stage is the country's inward-facing running culture and in particular the intense focus on ekiden. As we've seen, comparing half-marathon times in Japan with half-marathon times elsewhere is really like comparing training sessions with serious races. To see what Japanese runners are really capable of, to catch them in full flow, in the races they really care about and prepare for, we need to extrapolate their performances from ekiden races.

While events such as Hakone and the New Year ekiden remain virtually unknown outside Japan, their best performances will continue to go unnoticed by the rest of the world.

As I finish up my run across the old familiar fields, the sky a pale, fading blue, my face flushed from the fresh February air, I wonder how my own approach to running has evolved since I left for Japan all those months ago. Did I learn any secrets? The truth is, more than anything, in Japan I learned what not to do. Run less on concrete, run without fear, without stress, without fixating on the watch. In Japan, the impressive numbers of fast runners is largely down to dedication, good support and hard work. But hard work is also the cause of many of the problems. With the future of Japanese running in mind, and in particular the 2020 Tokyo Olympics, finding the right balance between the willingness to work hard, and the intelligence to know when to rest, is something Kenji and others are working on.

The one thing I hoped to learn in Japan, but never quite managed, was whether running as part of a team could rouse my racing spirit to new heights. In one final attempt to understand and experience the pressure and responsibility of running in an ekiden, a few months after returning to the UK I enter the South Downs marathon relay in southern England. Long-distance relay races do exist in the UK. They're not closely followed like ekidens in Japan, and are usually considered 'a bit of fun' for club runners, something a bit different, but at a basic level, they're the same. A team of runners each running a leg of a long-distance race.

The South Downs race is a marathon in total, split between four runners. I want my team to be competitive. If I'm going to recreate what I would have experienced in the Fuji ekiden, I'm going to need some good runners on board. We need to be near the front, challenging for victory. Everything needs to be riding on me when I take the tasuki – although I'll have to imagine the tasuki, as in relay races in England it's simply a matter of one runner finishing and the next one starting, without any symbolic ribbon to hand over.

First on my hit list for my team is an occasional training partner from London, Tom Payn. He's pretty much the fastest British runner I know. I first met him in Kenya, where he was training in the hope of making the 2012 Olympic marathon team. That didn't happen, but he has run a speedy 2 hours 17 minutes for the marathon. When I ask him if he'll join, he says yes.

The second runner on the list is Ceri Rees. A former English schools cross-country champion, he's still running strongly and winning big races in his forties, especially trail races. He has big, wild hair and says he hates running on concrete. He once took me on a twenty-four-mile jaunt across Dartmoor that left me in A&E. It's a long story, but let's just say my advice is never to try to outrun him in a hailstorm.

The final member of the team is a runner at my local club, Torbay AC, called Simon Longthorpe. While not quite as fast as Tom and Ceri, he has run 2 hours 40 minutes for the marathon, and has been in great shape since I got back from Japan, flying along at the front at our club's regular Tuesday-night sessions.

I'm the slowest member of the team, but I'm also, somehow, hitting top form just now. I'm not sure why, or how, but I've returned from Japan faster than ever. My injury, it turns out was nothing but a tight IT band, the fascia that runs up the outside of the upper leg. After stretching it regularly for a few days it gets better. Yet despite this injury preventing me from running for most of the last two months of my stay in Japan, now I'm back, I'm whizzing along. My win in Osaka, it turns out, was no fluke.

At one 10km road race on the edge of Dartmoor, not long after getting back to England, I arrive at the start with low expectations. The wind is blowing hard and the sky is spitting spiky rain at us. The course is also fairly hilly, so with no thought for times I decide to run without my watch.

About 2km into the race we turn up a steep hill. I'm just behind one of my regular local rivals, a man I've never beaten in a race before. Without even trying, however, I race away from him up the hill. At the top I'm still full of running and I can feel myself opening up. The two race leaders are in sight and I begin to think about chasing them down. Then my car key falls out of my pocket.

My first thought, when I hear it clink on the ground, is to leave it. I'm feeling too good to stop. The wind is behind me, blowing hard, so I run on for a few seconds, before I realise that I can't leave my car key on the ground in some country lane. That would be stupid. How would I get home? I stop, turn, and run back.

As soon as it's back in my pocket, I'm off again, streaking back past my rivals, chasing the leaders again. Then, down a steep hill a few minutes later, the key falls out again.

I later realise I was using the wrong pocket. My shorts have one pocket with a zip for important things such as keys, and a more open, wider one for energy gels. I put my key in the wide one. The second time, I at least recoup my key quickly, and then run on holding it in my hand. But I've lost more precious seconds and have been caught by a small group of runners from behind.

We run the last 5km together into a 30mph headwind, like a chain gang, following each other in single file, taking turns to lead into the wind. Like a peloton, we haul in a few competitors who got caught out running in the gale alone, and before I know it we're rounding the last corner. The clock has only just ticked past 35 minutes. I race to the line, crossing it in 35:20, a big personal best by over 30 seconds, despite the wind, the hills and the farce of the key-dropping.

It is hard to know what is driving this new improvement in my times. In most aspects, my running regime is unchanged from the days before I went to Japan. Yet a few weeks after the 10km PB, I win a local 10-mile trail race. That's two wins for the year already. After never winning anything in all my previous years of running, in a few short months I've won three trophies, two bottles of wine and two sports vouchers.

The only real difference in my running since Japan has been the improvement in my form. Since that fateful day with the TV presenter on the track at Ritsumeikan University, when I realised I was doing it all wrong, I've been working on my technique, squatting like mad and building up my core strength to stop my form collapsing halfway through each run. It seems to be working.

26

The night before the South Downs marathon I get a call from Ceri to say he's injured. He can't run. Without a fourth member, none of us can run. This is the problem with teams, you're relying on other people. In Japan, they always get you to have a replacement lined up in case something like this happens, but I'm not that organised. I'm meeting Tom in London, ready to drive down to the race in Sussex that evening. When he arrives, I give him the bad news. How are we going to find a fourth runner at such short notice?

Tom's life is running. He works as an agent for a team of mostly Kenyan runners called Run Fast. He scrolls through his phone.

'I wonder if James Ellis is free,' he says. 'He lives in the South Downs. I'll call him.'

After a quick chat he hangs up. 'He's in,' says Tom. As easy as that.

'Great,' I say. 'Is he any good?'

'He just won the Hampshire 5,000m champs,' Tom says. 'So he's not bad.'

*

We spend the night before the race in the stripped-down glamour of the Premier Inn beside the A27 near Arundel in

West Sussex. After a drink in the warm evening, sitting on a bench under the streetlights, Tom hands us all matching running kit – black shorts and vest. I still have the running hats I was given by the organisers of the Fuji ekiden. I hand them out too. In memory of Nomura, Kashara, Kono and the Professor, we've named our team The Ekiden Men.

'OK, time to turn in,' says Tom. 'Big day, tomorrow.'

I'm surprised, as I was with my Japanese team, by how seriously everyone is taking it. I guess this competitive streak is partly what makes them such fast runners. For me the fact it is a team race makes it seem less serious. The pressure, rather than being greater, seems to be dispersed among the team. By sharing the responsibility for how we run, we each have less of a burden individually. That's how it seems to me. In any case, I'm not getting the usual pre-race nerves, even though I'm running the final leg. This may seem counterintuitive, putting the slowest runner on the last leg, but it is what Kenji recommended when I asked him about it.

I'm not totally convinced. Given the choice, I'd rather be a fast runner chasing down a slower runner at the end, than the slower runner getting chased down. But what do I know? Kenji's the expert, and so it's agreed: Tom goes first, and I go last.

*

The morning of the race is hot and sunny. Too hot for tracksuits, so we all get into Tom's car in our black running outfits. The car itself is a black 4x4 with tinted windows and the words Run Fast printed along one side. We make quite a sight as we pull into the car park at the race, slide the doors back and leap out. The Reservoir Dogs of running.

'Oh, you look fast,' one woman comments. 'Are you going to win?'

We don't answer, instead looking at each other nervously as though we're a bunch of spies who have just been told we look like spies, and then asked if we really are.

'Oh my god,' she exclaims when we don't instantly profess to be hopeless, which is the usual British response to such a question. 'You are!'

'I need the loo,' I say, to avoid any further interrogation, and jog off to find one.

We have a complicated arrangement for getting to the various starting points, which involves two cars and lots of driving. So, while James drives to the first changeover point, Simon and I watch Tom start the first leg. There are around a hundred teams in the race, which begins across the manicured lawns of Slindon College near Arundel. Even by the first corner, Tom is clear at the front. He grins at us as he shoots by. The Ekiden Men are go. Simon and I climb into the second car and head off to our positions.

*

I arrive at the start of the final leg as the organisers are still setting up the changeover zone. It's on the top of a hill overlooking the Sussex countryside. People are out walking and cycling, enjoying the sunshine. A boy with a plastic bow and arrow is shooting it up into the air and chasing after it. There is no sign of any other runners.

People passing stop to talk to the race organisers.

'What's this then?' they ask. 'A bike race?'

'A marathon relay,' the man setting up says. 'The first runners won't be through for a while yet, though.'

They stand looking along the path that stretches off into the distance. 'Well, rather them than me.'

It's nearly midday by the time a few other final-leg runners appear at the changeover point. The sun is heating my black kit, and scorching my shoulders. One of the other runners sees my team race number, 22.

'Your guys are going well,' he says. 'They were five minutes ahead at the start of the third changeover.'

'Team 91 is leading,' says the man who was setting up. 'That what I hear on my radio.'

'Can't be,' says the other runner. 'Unless something strange happened. These guys were well ahead.' He's pointing at me. I have no idea.

All this speculation is making me feel tense. Has Simon got lost? Has he fallen and hurt himself? Suddenly he appears, rushing out from the trees, his face etched in pain, just like a real ekiden runner.

'Don't start too fast,' are his parting words as I speed off down a steep slope.

The effort etched on Simon's face seems to follow me through the trees. This is serious. I can suddenly feel the hopes of the team breathing warm on my neck. But rather than hurling me into a headlong rush down the track, it holds me back. I don't want to fall over. They've done their bit, and now it is just me. I don't want to be the weak link, losing the lead, and trailing in telling them I tried my best.

Showing them the cuts on my knee where I fell wouldn't be much of an excuse.

At the same time, I need to be quick. What if the person behind me is much faster? I don't want him to catch sight of me, that will only give him confidence. I need to keep pushing, keep the gap. Every second counts.

It's a lonely trail. The course follows a well-trodden footpath, but there are not many signs that a race is going on. The few walkers I meet coming the other way seem to regard me with bemusement. I'm red-faced, pushing hard, much harder than a man on a normal Sunday run. I must look like an escaped fugitive, constantly glancing behind, a look of fear in my eyes. Except I'm in full running kit, with a number pinned to my chest. By the time the second and third runners come by, they'll get it and step out of the way, perhaps even cheer them on. But me, I'm just a madman in black, racing myself along the trail.

In the quiet stretches, I keep hearing things. At one point I think I hear footsteps racing up behind me, and I glance around in panic, but it's just my own race number flapping. I look behind again, but there's no sign of life.

As much as I want to push on, I need to be careful, too. When I start getting a stitch, I slow down. A stitch can be debilitating, better to slow a little so it goes away than to be struck down by it. But then I worry I'll be giving up precious seconds, so I push on again.

I'm not sure all this worry about what's happening behind me is helping my running, especially as I've no idea of the gap. Part of me suspects the gap may be huge, and that really I don't even need to try. But that's a dangerous thought.

Every time I have it, the fear of blowing everything, despite starting with a big lead, comes rushing back. My team-mates called this the glory leg, as though there could only be one outcome. The other one is unthinkable. I race on, speeding up again.

I remember the words of a runner speaking to me after the Hakone ekiden. It was one of the Toyo runners. 'In ekiden,' he said, 'you can't always see your rivals, so you need to push on regardless. Fear of what they *may* be doing pushes you on to keep running faster.'

In the end, I stagger through the hazy heat to the finish still in first place. Only Simon has made it to cheer me across the line. I haven't seen another runner the entire way, and here it's almost as quiet. Just a big arch with the word 'Finish' on it, and a man with a microphone garbling something about the first team home.

I collect four goody bags at the end, as the women handing them out congratulate me. Tom and James have now arrived. We all hug. We did it. I think we knew we would.

We stand around waiting for the next team to arrive. Tom says he went the wrong way, but still managed to get back on the course and win his leg. From there the lead just grew and grew. It turns out Simon handed over to me fifteen minutes ahead of second place, and I managed to extend that by another five minutes. It was a huge win.

As I sit on the grass after the race, I wonder whether I finally experienced the essence of ekiden, the game-changing dynamic of running for the team. I definitely felt the weight of expectation this time, the sense of responsibility, the need not to mess things up. I ran scared, looking behind me, pushing on, being chased by invisible foes. If fear can lift you to greater heights, then perhaps it worked. I gained another five minutes on our nearest rivals over a six-mile leg. That's not bad going.

When we go up to collect our prizes, the announcer mangles the name of our team, getting stuck on the word ekiden. The man handing out the trophies, however, is Mike Gratton, who won the London marathon back in 1983. He shakes his head at the announcer's fumble. 'You're obviously real runners,' he says. 'You know what ekiden means.'

I nod politely. Yes, finally, I think I do.